A Christian's Guide to Effective

JAIL & PRISON MINISTRIES

Dale K. Pace

A Christian's Guide to Effective JAIL & PRISON MINISTRIES

Foreword by Myrl E. Alexander

Fleming H. Revell Company
Old Tappan, New Jersey

Scripture quotations not otherwise identified are from the King James Version of the Bible.

Scripture quotation identified PHILLIPS is from THE NEW TESTAMENT IN MODERN ENGLISH (Revised Edition), translated by J. B. Phillips. © J. B. Phillips 1958, 1960, 1972. Used by permission of Macmillan Publishing Co., Inc.

Scripture quotation from the New American Standard Bible is Copyright © THE LOCKMAN FOUNDATION 1960, 1962, 1963, 1968, 1971, 1972, 1973.

Library of Congress Cataloging in Publication Data

Pace, Dale K
A Christian's guide to effective jail and prison ministries.

Bibliography: p.
Includes index.
1. Church work with prisoners. I. Title.
BV4340.P3 259 76-41797
ISBN 0-8007-0844-X

Printed in the United States of America

Contents

List of Abbreviations

ACA	American Correctional Association
AEIC	Association of Evangelical Institutional Chaplains
APCCA	American Protestant Correctional Chaplains' Association
CPE	Clinical Pastoral Education
LEAA	Law Enforcement Assistance Administration
NCJI&SS	National Criminal Justice Information and Statistics Service
NCJRS	National Criminal Justice Reference Service
NILE&CJ	National Institute of Law Enforcement and Criminal Justice

Acknowledgments

This book was made possible through the cooperation of many people. It has drawn heavily upon materials prepared for the Good News Mission's course on the correctional chaplaincy. Those who wrote materials for this course and those who taught in it are identified in note 7. Their materials were indispensable. Gerald Adams, John Boon, Mary Pace, Frank Scholte, and Stuart Vivenzio graciously increased their work loads by assuming my normal responsibilities during the months that the Good News Mission assigned me full-time work on this book. Numerous volunteers at the Mission's Arlington and Richmond offices typed drafts of the manuscripts. Jack H. Goodwin, librarian of the Virginia Theological Seminary Library, allowed me special use of materials which I needed. Dr. Dale Keeton took time from his busy schedule to review the chapter on counseling. Chaplain David Duley and Dr. William L. Simmer also reviewed extensive portions of the manuscripts in their early development. A word of special appreciation is due to the many who prayed for me during the writing process that the book might be useful in the service of our Savior, and my family was most helpful during the writing process.

Charts and Tables

Foreword

American corrections is in the midst of its most rigorous reexamination in a century. The market is deluged by a flood of professional corrections books authored by social scientists: psychologists, sociologists, educators, social workers, anthropologists, political scientists, architects, administrators. The new literature and research reports have been most useful in university classrooms, to correctional administrators, to the public.

But the voice of the Church has been noticeably inarticulate despite its historical role of innovation and deep concerns about human deviant behavior, especially where incarcerated youth, men, and women were involved.

It was the Church and her representatives who created the "house of penitence": the penitentiary. It was the chaplains who initially developed libraries, schools, counseling, individualized treatment, and recreation in prisons and jails. The first youth institution, Saint Michael, was established in the eighteenth century in Rome by the Church. Elizabeth Fry, the "Quaker Heroine" in the early nineteenth century, spearheaded the vast change in English prisons through the great strengths of her deep religious belief and convictions. It was a clergyman, Dr. E. C. Wines, who became the moving spirit of the first National Congress on Penitentiary and Reform Discipline at Cincinnati in 1870, as well as the first International Congress at London in 1872. The world was thrilled in more recent years when Pope John chose to celebrate his first Christmas Mass at a prison in Rome.

Now comes this book which challenges the Church, chaplains and the laity, to engage in a renewal of that ancient interest in ministry to offenders. It is a needed and welcome addition to the flood of new publications in corrections. The book deals in specifics with the roles of the Church and her ministers who work as chaplains behind prison bars. It provides an answer to an oft-repeated question: What in the world do correctional chaplains really do these days now that other professionals have taken over the tasks of libraries, education, counseling, recreation?

Dr. Dale Pace, formerly a member of the senior staff of Johns Hopkins University Applied Physics Laboratory, and whose doctoral dissertation was written on the correctional chaplaincy, is the uniquely qualified author of this book. As an associate of a unique organization, the Good News Mission, he has worked with a wide array of correctional institutions, administrators, judges, parole and probation officers. He understands through experience the problems and needs of offenders, administrators, and chaplains. I have watched the Good News Mission grow and develop in its competencies, commitments, and influences since 1969, when I participated in the first course given by the Mission for ministers, chaplains, theological students, and interested officials. Dr. Pace's experienced philosophy and observations are written with a unique pragmatism deserving of wide and full attention.

Corrections is a complex and difficult field. The specialized role of the chaplaincy fully shares in those complexities. It isn't necessary that the reader fully agree with all the views reported by Dr. Pace, but they are surely thought-provoking views that should become an integral part of contemporary correctional literature. Finally, it is to be hoped that his writing will provoke and stimulate a flow of new literature and contribution about this historic and critical area of corrections.

MYRL E. ALEXANDER
Former Director of the
United States Bureau of Prisons

Introduction

Driven by a conscious obligation to bring the Gospel to all men (*see* Romans 1:14–16), the evangelistic missionary zeal of the early Church quickly spread Christianity throughout the Roman Empire. Then the vision of reaching all men with the Gospel of Christ waned, and more than a millennium passed before the Church began to expand its borders outside the "Christian" nations and those once-Christian lands lost to Islam. Even then, the expansion in the beginning of the modern era of missions (both Catholic and Protestant) simply followed the commercial and colonial interests of the European powers. It took the Evangelical revivals of the eighteenth century to renew the vision of the obligation to evangelize all men, a vision which culminated in the great missionary outreaches of the nineteenth and twentieth centuries.[1]

The history of the Church's interest in ministry to prisoners is somewhat parallel to its interest in missions. Modern penology's roots lie in the sense of obligation to prisoners of some of God's people, such as John Howard and the Friends in Pennsylvania. Most of these were Evangelical. Their actions were largely responsible for many changes in the criminal justice process at the end of the eighteenth and beginning of the nineteenth centuries. But then the vision of this responsibility waned, and for the past century the Church has done little more than provide for prisoners the religious services sought by the state. Today there seems to be a renewal of vision by the Church of its obligation to prisoners. May God cause this to result in a great missionary outreach of the Church into our nation's jails and prisons comparable to the missionary endeavors of the nineteenth and twentieth centuries.

Such an outreach into our nation's jails and prisons will not occur until God's people are impressed with a *sense of urgency* for this ministry. Our jails and prisons are crowded to capacity and beyond. Today most correctional administrators will open their institutions for Christian ministry. *Now* is the time that the Church needs to reach prisoners.

Yet the ministry needed behind bars cannot develop until the Church is willing to commit itself to the great demand of this responsibility. Token ministry in jails and prisons will not fulfill this obligation. It will take a major effort by the people of God and will require many ministers as chaplains, many laymen and women as volunteer workers, and a substantial amount of money.

Why Is This Book Needed?

Very simply, there is a need to expand the Christian ministry to offenders. More than 40 percent of the nearly 4,000 jails in the United States have *no* religious ministry,[2] and 21 of the 592 state prisons in our country have no religious ministry.[3] Often those correctional institutions which have religious ministry do not have an evangelical Christian ministry within them from the Church outside.

There is also a need for more correctional chaplains. Only 15 percent of our nation's jails have chaplains or adequate spiritual leadership for extensive religious programs.[4] In order to have the number of chaplains recommended by the ACA's *Manual of Correctional Standards* to serve the quarter of a million inmates in our nation's prisons, the number of chaplains serving our prisons must triple.[5]

Fortunately, there is a growing interest in ministry to offenders. In part, this is a result of the soaring crime rate; in part, it is due to jail/prison unrest and riots (especially at Attica and Huntsville); and in part it is a response to the Watergate scandal. The number of books and articles about ministry to offenders and inmate converts has increased substantially over a decade ago.

Many new organizations and groups have begun to minister to prisoners.

The purpose of this book is manifold: First, it is to set forth in a brief but comprehensive fashion the obligation of the Church to minister to prisoners. Second, it is to describe the work of the correctional chaplain in such a way that pastors and ministerial students may understand this ministry—and hopefully God will use this description to call many into this ministry. Also, many pastors will find this book helpful when someone connected with their churches runs afoul of the law. Third, its broad perspective is designed to help chaplains (both new and experienced) to be more effective, a matter of concern to the correctional administrator as well as to the Church. Effective chaplains contribute significantly to the peace and well-being of the institution by turning inmates to godliness and by providing for nondestructive releases of tension through the chaplains' programs. Fourth, it has practical suggestions that should benefit anyone ministering in jails and prisons. Finally, it is hoped that this book will help all professional workers in the criminal justice system to understand and appreciate the Christian ministry to prisoners.

This book is oriented primarily to the Christian ministry in jails and prisons, both adult and juvenile.[6] Its consideration of Christian witness and endeavors in other parts of the criminal justice system (courts, halfway houses, etc.) is of necessity very limited.

Until training for the correctional chaplaincy becomes a part of normal ministerial training in Bible colleges and seminaries, it is unlikely that the number of chaplains needed will be recruited from the ranks of American ministers. Therefore, this book has been designed with college and seminary use in mind. Its content is arranged in a logical study order. An extensive annotated bibliography and a directory of agencies involved in ministry to offenders identify resources needed by the serious student.

Sources

Unfortunately, published materials about ministry to prisoners are very limited, compared with those in most other areas of Christian ministry. Of the widely published materials drawn upon, Hoyles' *Religion in Prison* (1955) and *The Church and the Criminal* (1965), Garmon's *Who Are the Criminals?* (1968), and *Ministering to Prisoners and Their Families* (1968) by Cassler and Kandle have been the most substantial. The materials developed for the graduate-level accredited course on the correctional chaplaincy conducted each January since 1972 by the Good News Mission have been used extensively, as have the critiques and comments of students and instructors from the course.[7] Results from two extensive surveys of chaplains have been used heavily: Hylon Vickers' master's thesis (1971) and the author's doctoral study (1974).[8]

This writer has drawn freely from the experiences of Good News Mission staff members and of members of the AEIC and of the American Correctional Chaplains' Association as well as from his own ministry in more than a dozen correctional institutions (jail, juvenile, penal, and halfway houses) and his supervision and evaluation of chaplains in several dozen more institutions.

Two Comments

In this book a number of things are said which may not please those with vested interest in areas which are critically evaluated or those committed to doctrinaire positions. However, as Robert Browning noted, "Facts are facts and flinch not."

When Jesus saw the multitudes "as sheep having no shepherd," He said unto His disciples, "The harvest truly is plenteous, but the labourers are few; Pray ye therefore the Lord of the harvest, that he will send forth labourers unto his harvest" (Matthew 9:36–38).

There exists no more appropriate application for these words than to those sheep without shepherds in our nation's jails and prisons. May the Lord of Harvest use this book as a means of bringing laborers to the harvest, and may He endow each laborer with His power.

A Christian's Guide to Effective JAIL & PRISON MINISTRIES

1

The Challenge of Ministry to Offenders

The Church of Jesus Christ has an unfinished task. Jesus commanded His Church to bear witness of Him to men everywhere (Acts 1:8), to make disciples of all people (Matthew 28:19,20),[9] and to succor those in need, especially the brethren (Matthew 25:31–40; Luke 10:25–37). The potential for fulfilling these commands of Jesus resides in His sufficiency: His death to reconcile all things to Himself (Colossians 1:20), His authority over all things (Matthew 28:18), and His provision of the Holy Spirit to empower His Church to know and obey His will (John 15:26,27; Acts 1:8).

The purpose of this chapter is to focus attention upon one aspect of the Church's unfinished task. That aspect is the ministry to offenders. This chapter looks at the challenge of ministry to offenders from four points of view: (1) biblical imperatives for such ministry, (2) the great difficulty of developing significant and effective ministry among offenders, (3) the practical necessity for such ministry, and (4) the great opportunity before the Church for such ministry.

Biblical Imperatives

God's program often exceeds man's expectation. So it is with God's plan for the Church in its ministry to offenders. Biblical imperatives set forth a threefold ministry for the Church. First, the Church should minister to prisoners in their confinement. Second, the Church should seek to prevent crime. And third, the Church should seek reform of the criminal justice system. Although this book concentrates on the ministry in jails and prisons, each of these aspects of the biblical imperatives is discussed below.

Ministry to Prisoners

Early in His public ministry, Jesus preached in the synagogue of His hometown, Nazareth, from the text in the prophecy of Isaiah which describes the ministry of the Messiah. Jesus used this passage to explain His purpose and activities because it spoke of Him:

> The Spirit of the Lord is upon me, because he hath anointed me to preach the gospel to the poor; he hath sent me to heal the brokenhearted, to preach deliverance to the captives, and recovering of sight to the blind, to set at liberty them that are bruised, To preach the acceptable year of the Lord.
>
> Luke 4:18,19

These things Jesus did while on the earth bodily. His Body on earth now (i.e., the Church) should continue these same activities. And they find perhaps their greatest fulfillment in the Church's ministry to prisoners. Most prisoners are poor.[10] They desperately need good news, and the Gospel of Jesus Christ is good news. It is hard to imagine any group more brokenhearted than inmates, and more in need of comfort and healing of depression.[11] Inmates are not only physically captive; many are also in bondage to drugs, alcohol, lust and sexual perversion, hate, and need the deliverance that can be found in Christ. Most inmates suffer from spiritual blindness caused by bitterness, rejection of authority, and evil. They need to allow the Light of the World to bring them a recovering of sight. Bruised by the bureaucracy of the criminal justice system and by violence from brutal inmates, prisoners need the liberation of Jesus, for free indeed are they whom the Son makes free (*see* John 8:36). They need to hear the proclamation of the acceptable year of the Lord—that now is the time to accept Him and to become acceptable to Him through Jesus Christ (*see* 2 Corinthians 6:2; 5:21).

The ministry of Jesus on the earth was under the anointing of God's Spirit; likewise, as the Body of Christ continues that ministry and reaches in to prisoners, the guidance and power that come from the anointing of God's Spirit are essential.

Near the end of His ministry on earth, Jesus taught His disciples about His judgment of the nations at His return in His glory (Matthew 25:31–46). The separation of the sheep, the blessed of the Father to inherit the kingdom, from the goats—destined for everlasting punishment—will be on the basis of their treatment of "the least of His brethren": the hungry, thirsty, estranged, naked, sick, imprisoned. Jesus is clear: Whatever was done or not done unto the least of His brethren was done or not done unto Him.

It is not necessary to resolve the exegetical controversies about the interpretation of this passage. Its application is undisputed. Jesus wants His sheep to be concerned about prisoners and minister to them, and He will reward His sheep for so doing.

The use of "brethren" in this passage is a striking reminder that there are believers behind bars. Some inmate believers became brethren after confinement. Others were Christians before incarceration but were living in ungodly disobedience to the biblical pattern. A few are in prison even though they had been living godly lives. For example:

> Samuel[12] was a born-again Christian, active in his church. As a businessman involved in extensive real-estate transactions, he was charged with fraud when one of his business associates embezzled such a substantial amount that the entire business operation collapsed. Since the embezzler had absconded, angry creditors and investors initiated prosecution of Samuel, who was incarcerated for a prolonged period before his innocence was established at his trial.

Life behind bars is hard—especially for the brethren. Some face the dismal prospect of long years in prison. They have to face the same pressures that confront all inmates, but without resorting to many "con" ways of self-protection. Other inmates will test the brethren to see whether they have jailhouse religion or a living relationship to God:

> Stu, an inmate at a convict work unit in Virginia, had been a Christian for about a year. His testimony for Christ had been consistent and open. One day his fellow inmates nailed his boots to the floor to see how this "Jesus boy" would react.

Some brethren will be persecuted simply because evil men dislike a godly life:

> John, age 19, converted a month earlier, had developed the practice of reading his Bible for several hours each day. He was transferred to another cellblock within the jail. Other inmates in this cellblock threatened to beat him if he continued to read his Bible. A few weeks before, these men had beaten a young man in that cellblock so badly that he lost sight in one eye and his kidney was damaged severely. John asked the chaplain, "What should I do?" The chaplain replied, "What do you think Jesus wants you to do?" John said "I guess I'd better go read my Bible some more."

The most challenging verse about ministering to prisoners is Hebrews 13:3, translated forcefully by the New American Standard Bible as "Remember the prisoners, as though in prison with them. . . ." Serious consideration of this verse should impel Christians into both intercessory prayer for prisoners, especially the brethren behind bars, and active ministry to prisoners.

The perspective of Paul the prisoner is needed to provide balance for meditation upon Hebrews 13:3; otherwise one can easily become maudlin. His confinement had helped the Gospel of Christ to penetrate even the Praetorian Guard (Philippians 1:12,13). Paul's life was Christ's, for Him to use as He chose. To live, in prison or free, was Christ (Philippians 1:21). Whatever life brought, abundance or emptiness, a lifetime in prison or immediate freedom, Paul was confident that Christ would supply his need and use him (Philippians 4:12,13). Every brother and sister in Christ, those behind bars and those not, needs this perspective.

It is significant that the last individual whom Christ addressed before His death was a criminal. To him Jesus said, "Today shalt thou be with me in paradise" (*see* Luke 23:43).

The Church dare not turn its back and ignore prisoners. Nor can the Church expect to please the Lord Jesus Christ with merely a token ministry to those behind bars. *Jesus expects His Church to minister to prisoners as if He were one of the inmates and they the others.* Such would be done with zeal, dedication, and thoroughness. This is the demand of the biblical imperative that calls the Church to minister in jails and prisons.

Prevention of Crime

The Church also has a biblical imperative to prevent crime. From the practical side, it is obviously wiser to prevent crime than to deal with the consequences of crime. American society has taken three basic approaches to crime prevention. The first of these is to remove some of the temptation (a) by making it more difficult to commit crimes (bulletproof glass isolating the bank teller from the customer and potential criminal, etc.) and (b) by attempting to reduce some of the causes for crime, principally poverty (various efforts to improve the living level and job opportunities of ghetto residents, etc.). This pattern of crime prevention has a precedent in the Old Testament. The Mosaic law prescribes:

> . . . a society in which temptation to commit crime was reduced to a minimum. The Mosaic code included laws to protect the poor (Exodus 22:22–27; 23:6; Leviticus 19:13; Deuteronomy 24:12–15), to lessen the pains of their poverty (Exodus 23:11; Leviticus 19:9–10; 23:22; 25:35–37; Deuteronomy 14:28–29; 15:7–11; 16:10–14; 23:24–25; 24:19–21; 26:12), and to prevent it from becoming permanent (Leviticus 25:8, 34; Numbers 27:8–11; Deuteronomy 15:1–3; 19:14) . . . Likewise there were laws to protect the physically handicapped (Leviticus 19:14) and the stranger (Exodus 22:21; Leviticus 19:10, 33–34; 23:22; Deuteronomy 14:29; 16:11,14; 24:19–21; 26:12).[13]

The second approach to crime prevention that American society has taken has been to improve the efficiency of law enforcement (more police personnel, computer networks linking law enforcement agencies to control-data banks, etc.).

The third approach has been to decriminalize (or at least begin to talk about decriminalizing) a number of offenses which have widespread public sympathy. These offenses are often labeled "victimless crimes" and include drunkenness, prostitution, homosexual acts between consenting adults, and the use of marijuana.

The Church has a unique capacity to play a major role that can complement the crime-prevention efforts of society. Furthermore, the disciples of Jesus as the "salt of the earth" (Matthew 5:13) have a responsibility both to preserve the good in society by preventing decay and corruption and to bring forth the best of society—else, as unsalty salt, the disciples are "good for nothing, but to be cast out, and to be trodden under foot of men."

The Church can realize its crime-prevention potential by endeavors in three areas. The first two prevent crime from members of the Church and its families; the third addresses the community:

1. The Church should encourage its members to be law-abiding citizens (Romans 13:1–7; 1 Peter 2:13–15) and train its members in godly living (Ephesians 4:28; 1 Peter 4:15; etc.) so that they "may be blameless and harmless, the sons of God, without rebuke, in the midst of a crooked and perverse nation, among whom [they] shine as lights in the world" (Philippians 2:15). While statistics are not conclusive in this area, this author has met few offenders among the thousands whom he knows who were (1) born again, (2) active in an evangelical church, and (3) maintaining a daily time of prayer and Bible study when they committed the offense which brought them to jail.

2. The Church should assist the families of its members to be stable, wholesome families. This will prevent crime. The most significant single societal factor affecting the likelihood of criminal activities in a young person's future is the home environment. Broken homes, homes with a parent or two who abuse alcohol, drugs, or sex,[14] homes with an emotionally disturbed parent—from such come the majority

of delinquents and subsequently criminals.[15] With the divorce rate approaching a divorce for every two marriages, American families are becoming rapidly less stable, compounding the potential for crime.

Christian families have the capacity to be stable and wholesome. They have guidance for right living from God's Word. They have power for right living from God's Spirit. They have encouragement for right living from the love and concern of God's people in the Church. And they should have incentive for right living from the disastrous consequences of ungodly living all about them.

3. The Church should evangelize its community and bring the new converts into the fellowship of the Church, initiating the two crime-prevention approaches above. Such evangelization will reduce the number of "potential" offenders in the community.

By the above threefold approach the Church can play a major role in crime prevention.

Reform of the Criminal Justice System

It has ever been the duty of God's people to call upon their society, and especially its leadership, to behave righteously. In the Mosaic law, justice was commanded both in the market (Leviticus 19:35,36; Deuteronomy 25:13–15) and in the courts (Exodus 23:6–8; Deuteronomy 1:16,17; 16:18–20).[16] Nathan rebuked King David for his unrighteousness (2 Samuel 12:1–7), and Isaiah, Jeremiah, and other men of God did likewise to their society. The Church has a responsibility to call our society to righteousness—including that part of our society in the criminal justice system.

The need for reform is evident,[17] and the Church should have a major role in it. Historically, the "better part" of improvements for prisoners has derived from the Christian ministry among prisoners,[18] including development of schools, libraries, vocational training, and recreation programs in correctional institutions.[19] Most of the one-on-one volunteer counseling programs (Job Therapy, Volunteers in Corrections, etc.) were started by Christians and drew volunteer counselors mainly from the churches.

However, the Church has lost its leadership role in this work. The entry of vast numbers of secular professional workers into the correctional field has pushed aside the role of the Church as innovator and leader. For example, in reference to dealing with mentally disturbed offenders, Hoyles observes "now the chaplain has been pushed out of a realm in which he once had exclusive rights." [20]

There are four reasons that the Church has become a distant follower instead of a leader in the reform movement:

First, the Church has failed to develop a contemporary comprehensive philosophy of penology or correction. Evangelicals are indebted to Professor Gary Williams for the first step in this process by his summary of the penology contained in the Mosaic law.[21] Now the process needs to be completed so the Church can suggest positive directions for reform to take rather than merely decrying the problems of the present.

Second, correctional chaplains have failed to provide the leadership needed to call the Church's attention to its responsibility to minister to prisoners as it should.[22]

Third, the Church may have steered away from reform of the criminal justice system because the job is difficult and unrewarding. There are no easy solutions to the problems of our criminal justice system.

Fourth and finally, the Church may have hesitated to initiate the call for reform of the criminal justice system because it would have offended so many of the respected establishments of American society. For example, the legal and judicial community would have to be criticized for its emphasis upon legalism to the neglect of justice. John Brabner-Smith, former dean of the International School of Law, traces the cause for this to a change in the curriculum for law school students that eliminated the study of justice and concentrated simply upon study of the legal code.[23] Likewise, the law enforcement and correctional systems would have to be criticized for their unwillingness to punish their members who were guilty of crimes. This can be illustrated by the failure of the State of Arkansas even to investigate the suspicious deaths of a large number of inmates (possibly as many as two hundred) over the years.[24] Since the earliest colonists arrived from Europe, the Church in this country has been a prime supporter of the institutions of government and respectable society, which may have influenced the delay of the Church in its call for reform.

It may be that the Church will not regain the position of leadership that it once held in penology, but this does not negate the Church's responsibility to call the criminal justice system to reform. It will help the criminal justice system to take the Church's demand for reform seriously if (1) the Church will confess that it has not done its proper part in ministry to prisoners this century, (2) the Church begins to provide the needed ministry to prisoners, and (3) the Church presents a contemporary comprehensive philosophy of corrections.

The Church should not suppose that reform will come easily, if indeed it comes. Many have vested interests in the criminal justice system *as it is now*—and resist change stubbornly.

Restrictions on employment of ex-convicts illustrate the difficulty of reform. In spite of the fact that nearly everyone agrees that inappropriate restrictions on job opportunities for offenders should be removed—and despite extensive efforts of the American Bar Association and associations of ex-offenders and of various professionals within the criminal justice system—up to 1976 (about five years and many dollars after this effort began), fewer than twenty states had reformed their laws in this respect.[25]

Therefore, as the Church considers its responsibility to call for reform of the criminal justice system, it is necessary that it understand it should expect reform to come only after much persistent effort. Two lines from an epigram by C. S. Lewis express this warning precisely:

> Do not for the dregs
> mistake the first bitter drop.[26]

Summary

God's Word lays a threefold responsibility upon the Church: minister to prisoners, prevent crime, and reform the criminal justice system. Compliance is not optional but essential, if the Church of Jesus Christ is to please its Lord.

Difficulty of the Task

The challenge of ministry to prisoners does not set before the Church an easy task. Compared with the Church's endeavors in the recent past, the task is colossal. At present there are only four to six hundred full-time correctional chaplains (including both Catholic and Protestant chaplains) in the entire United States. Less than a hundred of these chaplains are supported financially by the Church, the rest being on government payrolls.[27] About two thousand full-time correctional chaplains are needed to provide the number warranted by the present (1976) inmate population![28] The majority of the fifteen hundred new chaplains needed will have to be supported by the Church. The state is unlikely to increase its support for chaplains and may even decrease its present support in the near future. Thus the Church will have to increase the number of ministers committed to this ministry as chaplains by nearly 400 percent and its financial commitment by 1,500 percent! Realistically, the financial support of some fifteen hundred chaplains will require at least twenty million dollars a year from the Church, and more likely *thirty* million a year.[29]

The discussion thus far has used the number of full-time chaplains to indicate the scope of the ministry needed, because (1) chaplains should provide spiritual leadership for the ministry in jails and prisons and (2) more quantitative information existed about chaplains than the other aspects of Christian ministry behind bars. This does not minimize the need for volunteer workers (both clergy and laity), for organizations and ministers other than chaplains providing religious services in correctional institutions, or for support contributions such as Bibles from the Gideons and American Bible Society. A substantial increase in all of these is also required for the Church to fulfill its responsibilities of ministry to inmates, their families, and friends.

Every inmate is important, and the salvation of a single prisoner is significant in God's eyes (*see* Luke 15:7–10). Yet the Church dare not be content with the fact that inmates are being saved when many inmates are not evangelized and ministered unto. The Church needs the vision of reaching every "reachable" inmate for Christ.

The challenge of ministry in jails and prisons is a difficult task not only because of its mammoth size but also because of the stumbling blocks which the Church has placed in the way of such ministry.[30] The stumbling blocks are three in number: First, many inmates have been offended by the hypocrisy of people in the Church (e.g., preachers and deacons involved in adultery and alcohol abuse), and a large number of inmates have had bad experiences personally with the Church prior to their incarceration. Second, many churches are not receptive to offenders or their families. They do not want them in their congregations. As one pastor told this author, "I hope God blesses your work, but don't send any of those converted crooks to my church." Third, the divided nature of Christendom hinders the ministry behind bars.[31] There is no satisfactory answer to the inmate who asks, Why are there so many different churches? Skeptics and others have used the divisions within Christendom as an argument against Christianity and as a reason to reject Christ. The chaplain who is asked this question can only confess that the Church is yet imperfect and that our sinful blindness is what divides those who belong to Christ; but the chaplain can also point out to the inmate the blessed unity that all true Christians have in the Body of Christ, the Universal Church (*see* Ephesians, Chapters 4 and 5).

The task of ministering to prisoners is difficult because it must be conducted in adverse situations. The audience is hard. Inmate populations include many who have committed atrocities, who have seared their consciences by repeated evil, who have injured their minds by alcohol and drug abuse. The atmosphere is hostile to the Gospel because fear and depression dominate jails and prisons. The facilities are often limited. Only 70 percent of chaplains reported having chapels at their prisons.[32] At the rest of the prisons, services have to be held in a multipurpose room, a classroom, or some other such space. Often the surroundings are not conducive to worship. In jails, the situation is even worse. Only

59 percent of jail chaplains reported any kind of room that could be used for religious services. In other jails, the services have to be held at the tiers and cellblocks where inmates are housed. The problems of such as these are manifold.[33]

When these difficulties are considered, it is helpful to remember that "with God all things are possible" (Matthew 19:26). The same God who began with a handful of Jewish converts in Palestine and before the end of the first century had spread Christianity through the Roman Empire can surely overcome the present obstacles. The number of chaplains needed is only about 2 percent of the evangelical ministers in this country. The money needed to finance their ministry is less than 0.1 percent of church income in 1974.[34]

It is appropriate to close with a comment by the apostle Paul: "Who is sufficient for these things? . . . our sufficiency is of God." (2 Corinthians 2:16; 3:5).

Practical Necessity for This Ministry

The crime problem and inmate populations are increasing. Most inmates return to the community. In fact, well over 99 percent return to the community at some time, if jail inmates are considered as well as prison inmates. Unchanged they represent a substantial threat to the community. Secular efforts at rehabilitation have not been effective in preventing released offenders from committing new crimes. But Christ can rehabilitate anyone by regeneration. Thus, extensive ministry with inmates will make the community safer, because *some* of those returning to the community will have been transformed by the power of Jesus. Also, godly lives of inmate converts will help reduce the explosive potential of overcrowded jails and prisons. Thus the Church has a very practical reason to provide extensive ministry to prisoners: It makes the community safer and reduces the likelihood of penal riots.

The increasing crime problem is alarming—and churches too are victims.[35] Among its causes are an increasing rebellious attitude against established authority among American youth (thought by many to be the natural consequence of excessive permissiveness in their rearing), continuing deterioration of family stability, and possibly an intensification of "last day" characteristics such as described in 2 Timothy 3:1–5 as a prelude to the return of Christ.

A relentless growth in inmate populations is likely to continue for the rest of this century. The reasons for this are simple and clear.[36] The population accounting for most inmates (i.e., young men from lower-income urban neighborhoods) is large, and it will grow for the rest of the century. Extensive use of probation during the latter half of the 1960s and early 1970s brought a substantial decrease both in inmate populations and the ratio of inmates to the population at large. Many states, however, have already expanded their use of probation to about the maximum possible.[37] Consequently, inmate populations can be expected to rise sharply as the crime rate and the high-risk population both increase—especially if the current public opinion prevails that judges should "get tough" with criminals.

Many released offenders will commit new crimes.[38] Secular efforts at rehabilitation within correction facilities have failed to demonstrate their effectiveness in reducing recidivism.[39] As this fact became more firmly established by correctional research in the 1970s, a shift has begun from "required" participation in rehabilitation programs to an emphasis that makes them completely voluntary. It is too early to tell what long-term effect such a change may have. It should be remembered that rehabilitation programs in correctional institutions have other benefits (reducing inmate tensions through constructive activities, providing sheriffs and wardens with additional privileges that may be given or withheld, providing jobs for teachers, psychologists, counselors, etc.).[40] It must be remembered also that *every* rehabilitation program has helped some inmates become better, even if the impact has been statistically insignificant.[41]

Secular rehabilitation efforts have been unsuccessful in changing the recidivism. Has Christianity done better? This is a fair question and deserves a careful, honest answer. A doctrinaire answer on the basis either of theology or secular prejudice is inadequate. First, it should be established that Christ can change men. Then, the kind of men that Christ can change must be established. Finally, the statistical impact of Christian conversion on recidivism needs to be considered.

Can Christ Change Men? The Christian answers a resounding *yes.* The New Testament abounds with illustrations of men changed by Jesus Christ: Matthew and Zacchaeus, tax collectors (Matthew 9:9,10; Luke 19:1–10), Saul of Tarsus, zealous Pharisee, into the apostle Paul (Acts 22:1–21), and others. The history of the Christian Church abounds with examples of men changed by Christ: the profligate Augustine, slave-trader John Newton, alcoholic songwriter Stuart Hamblen, syndicate gadgets man Jim Vaus, Harlem gang leader Tom Skinner, etc.[42]

What Kind of Men Can Christ Change? The grand promise of the Christian Gospel is "if any man be in Christ, he is a new creature" (2 Corinthians 5:17). Christ can change all kinds of men. The ones at Corinth who had been transformed by the power of Christ included those involved in the sexual immorality of fornication and adultery, homosexuals, thieves, drunkards, extortioners, agitators, greedy ones, and idolators (1 Corinthians 6:9–11). The power of Christ has not diminished (*see* Hebrews 13:8). He still changes and transforms all kinds of men, as has been illustrated in the lives of Floyd Hamilton, last of the Bonnie and Clyde gang; Chuck Colson, hatchet man for the president; and many others less well known. The three examples of changed men which follow illustrate a wide variety of backgrounds and crimes. In each of these cases, the man has lived a lawful, godly life for at least five years since his conversion and subsequent release from imprisonment.

> Sam, a man of violence and involved extensively in immoral and illegal activities, convicted of molesting a young girl, has become an effective evangelical minister of youth for a church in the area where his crime was committed.

> Ganni, though from a prominent family, destroyed his mind by ten years of heavy use of LSD plus other drugs and alcohol, regained sanity after regeneration and has become a businessman. Hospitalization in mental institutions and extensive psychiatric treatment had been unable to provide the mental soundness that Ganni found in Christ (cf. 2 Timothy 1:7).

Harry, who wrote many thousands of dollars of bad checks, found Christ in jail, has become a lay leader in his church and has played an extensive role for years in ministry to inmates.

As Arthur Hoyles concludes, "many a criminal has been so completely transformed by the power of God that all desire to break the law has been eliminated. Evangelical religion is a social asset." [43]

Does Christian Conversion Reduce Recidivism? The natural inclination of the evangelical Christian is to posit a yes to this question, but care is needed. In his careful look at religion in prison, Hoyles commented that "even when great emphasis was laid upon evangelism as a means of curing criminals, the success was not spectacular." [44] This question has been a matter of concern for a long time. For example, in 1851 the Prison Discipline Society (founded a quarter of a century before at Park Street Church in Boston) inquired of the prison keepers in Massachusetts about the religious programs in their institutions. Among the questions asked were these: Are there now in the prison cases of reformation? Have there been persons discharged who have indicated by their lives, since their discharge, the reality of their reformation? [45]

The answers to these inquiries varied. One reported, "We have no cases of permanent reformation." [46] Another, Sheriff John Lincoln of Worcester, cautiously noted:

It would be unsafe to rely on any professions of reformation made by a prisoner when in confinement, and it would require continued good conduct after . . . discharge to satisfy the public of a reformation. Such instances we have amongst us.[47]

N. Muzzy, superintendent of the Sabbath School in Sheriff Lincoln's institution, expressed his feelings on this subject with less reservation:

Two among the number of prisoners, within a few weeks, have given pleasing evidence that they have truly humbled themselves before God, and found peace in that precious

> blood which has been shed for the guilty, and seem to view their confinement in Prison, where the truths of the Bible have been kindly brought home to their hearts, as among their richest blessings.[48]

Today as then, the evidence is mixed. Many criminals profess to be Christians but still commit crimes. In fact, some claim that atheists have the lowest incidence of crimes.[49] The problem is that it is difficult to measure a convert's relationship to Christ. The only factors easily accessible to the researcher are church affiliation, professed beliefs, and the extent of involvement in the church. Some studies show that crime seems to be more prevalent among those without connections to a church; others do not.[50] Consequently, data do not exist at present which demonstrate conclusively the effect of inmate conversion on recidivism.

The Church should seek to develop the data to provide an empirical answer to the question of conversion's effect on recidivism.[51] In the meantime, it is important to remember that Christ is the answer for each one who will receive Him. Every convict truly converted by Christ is much less a menace to society than he was prior to his conversion, even one whose life never becomes very good. Thus the Church has a practical necessity for ministering to prisoners in addition to the biblical imperatives. Together they form an undeniable mandate.

Great Opportunity

While jails and prisons are caldrons of evil, many inmates within them are open to the Gospel because of boredom and desperation. Some, when free, were too busy to give Jesus a second thought. Now that they are forced into idleness, they are willing to listen to God's Word—and some will be converted. Other inmates are so desperate that they will try anything, even religion, in the hope that it may help them. Some of these, also, may be converted.

An amazing aspect of the New Testament message is that God does not care what motivates a man to come to Christ, He cares only that the man comes—because when one truly comes to Jesus, he is changed. This fact is illustrated by the parable of the prodigal son. He came home because his luck ran out and he was hungry (Luke 15:11–32).

Correctional administrators are open to constructive help from the community. During the past decade, jails and prisons have become much more open to all kinds of programs, both those conducted by the institution's staff and those conducted by volunteers from outside. While the doors to most jails and prisons are wide open to Christian ministry, three facts should be remembered: First, correctional administrators may be skeptical of inmate conversions (as expressed in the reserved comment of Sheriff Lincoln quoted earlier). Second, correctional administrators properly insist on control over all programs within their institutions, but at times may impose (or try to impose) unwarranted restrictions upon the religious programs.[52] Third, correctional administrators normally do not appreciate criticism of their institutions, even when the criticism is just and true.

The growing interest in jails and prisons makes now the time for God's people to begin expansion of the Christian ministry behind bars. There are four steps that the Church must take if it is to take advantage of the great opportunity before it:

1. Capable leadership for jail/prison ministry must be sought from among pastors and ministerial students. This means that jail/prison ministry and its leaders (especially correctional chaplains) must be honored as highly as the pastoral ministry and its leaders. At present, this is not the case. Ministry to prisoners is looked down upon by most of the churches.[53] The attitude limits recruitment of the leaders needed for this ministry. Recruitment of adequate numbers of chaplains and other leaders also means that training for jail and prison ministry must become a regular part of ministerial training. Until it becomes such, adequate numbers of leaders will not be available to meet the need.
2. Organizations ministering to prisoners need to be expanded and new ones begun. Otherwise it will not be possible to provide the ministry needed.
3. Church leaders must come to understand how the crimi-

nal justice system works and how the ministry to prisoners should be performed.

4. The Church must provide adequate support for the jail and prison ministry (prayer, people, money).

Chapter Conclusions

Jesus never gave His followers any options about obedience. He expects all who love Him to obey him. In this, He is a hard master (*see* Luke 9:23–27; 14:25–35; 19:22). He has given His Church a task. We dare not be slack in performing it. Let us be at it.

2

An Introduction to the Criminal Justice System

Much of the ministry to offenders is conducted in a foreign mission field: the criminal justice system. The adjective *foreign* is used advisably. The criminal justice system is poorly understood by most in the Church. Therefore it is appropriate to provide an introduction to the environment in which most of the ministry to offenders occurs.

This introduction to the criminal justice system will provide a brief orientation to the functions and operations of law enforcement, courts, correctional institutions, probation and parole, community programs, inmate treatment, and consider a few general theories and clichés about the criminal justice system. For a more thorough and detailed exposure to the criminal justice system, the reader should turn to one of the numerous texts and references on this subject.[54]

Chart 1 provides a general illustration of processing through the criminal justice system and an appreciation for the interconnected functions of law enforcement (mainly police), courts, and corrections in the tortuous arrest-to-freedom process of the administration of "justice." [55]

Law Enforcement

There are over half a million law enforcement officers in this country, most of them police personnel.[56] Over 80 percent of these

CHART 1

A General View of the Criminal Justice System

This chart seeks to present a simple yet comprehensive view of the movement of cases through the criminal justice system. Procedures in individual jurisdictions may vary from the pattern shown here. The differing weights of line indicate the relative volumes of cases disposed of at various points in the system, but this is only suggestive.

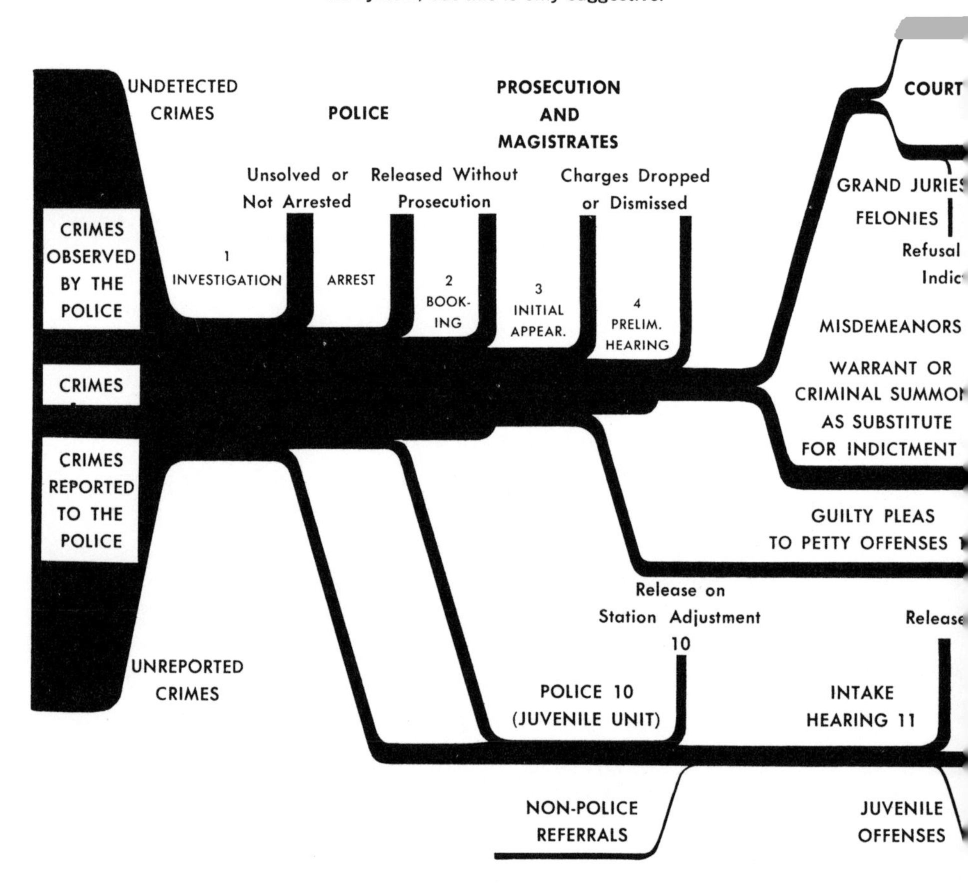

LEGEND

1. May continue until trial.
2. Administrative record of arrest. First step at which temporary release on bail may be available.
3. Before magistrate. Formal notice of charge, advised of rights. Bail set. Summary trials for petty offenses usually conducted here without further processing.
4. Preliminary testing of evidence against defendant. Charge may be reduced. No separate hearing for misdemeanors. Preliminary hearing in District Court for felony cases.
5. Charge filed by solicitor on basis of information submitted by police or citizens. Alternative to grand jury indictment. Often used in felonies, almost always in misdemeanors.
6. Reviews whether government evidence is sufficient to justify trial.
7. Appearance for plea; defendant elects trial by judge or jury (if available). Counsel for indigent usually appointed here in felony cases, often not at all in other cases.
8. Charge may be reduced at any time prior to trial in return for plea of guilty or for other reasons.

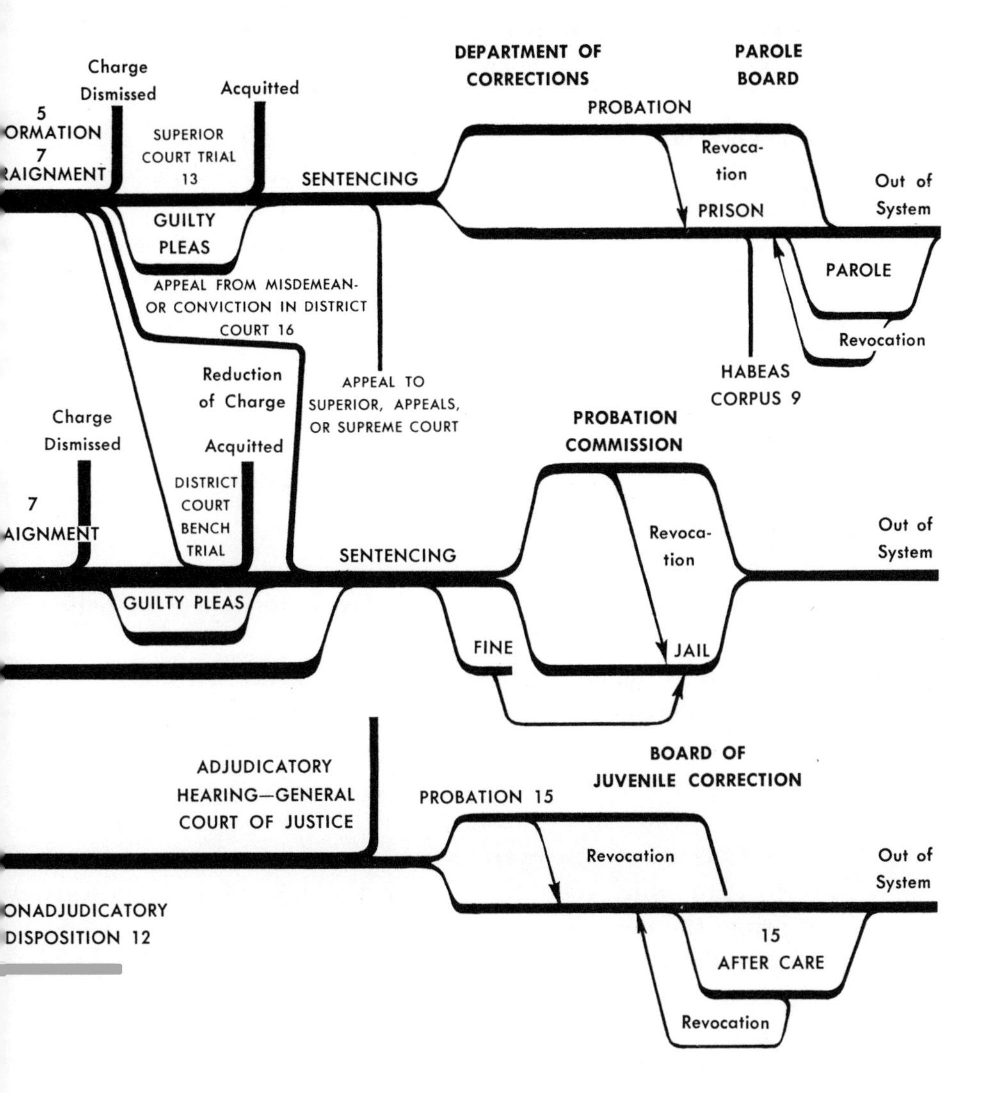

9. Challenge on constitutional grounds to legality of detention. May be sought at any point in the process.
10. Police often hold informal hearings, dismiss or adjust many cases without further processing. The subsequent course of processing juveniles is in a General Court (or even in a Juvenile Court), with felony suspects tried in a Superior Court and misdemeanants and petty offenders in a lower court. Only a few of the larger urban police departments have separate juvenile units.
11. Probation officer decides desirability of further action.
12. Welfare agency, social services, counseling, medical care, etc., for cases where adjudicatory handling not needed.
13. Superior Court trial in such instances as capital cases.
14. Guilty pleas to misdemeanors with punishment of $50 or 30 days or less in jail and certain traffic offenses may be taken by a **Magistrate.**
15. Department of Public Welfare.
16. Appeal from misdemeanor conviction in Lower Court is by trial **de novo** in Superior Court. No further indictment is necessary.

serve in the more than 40,000 local jurisdictions.[57] The rest are split 60 and 40 percent between state law enforcement agencies (e.g., state police) and federal law enforcement personnel (FBI, Secret Service, etc.).[58] Most urban areas will have a patchwork of local law enforcement agencies (more than a hundred of them in some large metropolitan areas) whose efforts and policies are at best loosely coordinated and at worst in opposition to one another (bad feelings and destructive rivalry exist between many law enforcement agencies, unfortunately). Infusion of large sums of LEAA funds during the early 1970s has helped such law enforcement agencies to develop communication systems that can better coordinate their efforts and significantly improve the quality of law enforcement personnel, increasing their professionalism.[59] All of this is much needed, since contact with law enforcement personnel is the point at which most citizens encounter the criminal justice system.

An offender's processing through the criminal justice system normally involves five steps [60] in the law enforcement or police section of the system: [61]

First, *arrest*. Where a police officer has witnessed a crime or has reasonable cause to feel a felony [62] has been committed and believes the suspect to be responsible, he may make an arrest without a warrant. In such a case, the arrest should be made as quickly as possible and a warrant issued at a later date. Normally an arrest occurs after a warrant has been obtained, the result of investigation which identifies a suspect as the culprit. The warrant brings the court into the process. A judicial officer, normally a magistrate, reviews the basis for the proposed arrest and either disapproves it or approves it with the issuance of the warrant.

Second, *booking*. Booking involves a formal charge at a police station with specific violation(s) of the law, fingerprinting, recording of the circumstances of the arrest and descriptive personal data on the arrestee, and completion of other paperwork.

Third, *interrogation*. Somewhere, and at no specific time in the processing procedures, a point is reached when the police officer will want to question the arrestee regarding his possible involvement in the alleged crime. Prior to any interrogation associated with the arrest, the officer is obligated to advise the suspect of his civil rights concerning confessions. These are: [63]

- You have the right to remain silent.
- Anything you say can and will be used as evidence against you in court.
- You have a right to consult with a lawyer of your own choice before you answer any questions and to have that lawyer present while you answer any question.
- If you are unable to hire your own lawyer and you want one, a lawyer will be provided for you before you are asked any questions.

Fourth, *appearance/presentment* (*"arraignment"*). Once the questioning is completed—or, if the arrestee demands it, immediately—he is taken for an *appearance/presentment* (popularly, but technically incorrectly, called an *arraignment*) before a committing magistrate, who determines upon the basic facts of the case (1) to release the suspect on his word that he will appear in court (recognizance) or (2) to remand him for confinement in the detention center, normally setting at that time the amount in cash or bond that the suspect would have to post in order to be released on bail until his court date.[64] The attorney may be appointed for indigent felony suspects at this time.

Except in traffic offenses, *a police officer has no authority to release an individual after an arrest has been made.* "From the moment of arrest, the subject is in the court's custody; and the police officers are merely *agents* of the court. The legality and duration of the confinement is a *legal question* to be passed on by a judicial officer." [65]

Fifth, the *lockup.* Once the suspect is ordered to be confined, he is placed in a holding cell, commonly called a lockup. Here he is held in custody until he has had a formal hearing on the next court day.

In some jurisdictions the lockup is staffed and maintained by the local police department. The preferable situation, however, is to place all confinement facilities under the control of the sheriff's office.

After the arrestee has been to court on his formal hearing, the police department's official responsibility toward him ceases. Of course, the arresting officer must present evidence in the case until it has been fully adjudicated. However, the onus for the care and maintenance of the prisoner now falls upon the sheriff or his equivalent in the particular jurisdiction involved.

The Courts

The judicial process in the United States is an outgrowth of the English common law transported to this country with the colonists, modified by legislative processes so as to make the law viable in our present complex society. In dealing with the judicial process, it is essential to realize that this country functions with a dual system of courts: federal courts to deal with violations of federal laws, and state courts to deal with violations of state and local laws.

While the particulars of the judicial process vary from one state to another and between federal and state systems, the following process is representative for *adult felony cases*. Misdemeanor and juvenile procedures will be treated subsequently.

The steps required to process an adult felony case through the courts are numerous. After the *appearance*, the accused with his attorney appears at the *preliminary hearing*, where the government must prove "probable cause" that the suspect is the culprit in order to have a *grand jury* examine the case. The function of the grand jury,[66] which meets in secret and hears only the government side of the case, is to determine if the evidence that the suspect is the culprit provides seemingly adequate reason (again "probable cause") to bring the suspect to trial. If it does provide such reason, an *indictment* is issued—the formal charge setting forth the specifics of the violation alleged—and the defendant is charged. This indictment provides the authority for the accused to be tried. Following the indictment, the defendant must enter a plea of guilty, not guilty, or *nolo contendere* [67] to the specific charges against him. This is technically his *arraignment*.

After this comes the *trial*. The defendant has the right to be tried by a jury, or he may choose to be tried by a judge. The basic elements of the trial are the opening statements, the government's or prosecution's case, the defense's case, the judge's charge to the jury (if there is one), and the verdict. If a guilty verdict occurs in a felony case, the judge will often postpone sentencing until a *presentencing investigation* has been completed by a probation officer.[68] The presentence report provides the judge with a verified social history of the defendant (prior record, family and marital history, educational and employment record, etc.) as an aid in determining the appropriate sentence. Normally the judge has a number of *sentencing* alternatives. He may impose a fine, give a suspended sentence (i.e., the defendant does not go to prison but may be sent to prison if there is subsequent misbehavior), place the person on probation with a suspended sentence, impose some treatment (e.g., participation in a drug halfway house program) as a requirement of the suspended sentence, or sentence the defendant to a correctional institution. Once the defendant has been sentenced to a correctional institution, the authority for his release from confinement passes from the hands of the court (with its requirements of due process and regard for the defendant's rights) into the hands of the institution's administration or parole board. The lack of "due process" requirements and other controls upon these—who determine how long an inmate actually remains incarcerated—is a matter of increasing concern to penal reformers.[69]

Most defendants are not tried. For example, of nearly 50,000 defendants before United States District Courts in 1972 (fiscal year), less than 7,500 were tried by a judge or jury. Over 85 percent of those convicted pled guilty.[70] This is a result of the phenomenon of *plea bargaining,* basically a negotiation between the prosecution and the defense for a guilty plea by the defendant to a lesser charge or to a specified sentence. In this process, justice and truth may easily be disregarded.[71]

The American criminal judicial process has not been noted for its speed. The arrest-to-sentencing period for serious offenses runs, in much of the country, from three to six months, and in some places even longer. If the defense attorney seeks continuances of the case (at times as part of his negotiation strategy in plea bargaining) or if an *appeal* of the conviction or sentence is entered, the interval from arrest to final disposition of the case may stretch well beyond a year. Efforts are being made to cut the arrest-to-sentencing interval so that defendants may indeed have speedy trials.[72]

In general, there are several levels of courts within a system of courts: a low court and a high court for normal trial processes (the low court handling misdemeanor cases and the initial processing, e.g., preliminary hearings, of felony cases),[73] a *Juvenile and Domestic Relations* (*JDR*) court, appellate court, supreme court, plus the noncriminal courts. Adult *misdemeanor* cases are normally handled completely within the lower courts (unless a decision is appealed), and the steps in the processing are much simpler than for a felony case (which is normally simply a trial resulting in a verdict and sentence without preliminary hearing, presentence investigation, etc.).

The JDR court (in reference to juvenile offenders) has a different purpose than adult criminal courts. The welfare of the child is of paramount concern, as long as it can be accomplished in the best interests of the state, thus placing emphasis upon prevention, treatment, and rehabilitation, as opposed simply to confinement:

> To assist the courts in carrying out this responsibility, the court is given jurisdiction over the custody, support, control, or disposition of a child whose parents are unable or neglect or refuse to provide proper or necessary support, education, or medical, surgical, or other care necessary for his well being; a child who is without proper parental care, custody or guardianship; or who was abandoned by his parents or whose parents for good cause desire to be relieved of his care and custody or whose custody and support is a subject of controversy; or whose occupation, behavior, environment, condition, association, habits, or practices are injurious to his welfare; or a child who deserts his home or is a fugitive therefrom or who is habitually disobedient or beyond the control of his parents or who is incorrigible; or truant; or who violated any laws; or one whose welfare demands adjudication as to his disposition, control, and custody, or is in need of commitment, being mentally defective or mentally disordered.[74]

Correctional Institutions

Correctional facilities in the United States comprise a plethora of institutions: about 4,000 jails, about 800 juvenile institutions (including halfway houses and group homes), about 600 state correctional institutions (including over 150 community centers), and some 50 federal correctional institutions.[75] These are operated by governmental units at the local (city or county), state, and federal levels. On any given day, about half a million persons are confined in these institutions, but several million inmates will pass through them in the course of a year. Although funding for correctional facilities has improved significantly during the 1970s over previous years, for many institutions (especially jails) funds still tend to be very limited. Historically, expenditures per inmate per day have been lowest for jail inmates, being only about half of those for inmates of state institutions and a fourth as much as for inmates in juvenile and federal institutions.[76] A brief discussion of these institutions follows:

Jails [77]

Most jails are small. Three-fourths of them have 20 or fewer inmates; fewer than 3 percent of the jails have 250 or more inmates. Facilities are extremely limited in most jails, with about two-thirds of the jails serving meals to inmates in their cells and two-fifths of them having no forms of recreation or entertainment. Religious services, the most common program in jails, were conducted in less than 60 percent of the jails in 1972. As late as 1970, forty-seven jails in the country were without toilet facilities! [78]

Juvenile Institutions [79]

The most numerous of juvenile institutions are detention centers, averaging about 40 youngsters in each. Next in number are the training schools, averaging between 150 and 200 juveniles, and then come the ranch, farm, forestry camps, with an average of 50 or so. Shelters, halfway houses, and group homes each normally hold 15 to 20 youngsters. The few reception/diagnostic centers are large, averaging about 150 juveniles. For all practical purposes, the detention centers are juvenile jails (average inmate stay, less than two weeks), and the training schools and ranch, farm, and forestry camps are juvenile prisons or reform schools (average inmate stay, six to eight months). Over 90 percent of juvenile facilities have programs of counseling, education, and recreation. Information on the extent of the religious programs in juvenile institutions is not available at this time.

State Correctional Institutions [80]

Inmates in state correctional institutions are classified in three categories of security: maximum, medium, minimum. About 40 percent of inmates are in maximum security status and a third in medium security status. The rest are minimum security status, especially inmates at community centers (halfway houses), forest camps, about half the road camps, etc. About 60 percent of inmates are in closed prisons (most of these facilities conform to the popular image of a prison). Most prisons have an extensive array of social and rehabilitative (including religious) programs, although these often exist in little more than name.[81] Almost all state correctional institutions have facilities for programs. About half the states have medical or classification centers for offenders.

Federal Correctional Institutions

By far the best financed and best equipped of adult facilities, the federal institutions include nearly a score of halfway houses, a number of traditional prisons (Atlanta, Lewisburg, etc.), and a few institutions described by critics (and jealous inmates elsewhere) as "country clubs."

Comments

In the prison world, there have been significant efforts to separate first offenders from hard-core criminals, and most states have at least one institution for first offenders (especially younger ones). Likewise, there have been intense efforts to get more inmates into community programs through community centers (about 5 percent of state inmates were in such programs in 1974) [82] and increased use of probation, parole, and alternatives to imprisonment. In jails, there have been efforts to separate misdemeanor from felony prisoners, and the untried from the convicted.

Probation and Parole

Normally, a person sentenced to prison may be released by parole before serving the full length of time to which he was sentenced.[83] Usually an inmate becomes eligible for parole after serving a fourth to a third of his sentence, depending upon the laws of the state in which he was sentenced. The authority to release prisoners on parole is vested in a parole board. In the majority of states, the governor appoints the members of the parole board. Half of the states have no requirements for parole board membership.[84] Parole is a conditional release from incarceration on the condition that the individual agree to abide by a specific set of conditions of good behavior and that he submit to the supervision of a parole officer. Probation is essentially identical to parole except that the individual is released by the court from *potential* incarceration before entering the penal system, in contrast to a parole board's releasing the offender from incarceration already in effect.

The probation/parole officer (usually an individual serves as both for adult offenders) has two functions: First, he serves as the *investigative* arm of the authority (court or parole board) considering the release of an individual to the community. For the court, this investigative function is normally employed to produce presentence reports. For the parole board, a similar report is prepared. It may also include confirmation and assessment of the inmate's prospective housing and employment situation should he be released. Second, the probation/parole officer serves as the *supervisory* arm of the releasing authorities in the control and treatment of conditional releasees within the community and within the limits of the release agreement.[85] The amount of attention that probation/parole officers give the offenders under their supervision varies with the caseload of the officers. Within recent years, court decisions have reduced the potential for arbitrary abuse of power by probation/parole officers by requiring more "due process" in probation/parole revocation. There are numerous volunteer programs providing assistance for probation/parole officers.[86]

Community Programs

Community programs overlap what has already been presented to some degree, but are treated here as a separate entity because of the great emphasis that has been placed upon them in current correctional planning.[87] The current scope of community programs includes work- or study-release and weekend-sentence programs,[88] halfway-house programs (both for those in danger of being placed into the jail/prison system and for those in the process of coming out of the correctional system),[89] diversion of some offenders to other institutions (e.g., alcoholic and mental patients, many of whom in the past spent long periods in jails and prisons) and other methods of pretrial intervention,[90] and increasing use of probation and alternatives to jail and imprisonment.[91] Community-based institutions and most community programs tend to be relatively small. The state community correctional centers average less than sixty residents each.[92] About 1,200 (or two-thirds) of the jails with work-release or weekend-sentence programs have twenty or fewer inmates in such programs.[93]

Inmate Treatment

During the past decade, court decisions about inmate rights have significantly affected the treatment of inmates by the correctional institution.[94] In general, court decisions arising from such litigation have increased the scope of inmate contact with the outside world (mail, lawyers, media) and have decreased arbitrary callous treatment of inmates by correctional staff (i.e., more "due process" has come into prison and jail discipline). During the past decade, the scope and variety of rehabilitation and social programs within correctional institutions have expanded immensely.[95] During this period also, an increasing emphasis was placed upon behavior modification as one of the general approaches to inmate treatment.

During the mid 1970s, two aspects of inmate treatment merit comment. A long-neglected need is being met by a major emphasis upon literacy training.[96] The other development is a growing trend to make inmate participation in rehabilitation completely voluntary by taking away some of the programs' "advantages" (e.g., impressing the parole board or classification committee). This trend has resulted from the careful analysis of various correctional programs, which revealed that recidivism was unaffected by treatment programs.[97] More emphasis has been placed upon inmates helping themselves and helping other inmates.[98] This emphasis is likely to continue.

Theories and Clichés

Most modern criminologists have given up on finding a simple cause for crime. No longer do the theories of phrenologist Franz Joseph Gall or of Johann Lavater, proponent of physiognomy, allow detection of criminals by the shapes of their heads or by their appearance. Likewise, most today reject Lombroso's ideas about "born criminals." Today it is widely thought that there is no single cause of crime. A number of factors are thought to enter the picture: [99] intelligence, poverty, group conflict (e.g., racial, social class), personality disorder, etc. Many feel that criminal behavior is a learned characteristic [100] which can be unlearned (applying the principles of behavioral modification). The perspective that crime arises from man's sinfulness has largely been overlooked. Whatever influence other factors may have upon causing crime, the root cause is man's sinful nature and his cultivation of sinful habits as a lifestyle. The Church needs to remind the criminologist of this truth.

The initiation of scientific investigation of the causes of crime is usually attributed to an Italian, the Marchese de Beccaria, in the late 1700s. His classical theory of crime as a *legal* act sought deterrence by fitting appropriate punishment to the crime. In American courts today, the punishment is made to fit the crime by the punitive bounds which legal codes place upon various crimes, but a more important principle in its application seems to be: let the punishment fit *the criminal.* Thus white-collar crimes are punished relatively lightly compared to "street crimes." An embezzler who steals $100,000 is very likely to be sentenced to a shorter prison term than a burglar who steals $5,000's worth of jewelry. In contrast to the biblical perspective "to whom much is given shall much be required" (*see* Luke 12:47,48), the American courts seem to follow a pattern of requiring little (i.e., lighter sentences) of those to whom much has been given (i.e., from a well-to-do family with good education and fine employment prospects). One cannot help but feel that this practice violates a basic biblical principle that a judge should not be a respecter of the status of a defendant (*see* Leviticus 19:15, Deuteronomy 1:17).

It is said that crime does not pay. That seems true for the offenders who are caught and convicted,[101] but apparently is not true for the hordes who perpetrate the majority of crimes (estimated at eight out of nine for reported crimes and *all* for unreported crimes!) for which the culprits are not apprehended and convicted.[102]

The American legal system is based upon the theory that one is innocent until proved guilty. As a practical matter, however, when an innocent person is confined in jail awaiting trial, it affects him as if he were guilty: the same separation from family and friends, the same confinement and loss of employment as a guilty person would experience.

Arbitrary exercise of discretion by judges in sentencing and by parole boards in their decisions is among the prime problems of the present criminal justice system, along with the *criminal delay* in processing criminal cases. The myth that prisons are for rehabilitation is a cruel jest on both public and offenders. Prison punishes and it keeps offenders out of society for a while. Prisons are much more effective as schools for crime than as reformatories.[103] Unfortunately, most American criminologists tend to neglect the proper role of punishment in both penology and justice.[104]

At present, the legal codes of the federal and state systems are a hodgepodge of antiquated confusion infused with modern complexity. A thorough revision of the law is needed—at least development of a uniform codification of existing laws, if not a bringing into some semblance of conformity the federal and state laws as they touch serious criminal activities—and an updating of the law to enable it to deal effectively with organized crime, white-collar crime, and the abuse of authority by officials, as well as with street crime.

Concluding Comment

This chapter has meandered through the criminal justice system, touching on many points. Two final observations are in order: first, our nation stands, in the minds of many, at a critical junction. The courts have been called upon, it seems, to solve all our social ills and criminal problems—and (in many cases) personal problems. By asking too much of the law, Judge Forer suggests, we have sounded the death knell for the law.[105] Second, law and its application need a solid foundation. The Word of God, its instruction about and its insight into man and society, can provide that solid foundation. But the Church must educate a society that is biblically illiterate—*even its educated leaders*—before that foundation can again undergird the law of our land and its application. The Church should also begin to provide a workable, biblically based approach to penolgy and the entire field of criminology. For such an approach to develop, this subject must become a matter of serious, intensive consideration in our seminaries and among our theologians.

3

Christian Ministry Within the Criminal Justice System

The criminal justice system is vast and complex. The Christian ministry within it is extensive and varied. This chapter describes many of the different kinds of ministry that exist at present within the criminal justice system. The chapter closes with a brief review of the present laws about religion behind bars.

Church-State Relationships

The Church-state relationship has three possible forms.[106] First, the state may dominate the Church and use the Church. Many inmates have felt such was the situation in their prison: the chaplain was the warden's lackey. Likewise, during the medieval period the Church was often used by the political forces of the state to bring charges against opponents which would result in their punishment. This condition of state dominance is also typical of the situation where the Church has little or no social and political status—as in the first two centuries of Church history and as in Red China today. In these cases, Christian ministry is done surreptitiously or by prisoners who themselves are Christian.

The second possible Church-state relationship is that in which the Church dominates the state and uses it to accomplish its ends, as it did in the medieval period.[107] This use of the state by the Church also manifested itself in the enforced religion that characterized the penitentiaries founded under Quaker leadership in

Pennsylvania at the end of the eighteenth century and in the experiment at the prison in Millbank, England, from 1816 to 1843, during which religion was forced upon the inmates and the chaplain for a while was also even the governor (warden) of the prison.[108]

The third possible form of Church-state relationship is a cooperative partnership (though often an uneasy alliance) between "equal" parties whose areas of authority are separate. This has been the predominate relationship in this country, although there has often been mistrust, harassment, and opposition from both sides. For example, Maud Booth had to appeal to President Theodore Roosevelt at the turn of the century for relief from both police harassment and opposition from the American Prison Association in reference to the Hope Halls established by the newly formed Volunteers of America as residences for those released from prison.[109]

Historical Glimpses

During the first few centuries of Christianity and at many times since then, the ministry to those in prison was mainly exercised by Christians who were themselves prisoners, as illustrated by Paul's imprisonments reported in Acts 16 and Philippians 1.

Apparently some Christians during this period ministered to the incarcerated, at least to those who were their friends. For example, the church at Philippi sent Epaphroditus to minister to the imprisoned Paul (Philippians 2:25–30), and Paul commends Onesiphorus' ministry to him (2 Timothy 1:16–18). The *Martyrdom of Ignatius* describes how several Christian friends stayed with Ignatius during his confinement prior to his death. Eusebius reports numerous letters as coming from imprisoned Christians of the second century, even letters from those on the verge of martyrdom, which shows the continuing contact of Christians with the incarcerated.[110] No doubt this form of ministry to and by imprisoned Christians continued,[111] not just during the first few centuries of the Church but during every period and place where the Church has been persecuted—whether by the state or by the "Church" (Waldensians, Lollards, Christians in Red China, etc.).

As the medieval Church became involved heavily in politics, it instituted ecclesiastical prisons as well as ecclesiastical courts. While it is a shame that the Church became a jailer (the last such prison was constructed in Paris in the sixteenth century[112]), it should be remembered that it was the Church prisons, with their individual cells for prisoners, that John Howard used as the model for prisons as the modern era of penology began.

Two groups merit mention for their enduring interest in offenders: the Salvation Army and an offspring from it, the Volunteers of America. Both have faithfully sent their officers into jails and prisons to preach the Gospel and to help the inmates in every possible way. Both have worked with inmate families and releasees from the last century to the present. *After Prison—What?* (Revell, 1903) by Maud Booth (a cofounder of the Volunteers of America) is a poignant apologetic for the Hope Halls (early halfway houses) and ministry of the Volunteer Prison League, both under the Volunteers of America. The scope of ministry of the two groups ranges from homes for unwed mothers and predelinquency programs to Bible classes in prisons, job assistance for ex-cons, and residential homes for alcoholics.

During the past quarter-century, Church interest in jail and prison ministry has increased—at least the number of religious organizations ministering to offenders has grown substantially. A few religious and church organizations in addition to the Salvation Army and Volunteers of America have been ministering to prisoners longer than twenty-five years, but most of the organizations listed in Appendix D have begun since 1950.

Varieties of Christian Ministry

The major emphasis of this book is ministry to inmates in jails and prisons. This section briefly takes a broader look at Christian endeavors and considers such ministry anyplace within the criminal justice system. These endeavors include: programs that are related to law enforcement, community programs, and programs within correctional institutions.

Law Enforcement–Related Programs

A number of clergymen (most on a very limited part-time basis) serve as police chaplains. The vast majority of these serve as little more than religious persons at official police functions. Some spend a great deal of time with the police officers, as illustrated in Robert Asmuth's *Preacher With a Billy Club* (Logos International, 1971), the story of a Florida minister who worked as a volunteer chaplain with police for fifteen years. The few full-time police chaplains in the country minister mainly in counseling and providing spiritual guidance for police department personnel. Such ministry is much needed. Police work is hard on the families of the officers, and few officers are active church members. A regular feature in *Law and Order*, a magazine for policemen, is the "Chaplain's Corner." It is usually a brief devotional message.

A second form of Christian involvement in law enforcement has been participation by religious groups in the various volunteer efforts at crime prevention and detection.[113] Such programs normally involve citizens in organized surveillance of their own community, with communication to the police of any suspicious or illegal activity. In some cases volunteers even ride patrol with police officers, but only as observers. The opportunities for the Christian to witness by example and testimony to police personnel and others through such programs are many.

In a number of communities, fellowships for Christians in the criminal justice field, especially for those in law enforcement, have been established. These go under a variety of names: Christian Law Enforcement Officers Fellowship, Law and Grace Fellowship, etc. Usually they consist of a breakfast or dinner every month or two, with a speaker (usually a Christian in law enforcement) who shares his testimony. Their purpose is to encourage Christians in this line of work to live as Christians should and to be bold in witnessing. The meetings also serve as occasions for

Christian officers to bring unsaved coworkers to hear how Christ can change lives.

Community Programs

In recent years a great deal of attention has been given to dealing with predelinquent youth in order to keep them from becoming offenders. The activities have included boys' clubs and similar organizations, summer camps, and special facilities such as Christian coffee houses to provide youth an alternative to activities with high potential for trouble (like loitering on the street). Church groups as well as civic groups and the criminal justice system have had a part in all these. A number of churches have initiated efforts to provide temporary homes for youngsters before the juvenile court (a few have established organized group homes, but most have used the homes of individual church members) so that the court does not have to place the child in a jail or juvenile detention home while it decides the disposition of the case.

Since the early 1960s a number of courts have turned to volunteers to help those on probation.[114] Many such volunteers are drawn from the churches. Their primary function is to be an encouraging friend and to provide an example of proper behavior for those on probation. These volunteers also free the probation officer to give more attention to his problem cases. In a few jurisdictions across the country, there have been efforts to provide a coordinated religious program for all "clients" of the criminal justice system: court, jail, etc.[115]

Since about 1960 there has been increasing emphasis on the use of halfway houses. The Church has played a major role in these for a long time—from the Isaac T. Hopper Home, established by the Quakers in New York City in the last century for released prisoners and still in operation, to the multitude of Christian-oriented halfway houses set up for drug addicts (e.g., Teen Challenge Centers) and homes for alcoholics. As indicated, many of the Christian halfway houses cater to those with a single special problem (drug addicts, alcoholics, ex-offenders, unwed mothers, delinquent girls or boys, etc.), but some have a completely open door to anyone who wants help and is willing to live by the rules of the house (e.g., New Life Center in Des Moines). In some cases these halfway houses are more of a commune, but they provide a transitional phase designed to help one go from a bad lifestyle to a good one.

A fairly new form of ministry is being provided in some areas for inmates of work-release centers. Patterned after "the crisis-oriented chaplain-on-call program implemented by Holiday Inns across America in recent years," the Florida Department of Corrections initiated a Chaplain-on-Call Program for its work-release centers in 1975.[116] In this program, the chaplain is a local clergyman who volunteers to make himself available to the staff and residents of the work-release center whenever needed. This program formalizes what is being done more casually and informally in a number of other places.

Another aspect of Christian ministry in the community that is related to the criminal justice system is the calling of the Church's attention to its responsibility in this area. This is being done within separate congregations by individuals sharing their burden for jail/prison ministry and their experiences in it. On a broader scale, it is being done through the newsletters, magazines, and pamphlets of those organizations involved in ministry to offenders and by articles in denominational journals.

The growing number of books and general magazine articles about inmate converts and ministry behind bars is also helping to focus the Church's attention on the need. Perhaps no one has done more in this connection than the Reverend Ray Hoekstra, better known as Chaplain Ray, of the International Prison Ministry, whose daily radio broadcasts on more than a hundred radio stations have created so much interest in prisons among Christians.

Programs Within Correctional Institutions

First and foremost among the programs inside jails and prisons are the religious services: worship, preaching, Bible classes, prayer meetings, showings of Christian films, distribution of Christian literature and tapes, witnessing to inmates at the cellblocks and tiers, musical programs, and religious dramas. These may be presented on an irregular or a regular basis. They may be part of a total religious program for the institution, coordinated by the chaplain, or the ministry may result simply from a call to the sheriff or warden for permission to hold the service.

Some of the religious activities within the institution will be indigenous—that is, inmate led. In addition to personal witnessing and *informal* Bible classes/discussions conducted by the inmates, there has been an increasing interest in *formal* Bible classes and services that are led by the inmates themselves.

In addition to these traditional religious activities, there are occasional programs that are very unusual. One example has been the few instances of the Cursillo program in penal settings. Basically these are marathon (three-day) group encounters that are intended to provide a short course in Christian behavior (or human interaction).[117] The Cursillo movement is Roman Catholic oriented.

Some institutions allow inmates to be released to attend or participate in special programs in the community—e.g., to give a testimony in a church. Normally the releasee must be accompanied by a responsible citizen and occasionally by a correctional officer as well.

Another example of an unusual program is the Discipleship Training conducted by the Good News Mission in the Chesapeake City Jail, Virginia. In this, a group of Christian inmates, all volunteers selected for their leadership potential, are housed together for two weeks of intensive training (daily classes morning, afternoon, and evening) in Christian living and service. Then these inmates are returned to the general inmate population to provide inmate leadership in spiritual areas. The program is conducted for six to ten inmates every two months. Graduates from the program are not only more effective witnesses for Christ, but a number of them have also become teachers of formal Bible classes within the institution.[118]

Occasionally prison chaplains have to conduct funerals for inmates who die while in prison. At times the jail or prison chaplain is the only minister well known by members of the institution staff and may be called upon to conduct a funeral for a staff member or for someone in a staff member's family.

A second area of Christian ministry within the institution is counseling. In addition to the formal pastoral counseling of inmates by chaplains and ministers, there are many counseling programs that use lay Christians. A major part of the counselors in the one-on-one volunteer counseling programs (Volunteers in Corrections, Offender Aid and Restoration, man-to-man and woman-to-woman phases of Job Therapy, etc.) have come from the churches. In many of these programs, the counselor is asked to commit himself to a weekly counseling session of an hour or so with an inmate and to continue such sessions for some months after the inmate is released and returns to the community. There are also counseling programs designed to disciple Christian inmates, such as the Good News Mission's discipleship counseling program, in which volunteers meet weekly with an inmate to take him through a program of discipleship training that involves tutoring him in Christian doctrine (using prepared materials), sharing Bible study with him, and providing supportive counseling.

Within many institutions, there are group counseling sessions. Some are led by institution treatment staff or chaplains, others by professionals (clergy and others) who volunteer their services. Some are group-sharing sessions, such as the Yokefellow groups.

In addition to conducting religious services and counseling, Christians minister in jails and prisons in a wide variety of social programs. Some Christian groups provide physical amenities (writing paper, pencils, deodorant, etc.) for inmates when these are not provided by or available from the institution. Others have donated and maintained libraries for prisoners. Books are still much needed, especially in jails. Other Christians work as volunteers in jail/prison educational and vocational programs, especially as literacy teachers. Some Christians are involved in casual, loosely organized education and literacy programs, others in programs more structured.[119] A number of church groups are teaching domestic skills (e.g., sewing for women inmates) and participating in recreational activities (e.g., church basketball team playing the inmate team at the institution).

Some religious groups help inmates earn money by arranging for the exhibition and sale of arts and craft objects made by inmates.

Organization of Religious Programs

In most state and federal prisons and in some jails and juvenile institutions, there will be a chaplain employed by the institution. Normally the chaplain will be in charge of the religious program of the institution and may use Christian individuals, church groups, and religious organizations (e.g., the Gideons or the Salvation Army) as volunteers in the religious programs—some occasionally, others on a regular basis. Some prisons also use "contract" religious workers. These are usually clergy paid for regular religious ministry within the institution.

In other jails, prisons, and juvenile institutions, the chaplain will be provided by a church or religious organization—that is to say, his salary is paid by such, but he will perform the same role as a chaplain paid by the institution itself. Many church and religious organizations provide chaplaincy services for a single jurisdiction; a few provide chaplains (i.e., those in charge of the religious programs within the institution) for a number of jurisdictions and institutions.

Those ministering in the jails and prisons come in many varieties. There are some who do so as individual Christians; others work as a part of the program of the institution's chaplain. There are some who go as representatives of their churches. There are many organizations that provide ministry to prisoners but not chaplaincy services. Some provide ministry in a single institution. Other organizations minister in many, usually holding evangelistic services or crusades or performing a wide variety of other services.

A multitude of organizations provide support for ministry in jails and prisons in terms of Bibles, Scripture portions, tracts, Bible correspondence courses, tapes, films, and other materials. These are often provided free or at very low cost.

Christian ministries in jails and prisons are limited only by the Church's imagination and its willingness to minister.

Religion Behind Bars and the Law

The past fifteen years have seen an avalanche of judicial interest in the rights of prisoners, including rights related to religion behind bars.[120] Much of the religious litigation has been related to the Black Muslim faith.[121] Prior to 1960 the court had followed a hands-off policy with regard to jail and prison operations. The avalanche of judicial interest culminated in the early 1970s. "The October 1973 term of the Supreme Court of the United States will probably have more impact on the rights of confined persons than any other previous term. . . . This massive intrusion into the correctional process seemingly sounds the death knell for the hands-off doctrine." [122] Thus the law about religion behind bars is much clearer now than it had been.[123] This section summarizes some of the more significant aspects of court rulings about religion behind bars.

The First Amendment to the Constitution of the United States provides that "Congress shall make no law respecting an establishment of religion, or prohibiting the free exercise thereof." In some court cases a distinction has been drawn between the right to believe in a religion (no limitations can be properly placed upon such) and the right to practice the tenets of that religion (limitations can be placed upon such right when a "compelling state interest" can be demonstrated).

At present, the institution must allow all inmates who desire to do so to attend services and may restrict attendance at services, or stop them, only where there is a clear danger of disturbances. In general, mandatory attendance at religious activities is improper. The institution is not required to provide (i.e, pay) chaplains or clergy to minister inside the institution—but if it does, it must not discriminate and foster one religious group over another (e.g., Muslim ministers must be compensated in the same way as Catholic, Jewish, and Protestant clergy).[124] This naturally raises the question of what a "religion" is, an issue that faced the courts in litigation from convicted thief Harry W. Theriault, founder of the "Church of the New Song," the inmate religion of Eclatarianity. Although the courts are reluctant to define religion, they use three basic tests to determine if a movement is a "religion": (1) the history and age of the group, (2) its possession of characteristics associated with traditional "recognized" religion, and (3) the sincerity of its adherents. Application of this kind of test has caused the Metropolitan Community Church (homosexually oriented) to be formally recognized by a California court and given the same access to the California prisons as other denominations.[125]

Ministers do not have an absolute right to enter correctional institutions to minister to the inmates. Regular chaplain reports on inmate religious activities to parole boards are frowned upon because they tend to coerce inmates into religious participation.

Institutions are not required to provide special diets for inmates on religious grounds, if the institution menu provides adequate nourishment by simply omitting the offending item (e.g., pork to Jews and Muslims). Wearing of religious apparel/jewelry and beards/hairstyles must yield to institution clothing and grooming regulations as long as such regulations are applied equally to all religious groups and have some relation to institution discipline and well-being.

In general, institutions will not interfere with religious mail unless (1) it comes in such volume to an inmate that it cannot be stored properly, (2) it goes to or comes from another inmate (inmate ministers of the Church of the New Song were not allowed to mail their "sermons" to others), or (3) it is clearly obscene (as in materials related to the sexual activities of some Satan-worship cults) or possesses clear agitation potential (as has been alleged of some Black Muslim literature).

4

Development of the Correctional Chaplaincy

Good leadership is essential for effective ministry. The rapid expansion of Christianity throughout the Roman Empire in the first century was under the leadership of God's men with vision for sharing the Gospel: Peter, Paul, Barnabas, Silas, and many others. Likewise, a major factor in effective ministry to prisoners will be the chaplains whom God raises up as leaders in this ministry within jails and prisons. This chapter provides background essential for a proper perspective on the correctional chaplaincy, namely historical highlights of the chaplaincy and a description of the present varieties within the correctional chaplaincy.

The Title *Chaplain*

The word *chaplain* is derived from the Latin *cappellan(us)*, a term used to describe the clergy who were assigned to the building where St. Martin's cloak (*cappa*) was preserved. The building came to be known as *cappella* from which the word *chapel* is derived. From the time of the Reformation forth, *chaplain* has been used for a clergyman associated with a chapel or involved in a specialized ministry (military, hospital, prison, etc.).

It is fitting that the term *chaplain* is derived from the tradition about St. Martin, bishop of Tours (316–397). One day, Martin met a beggar and, out of compassion, took his own cloak, cut it in two, and gave half to the beggar, keeping the other half for himself. Later in a vision, Martin saw Christ wearing the half of his cloak which had been given to the beggar. Consequently, the remaining half of the cloak became a relic.

St. Martin is a good example for the modern chaplain to follow. Martin was a tireless worker for Christ, winning many non-Christians to the faith. He believed that no one was so depraved as to be beyond the scope of God's ability to pardon. One of Martin's contemporaries wrote of him that "he judged none and condemned none and never returned evil for evil. . . . Nothing was in his mouth except Christ, nothing in his heart but piety, peace, and pity." [126]

Historical Highlights

The earliest formally organized ministry to prisoners began in 1488 when the Order of Misericordin ("Beheading of St. John") was formed to have its members "assist and console criminals condemned to death, accompany them to the gallows, and provide religious services and Christian burial." [127]

It is important to remember that imprisonment was not used extensively as punishment for serious criminal behavior until the end of the eighteenth century. Prior to that time, punishment consisted of fines, flogging, mutilation, execution, and banishment.[128] Consequently, the opportunities for extensive ministry to prisoners did not exist other than to succor them about the time of their judgment.

The need for such a ministry to prisoners was recognized by the English reformers. In a 1549 sermon before young King Edward, Hugh Latimer appealed that "such men as shall be put to death may have learned men to give them instruction and exhortation." [129] Latimer knew the need for such ministry, not only from his own visits to prisoners [130] but also from his own imprisonment and from the martyrdom of his friends during the reign of Queen Mary, especially Thomas Bilney in 1531. Latimer knew the urgency with which the Gospel should be presented to prisoners.

The initiative of other leaders in the English Reformation, especially Thomas Lever and Bishop Ridley, caused the "first house of correction" (i.e., a workhouse for misdemeanors as an alternative to whipping) to be established in 1552 at Bridewell; twenty-five years later similar establishments were ordered for each county in England.[131]

During the seventeenth and eighteenth centuries, a number of evangelical preachers became "chaplains" in a somewhat unusual way. Both in America and in England, some were imprisoned for religious reasons and had a major ministry to their fellow prisoners and others. Among the most notable of these were John Bunyan and George Fox.

> The ministrations of George Fox in the various prisons in which he was held form a prelude to the subsequent work of the prison chaplain. He discussed religion with clergymen who were brought to his dungeon at Carlisle. He addressed a crowd from the jail window at Lancaster. He visited the Friends in Reading Jail, declaring unto them the word of life and encouraging them in the truth. But his greatest joy was to witness to the debtors and felons amongst whom he was compelled to live.[132]

Fox had the privilege of seeing the jailer at Carlisle converted, a man who had beaten Fox with a cudgel. It was Fox's love, joy, and grace in spite of such treatment, and his singing even during the flogging, that opened the jailer to Christ.[133]

The roots of the modern correctional chaplaincy lie in the origin of Methodism. Around 1730, William Morgan and John and Charles Wesley, along with others from "The Holy Club" of Oxford, obtained permission to visit the condemned felons housed in Oxford Castle. Soon a plan of regular services was arranged. "It was this fondness for system which earned for the members of the Holy Club the name 'Methodists.' "[134] Later similar ministries were established under Methodist leadership in Newgate and other prisons.

The nature of this ministry is illustrated by the work of Silas Told in Newgate, which began about 1744 and lasted twenty-five years. Told had been converted four years earlier at the age of twenty-nine. "He knew enough of the ways of sin to be able to understand the feelings of criminals, but he knew something else: he knew that sin could be conquered" because he "had found a Gospel which could transform depraved men."[135] In Told's ministry:

> He preached the Gospel in the jail; he rode in the cart to Tyburn [the place of execution], singing hymns with the prisoners; he prayed at the gallows; he arranged for funerals, he cared for widows and fatherless children.[136] As the years went by, . . . even sheriffs as well as turnkeys and hangmen could be seen in tears as they listened to his exhortations and his prayers.[137]

The early jail ministry was not restricted to men. Often prisoners of both sexes were confined in the same quarters. Women played an important role in the ministry from the beginning. One of the earliest was Sarah Peters who ministered at Newgate also. John Wesley described her as "a lover of souls."[138] She died of jail fever (as typhus was then called). Ten days before her death she had led six men to a saving knowledge of Jesus Christ the day before their execution, probably contracting at that time the disease which brought her death. A century later, Elizabeth Fry, a notable member of the Society of Friends, became famous for her "systematic Bible readings in Newgate prison."[139] "Unquestionably the publicity given to Mrs. Fry's readings did much to focus attention on religious ministrations in penal establishments."[140]

The ministry described above was done voluntarily and unofficially, without financial support from the state or the established church. In the eighteenth century, jails were run for private profit, with the jailer allowed to collect fees from the prisoners for accommodations such as room, bed, blanket, and services such as food and alcohol—even a prostitute for a night "if the prisoner paid for her bed and tipped him [the jailer] a shilling."[141] Chaplain salaries were paid from such jailer's fees, and the chaplains were usually part-time because jailers objected to the decrease of their profits.[142]

From the beginning, there were conflicts between clergy of

the established church who were employed for the jails and those ministering to prisoners voluntarily. The character of the official chaplains was one source of the conflict. At that time, "any needy priest of damaged character was thought good enough to minister among rogues." [143] One, Dr. Forde, was called before a Parliamentary Committee to tell of his work in Newgate prison.

> His tale was merely a recital of the things he was not expected to do. He was not called upon to know anything about the moral condition of the establishment. It was not his business to visit the prisoners in private. He had no interest in the young convicts, though there were many under fourteen years of age. He had no responsibility for the sick until he was called upon to bury them. He then had to complain that an amateur chaplain, probably Silas Told, was frequenting the prison and cramming the prisoners with prayers and preaching.[144]

Such ministerial conflict can go to extremes. "It is on record that in 1825 the Anglican chaplain in Monmouth jail refused to allow a Nonconformist minister who could speak Welsh to attend a condemned prisoner who knew no other language." [145] Such conflict continues today, although not in such extreme manifestations. Cassler and Kandle contend "every prison chaplain has felt indignation at fellow ministers who storm the institution so eager to save souls they disregard his religious programs." [146] Sometimes the conflict arises from the chaplain's insecurity because he is doing an inferior job (as in Dr. Forde's case above), sometimes the conflict arises from uncouth behavior by the minister(s) from the outside. But most often the conflicts arise because there are significant and severe differences theologically and ideologically.

Another area of conflict that has been with the correctional chaplaincy from the beginning is the tension between the prison/jail administration and the chaplain. John Howard, who more than any other person laid the groundwork for modern penology, was concerned about this problem. It was his "avowed aim" to make "religious observance an integral part of prison life." [147] He wrote that the jailer should not hinder any prisoner from attending divine services.[148]

The nineteenth century saw substantial Church involvement in penology. The penitentiary approach instituted under Quaker leadership in Pennsylvania at the end of the eighteenth century became popular as the idea spread of using confinement, instead of corporal punishment, as a penalty for criminal behavior. In the penitentiary, a prisoner was confined in a single cell with a Bible and isolated from all others except clergy and others who might edify him so that he could do "penance." Unfortunately, many inmates went insane from the enforced isolation and lack of contact with others.

Another effort at what one might call "forced religion" began in 1816 in the prison at Millbank, England. The prison had been designed to keep religion in the center of its operations and to have the chaplain's ministry at the heart of prison life. In fact, for a time, the chaplain was also the governor (warden) of the prison. Yet by 1843 Millbank had been turned back into an ordinary prison. "The experiment could hardly be pronounced a success. . . . The lesson of Millbank was that unless a man voluntarily opened his heart to the love and power of God, not all the coercion of a penitentiary could make him religious." [149]

On the positive side, The Prison Discipline Society was founded in 1824 at Boston's Park Street Church and exercised a positive influence over prisoner treatment for many years. Likewise, during this period, chaplains and the Church began to develop the special programs that would mature into schools and other worthwhile activities within jails and prisons.

It was during this same period, the middle of the nineteenth century, that the full-time prison chaplain's role became better defined. "The man who was responsible more than anyone else for defining the chaplain's position in a prison was the Rev. John Clay. . . . It would almost be true to call him the patron saint of prison chaplains." [150] Chaplain Clay made the religious services attractive and conditions as much like worship in ordinary churches as possible, not following the contemporary pattern of isolating prisoners from communication with one another. He never preached down at the inmates, but had the habit of addressing them as "fellow sinners." He refused to make chapel attendance a part of the prison system and often had conflicts with prison administrators over needed reforms. His annual reports helped bring many needed improvements in prison discipline and operations. He tried to be a true friend to the prisoners, assisting in contact with their families, feeling that his preaching would do little unless the prisoners accepted him as their friend. He was devoted to the ministry to prisoners and put aside all other ambition. Always he maintained his belief in the power of the Gospel to reform criminals.[151]

Some nineteenth-century prison chaplains would be severely troubled by conditions in modern prisons. In his 1844 report to the inspectors of the Mount Pleasant State (New York) Prison, Chaplain John Luckey wrote, "What good could the chaplain do to these men, unrestrained by the discipline of the 'silent system?' "[152] He repeated this theme twelve years later in his report from Sing Sing. "The chaplains' labours are comparatively *useless, unaided* by a firm, vigilant and uniform discipline."[153]

Chaplaincy Developments in the Twentieth Century

This century has witnessed a number of changes within the correctional chaplaincy as this ministry has evolved. Within prisons and juvenile institutions, the chaplain's role has diminished from that of one responsible for all programs, whether religious, educational, recreational, or something else, to that of one whose almost exclusive concern is the religious ministry. This has been caused simply by the advent of a multitude of secular professional workers into the institutions: teachers, psychologists and psychiatrists, social workers, and others. These specialists have taken over almost all the nonreligious responsibilities that once characterized the chaplain's job. While this has the great benefit of freeing the chaplain to devote himself more to his primary duties, it has led to a long-lasting debate about the justification of a chaplain's position (at least on a state payroll) from his religious ministry alone.[154] Such evolution of the chaplain's role has not yet occurred within jails, because jails have not yet experienced the influx of the other professional workers. The entry of large numbers of social workers, etc., into jails is beginning, however, and will increase as more emphasis is placed upon community institutions and as more funds become available for them. At present, in most jails, the majority of the social programs, as well as the religious program, are under a chaplain's direction, just as they were in prisons a few generations ago.

Such a change in role should not threaten any chaplain whose ministry is producing changed lives through the regenerating power of God's Spirit in those inmates who come to know Jesus as their Savior and Lord. If such changes are not occurring through the chaplain's ministry, there is no way to justify his role as a religious worker. In fact, the evangelical chaplain should rejoice in such changes because it means that he can devote more time to his spiritual ministry and at the same time know that the social needs of the inmates (education, recreation, etc.) are being met.[155] A chaplain whose orientation is primarily that of the "social gospel" may, however, feel threatened, because in a real sense he has become extraneous.

In some cases, there is hostility toward chaplains from some of the other professional workers within correctional facilities. One prison chaplain reported, "There was considerable effort on the part of the social service personnel to discourage men from attending services." Such problems may be caused by adverse reaction of one who feels another is meddling in his affairs, as can frequently occur, because of the overlap of pastoral concern and the social sciences, or because of the growing hostility to religion of a society whose presuppositions are increasingly secular. At present most chaplains find little opposition to the religious programs from other professional workers in their institutions. However, chaplains may find the competition for inmate time and interest from the programs of these other workers to be very severe.[156]

A second way in which the chaplain's role has evolved in this century has been the shifting in the main thrust of his ministry. Early in the century, most chaplains gave primary emphasis to the preaching and teaching of God's Word in the religious aspects of their ministry. Then, in the middle of the century, the main emphasis in the ministries of many chaplains shifted to counseling. CPE began to be required in a high percentage of government-supported chaplaincy positions, and this provided additional emphasis to the counseling ministry of chaplains.[157] More recently, the emphasis for chaplains in many institutions has shifted toward coordination of volunteers performing religious ministry within the institution. For example, in a paper at the 1975 Congress of Correction, federal prison chaplain Richard Summer reported that eighteen years before, when he began in the chaplaincy, half his time was spent in interviewing new inmates, attendance at staff meetings, and writing reports. Now he spends but little time in these. At least half his time now goes to recruiting, training, and supporting volunteers and contract personnel (i.e., clergy paid to come to the institution to minister) for the religious ministry within his institution.[158]

Such a shift in emphasis also brings its problems. It means, in the words of Chaplain Summer, "The role of the chaplain now includes that of a broker of program options for all faith groups." [159] It should be emphasized that "all faith groups" includes not just the many varieties of Protestants, Catholics, and Jews, but also a host of Islamic groups, Eastern religions and a few "faiths" almost peculiar to the prison world, such as The Church of the New Song.

The movement of the chaplain into the role of being primarily a religious program coordinator is driven by two main forces. The first is the surge of interest in and emphasis upon the use of volunteers in all aspects of the criminal justice system. This surge began in the 1960s and has blossomed in the 1970s. The second comes with the great emphasis upon inmate rights that has gained judicial and correctional attention in the past decade. Inmates have the right to the religion of their choice (including no religion). Furthermore, the state cannot support or promote one religious persuasion over another. Thus, logically, the chaplain (as a state employee in many cases) runs the risk of putting the state in the position of promoting a religion if he does not promote *all* religious programs equally, that is, become a "broker" for all faith groups.

It seems likely that there will be a growing dichotomy between government-supported chaplains and those supported by churches and privately, mainly because government chaplains will be forced by future court decisions to move more and more into the role of religious program coordinator.[160] The church or privately supported chaplain will maintain the freedom to continue to minister in the tradition illustrated earlier by Silas Told.

The third development of the chaplaincy within this century has been in the area of standards for chaplains. Along with the glory of much faithful, fruitful ministry for Christ, the history of the correctional chaplaincy contains many blemishes. Dr. Forde of Newgate has already been mentioned. The chaplain who followed him, Dr. Cotton, showed no more concern for inmates than had Dr. Forde. In fact, the prison inspectors gave Dr. Cotton a "severe reprimand" in 1836. On the Sundays before executions, the condemned men had to sit in a center pew in full view of all present and with a coffin conspicuously beside them while Dr. Cotton preached from the text "God is not mocked." To endure this final humiliation was part of the punishment of those who were about to die for their sins. Also, the gallery of the chapel was open to visitors *at a charge of one shilling per head.*[161]

Most of last century and early in this century, chaplaincy positions were awarded to clergy with political connections to those operating the institutions. The ability or calling of such men to the chaplaincy was often a matter of little or no concern. In the 1930s, the performance and conduct of chaplains in federal prisons were so poor that the Federal Bureau of Prisons approached the Federal Council of Churches (now the National Council of Churches) for assistance in chaplain appointments: Either decent-quality chaplains would serve in federal prisons or else there would be no religious activities in those prisons.[162]

Since that time great progress has been made in developing standards for chaplains. No longer are political connections the prime prerequisite for one to enter the chaplaincy. There is debate at present over the appropriateness of some standards used for many chaplaincy positions, but the present situation is a great improvement over that of half a century ago.

A factor closely related to the matter of standards is the quality of men who enter the chaplaincy. In many ways, the correctional chaplaincy needs the best possible ministers—because they must minister to people of more varied racial, social, economic, and educational backgrounds, with more severe personal problems, and in a more adverse environment, than most pastors ever encounter. However, instead of drawing from the cream of the ministerial crop, the correctional chaplaincy tends to draw more from the dregs. A decade ago, Byron Eshelman noted, "Churches and seminaries show no enthusiasm for recruiting chaplains to go into prisons, and those that do go are usually motivated by personal reasons that arise in the midst of their ministerial careers."[163] In the mid 1970s, 16 percent of Protestant chaplains responding to a survey openly stated that they entered the chaplaincy because divorce had interrupted their pastoral careers, they were disillusioned with the Church, they needed jobs or more money, and other similar reasons. One might suspect that others also entered the chaplaincy for similar reasons but were not willing to admit it.

Part of the reason for less than the best clergy entering the chaplaincy lies in the attitude of most church groups toward chaplains. Often chaplains are omitted or excluded from the normal ministerial privileges in their denomination (e.g., voting privileges in denominational meetings):

> Frequently looked upon as something less than authentic clergy, presumably unfit for the parish, interested in the securities of public employment, the chaplains are not seen as a major resource of the church for reaching persons whom the ministry of the ordinary congregation and its pastor cannot touch.[164]

Whether such attitude is derived from the fact that chaplains do not lead congregations which will provide funds for the denomination's endeavor or from some other reason, *this attitude should be changed*—and the ministry of correctional chaplains recognized as authentic, regular ministry. Only when the Church honors correctional chaplains as highly as the missionary, the military chaplain, or the pastor, will there be adequate numbers of excellent clergy for the correctional chaplaincy.

A fourth development within the chaplaincy within the next generation is likely: Various groups will contest the legitimacy of government-supported chaplains in our correctional institutions, and the courts may begin to rule that such chaplains violate the required separation of Church and state. Such was the conclusion of a court case in Iowa in 1976.[165] If such rulings become common, both the burden and the opportunity for jail and prison ministry will fall fully upon individual Christians and local congregations as well as church- and privately funded organizations which provide leadership and chaplains for ministry to offenders.

Varieties of Chaplains Today

Before the varieties of chaplains can be addressed, it is necessary to ask: What is a correctional chaplain? (Some prefer the term *institutional chaplain.*) A formal definition is needed that will distinguish the chaplain from the volunteer religious worker and also from the clergyman who occasionally is involved in the ministry to offenders. The following is a formal definition of a correctional chaplain:

> The correctional chaplain is an ordained clergyman, endorsed or approved as a chaplain by the proper ecclesiastical authority and appointed or accepted by the governing body of a correctional institution, whose purpose is to minister to the religious needs of persons in the setting in which he serves. Although the primary concern of the chaplain is ministering to the inmates, he also serves their families, the institution's staff, and the community.

This definition should apply in general to most part-time as well as full-time correctional chaplains, although ordination should not be expected or required of ministers from religious persuasions whose spiritual leaders are not normally ordained, and ecclesiastical endorsement or approval should not be required of those who come from religious backgrounds outside the normal denominational structures.

It is most convenient to classify correctional chaplains by the institutions which they serve. When this scheme is adopted, there are three main classes of correctional chaplains: (1) jail chaplains, (2) juvenile institution chaplains, and (3) prison chaplains, both state and federal.

The three faith branches (Catholic, Jewish, Protestant) of the American Correctional Chaplains' Association have about five hundred members total. About a third of these are not correctional chaplains according to the formal definition above. These are retired chaplains, ministers who serve as denominational liaison for their denominations, and chaplains and ministers who function basically as visiting clergy in a correctional institution typically teaching a weekly Bible class or counseling regularly with an individual or two. There are four hundred to six hundred

TABLE 1

Number of Full-Time Chaplains

Denomination	Jails	Juvenile Institutions	All Prisons	Prisons	
				State	Federal
Assembly of God	—	—	4	4	—
Baptist	8	8	34	29	5
Church of Christ	—	—	6	4	2
Disciples of Christ	—	2	2	1	1
Episcopal	—	—	5	3	2
Lutheran	—	3	12	10	2
Methodist	2	2	9	7	2
Presbyterian	—	2	5	5	—
Other Protestant	—	—	5	3	2
Nondenominational Protestant	5	—	3	3	—
Roman Catholic	5	5	45	35	10
Total	20	22	130	104	26

NOTES:

(1) "Other Protestant" refers to denominations (e.g., Evangelical Free Church) not encompassed by the denominations named.

(2) "Non-denominational Protestants" refers to chaplains who are not related to a denomination. Usually the ordination of such a chaplain was by a single congregation (e.g., a community church).

(3) The distribution of chaplains among these denominations is almost identical to the distribution of church members in this country among these denominations, indicating the survey results are well balanced denominationally.

full-time chaplains serving correctional institutions in the United States. About 70 percent of these serve prisons. The rest are evenly split between jails and juvenile institutions. The distribution of chaplains among the various kinds of correctional institutions is indicated by Table 1, which is based upon the results of an extensive survey of chaplains in 1973. The 172 full-time chaplains indicated in the table represent about a third of the full-time chaplains in the country. It is interesting to note that the more liturgical churches have neglected jail ministry.

In addition to the full-time chaplains, there are a number of ministers who provide a part-time ministry in correctional institutions. No comprehensive statistics of any sort exist about them. The part-time chaplains responding to the 1973 survey followed the same denominational pattern shown for full-time chaplains.

It is also appropriate to look at the distribution of chaplains theologically. Orthodox Christians know that what a chaplain believes does matter. His beliefs affect his ministry. In fact, as will be seen in chapter 5, the most significant factor affecting inmate response to a chaplain's religious and counseling programs is the theology of the chaplain!

The 1973 survey of chaplains asked chaplains to identify themselves theologically. Five labels were suggested: Liberal, Neoorthodox, Evangelical, Conservative, and Fundamentalist. Space was provided for other labels, which were written in by 18 percent of the respondents—labels so chosen including *Biblical, Christian Humanist, Incarnational, Biblical Theological, Pragmatist,* etc. However, 23 percent of the chaplains responding to this survey could not or would not identify themselves with theological labels. The theological distribution of chaplains is as follows:

Theological Label	*Chaplains Choosing*
Liberal	17%
Neoorthodox	4%
Evangelical	13%
Conservative	13%
Fundamentalist	12%
Other (specified)	18%
Unspecified	23%
Total	100%

Chapter Conclusions

This chapter has presented highlights from the history of the correctional chaplaincy and traced some of its evolution to the present. The varieties of the chaplaincy have been presented as well as an indication of the distribution of chaplains theologically, denominationally, and among the various institutions of the criminal justice system.

A Japanese penologist commented on the importance of chaplains in his evaluation of American prisons during the mid 1960s. He said, "The institutions having social workers and psychologists, but no chaplains, are worse than the ones with chaplains and no social workers and psychologists." [166]

5

Contemporary Praxis of the Correctional Chaplaincy

What do chaplains do? This chapter answers that question.

Normally the chaplain's ministry is viewed as having three major emphases: (1) ministry of the Word and sacrament, (2) ministry of religious education, and (3) ministry of counseling (often termed "pastoral care").[167] For many jail chaplains, their ministry also has a social emphasis, since social programs such as jail libraries and educational and recreational activities are often the chaplain's responsibility, most jails not having treatment staffs.[168]

Another way to approach what chaplains do is to examine the various styles which chaplains bring to their ministry.[169] Some chaplains concentrate on the "chapel crowd," that group of inmates (usually few in number) who spend as much time as possible around the chapel and the chaplain. Some chaplains emphasize a big crowd at chapel services and ensure it by providing special attractions at the services (bands, women in the program, etc.). Some chaplains prefer to be primarily a "presence" around the institution.

This chapter takes a different tack. It simply examines what chaplains actually do—or at least what they *reported* that they do.[170]

Chaplain Time-Use and Activities

Table 2 describes how chaplains use their time, and Table 3 describes the activities under chaplain supervision. Discussion of

TABLE 2

Chaplain Time-Use (Hours per Week)

	Catholic Chaplains					Protestant Chaplains				
		Juvenile Insti-	Prisons					Juvenile Insti-	Prisons	
	Jail	tutions	State	Federal	ALL	ALL	Jail	tutions	State	Federal
Total Workweek	49.8	70.6	52.5	55.0	55.2	48.8	60.6	44.4	46.7	47.3
Total in Personal Contact with Inmates	21.5	36.9	28.4	26.6	28.4	27.6	30.3	22.7	28.2	25.2
Personal Prayer/Study	8.5	9.8	9.7	8.2	9.3	7.8	11.5	6.3	7.8	6.0
Worship/Preaching Services	5.8	3.9	4.8	6.4	5.2	2.5	2.6	1.1	2.6	3.2
Bible/Religious-Ed. Classes	0.3	–	2.1	1.7	1.7	2.4	2.9	1.8	2.5	2.0
Group Counseling/Discussion	0.3	2.5	2.7	1.7	2.2	3.0	1.7	3.3	3.2	3.4
Individual Counseling	10.0	23.8	14.2	15.6	15.5	14.1	12.8	13.4	14.9	12.8
Informal Inmate Contact	2.5	1.5	2.7	–	1.9	2.9	8.7	2.3	2.4	1.7
Administrative Activities	–*	8.5	9.3	7.9	8.2	8.1	7.3	7.5	8.2	9.2
Personal Contact with Releasees, Inmate Families and Friends	0.5	3.8	2.8	0.7	2.2	2.1	4.7	1.7	1.9	1.7
Recruiting, Training and Supervising Volunteers	6.5	2.5	0.9	2.0	1.6	2.6	3.3	3.6	1.7	4.3

* Although Catholic jail chaplains reported no administrative time, they must spend about the same amount of time as the other chaplains, since they wrote as many letters, made as many phone calls, and attended as many meetings as their Catholic colleagues in other institutions.

TABLE 3

Weekly Activities Under Chaplain Supervision

	Catholic Chaplains					Protestant Chaplains				
		Juvenile Insti-	Prisons					Juvenile Insti-	Prisons	
	Jail	tutions	State	Federal	ALL	ALL	Jail	tutions	State	Federal
Worship/Preaching Services	3.8	3.2	5.9	3.4	5.0	2.5	6.8	1.6	1.8	2.1
Bible/Religious-Ed. Classes	1.3	0.6	4.1	1.1	3.0	3.0	4.8	2.4	2.8	2.7
Religious Film Showings	0.5	—	0.3	0.8	0.4	0.8	2.6	0.5	0.4	0.7
Choirs	0.3	0.8	0.6	0.4	0.6	0.6	—	0.4	0.7	0.9
Individual Counseling Sessions	20.2	24.0	30.6	37.1	31.1	25.4	19.7	17.7	27.4	30.8
Group Counseling Sessions	2.3	3.8	2.6	1.5	2.4	2.0	1.8	1.9	2.0	2.6
Distribution of Bibles/New Testaments	8.3	5.2	10.2	5.6	8.4	15.5	24.2	12.8	13.5	17.8
Distribution of Pieces of Religious Literature	8	6	44	54	39	91	182	71	94	24
Volunteers (Religious Programs)	4.5	5.2	8.0	8.6	7.7	19.0	15.1	29.6	15.6	25.5
Volunteers (Nonreligious Programs)	1.3	1.8	2.0	2.3	5.8	6.5	7.2	7.8	4.3	13.6

information in these tables illuminates what chaplains actually do, i.e., the praxis of their ministry.[171] The similarities between the overall averages for Catholic and Protestant chaplains may amaze some.

Work Week and Personal Contact with Inmates

Catholic chaplains tend to work somewhat longer hours than Protestant chaplains. This may reflect the fact that priests, as single men, have more time for the ministry than those with families (nearly all Protestant chaplains are married). Age also plays a factor in the workweek. Younger chaplains work longer. The overall average age for correctional chaplains is 45.2 years. The two groups of chaplains who work longer than others are Catholic chaplains serving juvenile institutions (average age 33.8 years) and Protestant jail chaplains (average age 39.2 years). Chaplains of all varieties spend about half their time in personal contact with inmates (i.e., the sum of their services, classes, counseling, etc., and informal inmate contact).

Personal Prayer/Study

If a chaplain is to have a ministry with spiritual power, his ministry must be immersed in prayer. As E. M. Bounds noted, "What the Church needs today is . . . men whom the Holy Ghost can use—men of prayer." [172] The apostles recognized this. They selected others to care for the widows so that they could devote themselves "continually to prayer, and to the ministry of the Word" (*see* Acts 6:1–6). The result of such a commitment to prayer and study was that "the Word of God increased; and the number of the disciples multiplied in Jerusalem greatly; and a great company of the priests were obedient to the faith" (*see* Acts 6:7). A major weakness of the present chaplains is their limited commitment to prayer and study of God's Word. Until chaplains as ministers of God put their priorities straight and spend much more time in prayer and the Word of God, the Spirit of God will limit the power in their ministries.[173] Likewise, the limited study time is likely to produce mediocre messages and Bible lessons from chaplains.

Worship/Preaching Services

Catholic chaplains spend more time in worship than Protestant chaplains because they conduct about twice as many services per week as Protestant chaplains. Many Catholic prison chaplains celebrate Mass each day they are in the prison. Two to ten times as many inmates attend Catholic services as go to confession. Except for Protestant jail chaplains, comparison of Tables 2 and 3 suggests that chaplains are personally involved in every worship/preaching service under their supervision. Since many jails do not have a meeting room for services (only 44 percent of jails with Protestant chaplains reported they had such a room available), many worship/preaching services in the jails must be conducted at the inmate quarters (cellblocks, tiers, etc.). Consequently, Protestant jail chaplains appear to be involved personally in about only one-third to one-half of the worship/preaching services under their supervision—leaving the direction of the other services to other persons whom the chaplains have appointed to lead them. All prisons have meeting rooms or chapels for worship services. About 20 percent of the prisons served by chaplains even have separate chapels for each faith group.[174]

Most worship/preaching services in correctional institutions are interdenominational in character. When Communion is served in prison, it is "usually served in the Chancel area (Episcopalian, Methodist, Lutheran style) at an altar rail, with inmates invited to receive the elements in the manner closest to their own tradition: standing, sitting, or kneeling."[175] Because the liturgical churches have largely neglected jails,[176] Protestant services in jails tend to be more Baptistic in style and more conservative in theology than prison services.

Religious Education

Religious education in a broad sense includes Christian film showings and music programs as well as Bible and religious education classes. As much impact as audiovisual aids and music have upon people, it is surprising that both Catholic and Protestant chaplains avail themselves so little of these methods of communication. Only Protestant jail chaplains make extensive use of films. This in spite of the fact that jails have more limited facilities and only 6 percent of Protestant jail chaplains serve jails that provide movie projectors (compared to two-thirds of prisons and *all* juvenile institutions).

Among Protestant chaplains, Bible and religious-education classes are given about the same attention as preaching/worship services. On the other hand, Catholic chaplains spend three times as many hours in worship/preaching services as in Bible and religious-education classes—illustrating the continuing importance in the Catholic faith of performing the ritual of the Mass.

Distribution of religious literature is a form of religious education as well as a method of evangelism.[177] The attitude of many chaplains about literature distribution is very casual, and occasionally hostile. Responding to the 1973 survey, one chaplain wrote:

> What in the world does distributing tracts, etc., have to do with the chaplaincy? My approach is quite nonreligious per se. I am much more concerned with the qualitative impact of the chaplain on residents, staff, and the institution, than in performing certain religious tasks.

Another chaplain stated:

> It seems to me that the best chaplain in corrections today will be the one who primarily aims at renovating the system of justice, at all levels, and secondarily concerns himself with the trivia of Bible distribution and the like.

It is of interest to note that this chaplain possessed an earned doctorate, had extensive counseling training (more than two years of CPE), and worked very hard at his ministry (about seventy hours per week). Yet only 4 percent of the inmate population responded to the weekly worship/preaching services under his supervision. Apparently the inmates sensed how little he cares for "religious" activities.

Many juvenile and prison chaplains merely maintain a tract rack near the chapel or chaplain's office but have no plan for extensive distribution of Christian literature. A shockingly large number of inmates in jails and prisons served by chaplains have to write to organizations such as the International Prison Ministry or the Good News Mission in order to obtain a Bible or New Testament. A chaplain has been derelict in his duties if any inmate in his institution a week or longer has not been offered a Bible, or at least a New Testament, and if the chaplain does not attempt to place two or three pieces of Christian literature each week in the hands of every inmate in the institution.

Counseling

No other activity occupies as much time in a chaplain's ministry as does counseling. Jail chaplains spend the least proportion of their time in group and individual counseling (20 to 25 percent), juvenile chaplains the most (35 to 40 percent). Protestant chaplains do nearly all individual counseling (23 of the 25 sessions per week under their supervision); so do Catholic chaplains (29 of the 31 sessions per week under their supervision).

Administration

Administrative activities (letters, meetings, telephone calls, reports, etc.) take about a day per week of the chaplain's time. The administrative load seems to be about the same for all kinds of chaplains.

Recruiting/Training/Supervision of Volunteers

Most chaplains have a number of volunteers working under them, about twenty-five for the average Protestant chaplain and only a dozen or so for the average Catholic chaplain.[178] Some chaplains have more than a hundred volunteers under their supervision. The number of volunteers under the chaplain is likely to increase in the future as many chaplains (especially government-employed chaplains) become primarily religious program coordinators. Yet it is clear that most chaplains simply coordinate programs conducted by volunteers, as contrasted to using volunteers in programs conducted by chaplains. The couple of hours per week spent in training and supervision of volunteers is inadequate for a volunteer program that is indeed the chaplain's program.

Chaplains, as spiritual leaders, should use volunteers to teach

Bible classes, show Christian films, distribute Christian literature, to counsel and develop friendly, supportive relationships with inmates as well as to assist in social programs. The biblical pattern for spiritual leaders is to develop others to maturity and help them to use their gifts and abilities.[179] A chaplain who is content merely to preach, teach, and counsel by himself has abrogated his responsibility as a Christian leader.

It takes time to recruit, screen, train, supervise, evaluate, coordinate, recognize, appreciate, and (when necessary) dismiss volunteers. On the average, this author found that it took an average of a quarter-hour to half an hour per week of his time for each volunteer under his supervision inside a correctional institution.[180] In return, most volunteers put in two to four hours per week in ministry (teaching Bible classes, showing Christian films, doing one-on-one counseling, etc., plus serving as social volunteers, tutors, library helpers). At present, most chaplains do not use volunteers in *their* programs as much as they should.

Informal Inmate Contact and Personal Contact with Releasees and Inmate Families and Friends

As will be noted later, some inmates respond to the religious and counseling programs of certain chaplains much more than to those of others. One factor which has shown a high correlation with inmate response is the informal contact with inmates by the chaplain and the depth of the chaplain's personal interest in the inmates, illustrated by his contact with releasees and inmate families and friends. Only Protestant jail chaplains spend much time in these activities. Informal contact with inmates is a primary way in which friendships and the close bonds of Christian fellowship can develop between the chaplain and inmates. Failure of a chaplain to spend time in developing such relationships will reduce the impact of his ministry within the institution.

Influence of Various Parameters Upon Chaplain Praxis and Ministry

A variety of parameters characterize the ministry of every chaplain, including his denominational affiliation, his theological persuasion, his training, the type of institution that he serves. It is pertinent to ask what impact these have upon a chaplain's ministry.

Evaluation of such impact is not easy. No widely accepted measure(s) of chaplain performance exist—and if such did exist, the data about it (or them) might not be available. Therefore it is necessary to make maximum use of the data that we have.

The impact of eight parameters will be considered, some in more detail than others: (1) theological persuasion, (2) denominational affiliation, (3) level of academic education, (4) CPE training, (5) type of institution served, (6) employer (church or state), (7) facilities for ministry within the institution, and (8) prior parish experience.

Impact of Theological Persuasion. The 1973 survey of chaplains asked them to identify themselves theologically. Table 4 shows the percentage of chaplains with CPE, and the response of inmates to programs under chaplain supervision as a function of the chaplain's theological persuasion.[181]

Several points stand out immediately from Table 4. The first is the theological bias implied for CPE. This item will be discussed in more detail under the impact of CPE. Second, no single theological persuasion dominates the correctional chaplaincy. Chaplains are about evenly divided between those to the left and those to the right of theological center. The majority of privately and church-supported chaplains are theologically conservative (i.e., of evangelical, conservative, or fundamentalist theological persuasions). Liberal chaplains have a high level of representation among government-employed chaplains. Third, there is a definite correlation between a chaplain's theological persuasion and inmate participation in his religious programs, with three to four times as many inmates involved in programs of theologically conservative chaplains as in programs of liberal chaplains.

The reason for this phenomenon is simple, a reason which was observed by sociologists Rodney Stark and Charles Glock in their analysis of the large body of empirical data collected originally to investigate the effects of religion on contemporary anti-Semitism. They observe, "*A general corrosion of commitment*

TABLE 4

Comparison of Protestant Correctional Chaplains by Theological Persuasion

	Liberal	Neoorthodox	Evangelical	Conservative	Fundamentalist	Other (specified)	Unspecified	All Protestant	Roman Catholic
Distribution of Respondents	17%	9%	13%	13%	12%	18%	23%	100%	100%
Chaplains with CPE	89%	67%	50%	50%	33%	62%	75%	64%	37%
Percentage of the Inmate Population Involved Weekly in Chaplaincy Programs:									
Worship/Preaching Services	15%	18%	66%	32%	69%	29%	21%	34%	25%
Bible/Religious-Education Classes	6%	5%	55%	16%	56%	25%	17%	25%	8%
Bible/Religious Correspondence Courses	4%	8%	9%	4%	7%	6%	5%	8%	2%
Group Counseling/Discussion	7%	6%	22%	6%	25%	12%	9%	12%	7%
Individual Counseling	10%	17%	31%	25%	18%	17%	12%	18%	28%

presently accompanies the acceptance of a modernized, liberal theology" (emphasis theirs).[182] The result is:

> Only a minority of members of the liberal bodies feel that their religious perspective provides them with the answers to the meaning and purpose of life, while the overwhelming majority of conservatives feel theirs does supply the answers.[183]

Consequently, only theological conservatives have much success at attracting and activating the unchurched, which consist of (1) those "of low social class—people who are simply outside most of society's institutions [except correctional ones], the isolated, often itinerant, extremely impoverished underdogs" and (2) those "outside the church through conscious choice, [who] have rejected the basic tenets of religion." [184] The majority of inmates fit into that "unchurched" category. Thus, behind bars *as in society*, the "unchurched" respond most to conservative theology because it provides meaningful answers to life's most important questions, answers from the Bible, God's Holy Word.

Impact of Denominational Affiliation. The impact of a chaplain's denominational affiliation follows the pattern set by the impact of a chaplain's theological persuasion. Inmate participation in religious programs of chaplains from denominations that are conservative theologically (e.g., Assembly of God or Southern Baptist) is several times higher than for programs of chaplains from denominations that are theologically liberal (e.g., Episcopalian). As Stark and Glock noted, "In contrast to conservative denominations, the majority of members of liberal bodies are dormant Christians . . . . they have stopped attending church, stopped participating in church activities, . . . stopped praying, and are uninformed about religion." [185] This pattern follows also in religious programs behind bars.

Impact of Chaplain's Level of Academic Training. Table 5 shows the educational distribution of chaplains. Surprisingly, the group of Protestant chaplains attracting the highest percentage of inmates to their religious and counseling programs (about double the average) were those without the benefit of standard

TABLE 5

Comparison of Correctional Chaplains by Educational Level

	Catholic Chaplains				Protestant Chaplains			
	No Seminary Degree	Seminary Degree plus Master's Degree	Doctoral Degree	All	All	No Seminary Degree	Seminary Degree plus Master's Degree	Advanced Theological or Doctoral Degree
Worship/Preaching Services	12%	23%	49%	26%	32%	56%	29%	52%
Bible/Religious-Education Classes	2%	6%	19%	8%	27%	50%	10%	21%
Individual Counseling	8%	11%	49%	28%	18%	38%	21%	12%

Table shows the percentage of the inmate population involved weekly in the program indicated.

See Table 12 (Chapter 6) for the distribution of chaplains among the various educational levels. Since about ¾ of the chaplains had standard seminary degrees, the ALL column is representative of them.

seminary training. All of these chaplains were theologically conservative; most had attended Bible college; a few were ex-offenders. This suggests that a chaplain's theology is more important than his educational level.[186] The chaplain with advanced theological training (ThM or ThD) attracts many more inmates to worship/preaching services but not to his other programs. The chaplain with a master's degree (MA or MS) attracts even fewer inmates to his religious programs. Perhaps his interest is elsewhere.

Impact of CPE Training. CPE has been promoted as essential for correctional chaplains. The importance placed upon CPE can be illustrated by the following: (1) it is recommended by the ACA *Manual of Correctional Standards*,[187] (2) more than 50 percent of the prisons surveyed by Vickers required CPE,[188] (3) an ACPE chaplain supervisor can be granted certification as a correctional chaplain by the APCCA without having to submit any of the materials required of others for certification,[189] and (4) job advertisements for correctional chaplains sometimes indicate that a CPE supervisor can assume the head position of a correctional chaplaincy program without *any* experience in corrections.[190] Therefore, it should be expected that CPE-trained chaplains (37 percent of Catholic chaplains and 64 percent of Protestant chaplains) would be much more effective chaplains than chaplains without CPE. Unfortunately, Table 6—comparing chaplains with and without CPE—shows such is not the case.

For the Catholic chaplains, CPE or its absence has little influence on the chaplain's ministry except for the number of individuals counseled each week. For Protestant chaplains, the difference is striking. Although Protestant chaplains with CPE are paid about 25 percent more than chaplains without CPE, they work

TABLE 6

Comparison of Correctional Chaplains With and Without CPE

	Catholic		Protestant	
	With CPE	Without CPE	With CPE	Without CPE
Average Experience as a Correction Chaplain (years)	6	11	6	6
Average Workweek (hours)	57	57	49	60
Chaplain's Time Use (hours/week):				
Personal Prayer/Study	9.9	8.6	7.4	11.6
Bible/Religious-Education Classes	0.5	1.8	1.9	3.2
Group Counseling/Discussion	2.4	2.5	3.1	1.9
Individual Counseling	16.2	18.1	20.1	13.3
Number of Individual Counseling Sessions per week by the Chaplain	22	33	22	24
Percentage of Inmate Population Involved Weekly in Chaplaincy Programs:				
Worship/Preaching Services	29%	21%	27%	46%
Bible/Religious-Ed. Classes	5%	10%	20%	32%
Group Counseling/Discussion	6%	7%	12%	12%
Individual Counseling	31%	26%	16%	22%

eleven hours less per week and have a significantly smaller response by inmates to their religious and counseling programs. More than a third of chaplains with CPE spend *no* time in Bible/religious-education classes. Chaplains without CPE appear to be more concerned about spiritual matters (spending 50 percent more time in personal prayer and study). The 1973 survey also contained data suggesting that CPE-trained chaplains were less effective as administrators of programs than chaplains without CPE.[191]

It is appropriate to ask why inmates respond so much less to CPE-trained chaplains. Part of the reason is the theological impact of the higher percentage of liberal chaplains with CPE (*see* Table 4). But this is not the entire reason, as can be seen from Table 7, which compares chaplains of the same theological persuasions with and without CPE. The same kind of differences are seen: CPE-trained chaplains work fewer hours and have a significantly (*statistically significant*) smaller response to their programs by the inmate populations.

Since studies have indicated no significant personality differences between those who take CPE and those who do not,[192] it appears to be the CPE training itself which makes the difference, or at least a major part of the difference.[193] While the liberal influence [194] in some CPE training centers is greater than in others, all who go through CPE seem to be affected by the characteristic

TABLE 7

Selected Comparison of Chaplains of Evangelical or Fundamentalist Theological Persuasion With and Without CPE

	With CPE	Without CPE
Average Workweek (hours)	52	56
Percentage of Inmate Population Involved Weekly in Chaplaincy Programs:		
Worship/Preaching Services	41%	75%
Bible/Religious-Education Classes	33%	62%
Group Counseling/Discussion Groups	8%	28%
Individual Counseling	14%	29%

of liberalism that places the locus of authority not in theological or biblical doctrine, but vests it in the example of a religious life—either that of the CPE supervisor or that of the student.[195] Thus, the CPE training process seems to cause even evangelical and fundamentalist chaplains to shift their emphasis and trust (at least to some degree) from God's Word and His Spirit to the influence of their presence as persons.

CPE training may be part of the reason that correctional chaplains are viewed by many pastors as less than authentic clergy, because of a long history of hostility between CPE supervisors and denominational leaders [196] and because certified members of the Association for Clinical Pastoral Education spend significantly less time in denominational activities than do other clergy.[197]

Impact of Type of Institution Served. Tables 2 and 3 show chaplain time-use and activities under his supervision as a function of the type of institution served. Table 8 shows inmate response to chaplaincy programs.

Table 8 warrants a few comments. In some juvenile institutions, participation in religious services is mandatory, or at least coerced, by the juvenile's earning program credit by attendance. In some jails, services have to be conducted at the cellblocks or tiers where inmates are housed, thus exposing all the inmates in the cellblock or tier to the service. Likewise, most jails have so few programs that many inmates attend services simply because it is the only way to relieve the daily monotony of confinement. These factors explain in part the higher level of inmate response to programs of Protestant chaplains in jails and juvenile institutions. The very low percentage of jail inmate participation in the group counseling/discussion programs reflects the lack of facilities for such programs in jails. Only 36 percent of jail chaplains reported existence of a suitable room in the jail for group counseling.

Impact of Employer. Most full-time chaplains are employed by government agencies. Of the full-time chaplains responding to the 1973 survey by Pace, 97 percent of the Catholic chaplains and 88 percent of the Protestant chaplains were employed by the state. The breakdown of government-employed Protestant chaplains is: 40 percent of jail chaplains, 86 percent of chaplains serv-

TABLE 8

Inmate Response by Type of Institution

	Catholic Chaplains					Protestant Chaplains				
	Type of Institution					Type of Institution				
		Juvenile	Prison					Juvenile	Prison	
	Jail	Institution	State	Federal	All	All	Jail	Institution	State	Federal
Chaplain Average Age (years)	52	34	50	47	48	44	39	43	45	44
Average Experience (years) as a Correctional Chaplain	7	3	11	7	9	8	7	7	8	9
Percentage of Inmate Population Involved Weekly in Chaplaincy Program:										
Worship/Preaching Service	21%	22%	14%	44%	26%	32%	59%	69%	27%	22%
Bible/Religious-Education Classes	4%	2%	9%	14%	8%	27%	44%	71%	12%	8%
Group Counseling/Discussion	2%	5%	10%	10%	7%	12%	2%	45%	7%	43%
Individual Counseling	13%	10%	33%	26%	28%	18%	16%	27%	17%	7%

TABLE 9

Selected Comparisons of Protestant Correctional Chaplains Employed by Government and Private/Church Agencies

	Chaplain Employer	
	Government	Private/Church
Average Experience (years) as a Correctional Chaplain	6	7
Average Workweek (hours)	51	61
Percentage of Chaplains with CPE	72%	10%
Percentage of Inmates Involved Weekly in Chaplain Programs:		
Worship/Preaching Services	32%	42%
Bible/Religious-Education Classes	24%	31%
Bible/Religious Correspondence Courses	5%	9%
Group Counseling/Discussion	14%	7%
Individual Counseling	17%	20%
Chaplain's Time Use (hours per week)		
Personal Prayer/Study	8.5	12.4
Bible/Religious-Education Classes	2.2	3.3
Group Counseling/Discussion	2.9	1.8
Individual Counseling	18.7	13.7
Number of individual counseling sessions conducted by the chaplain each week	23	18
Percentage of chaplains conducting Bible/Religious-Education Classes	59%	86%

ing juvenile institutions, and 91 percent of prison chaplains. Table 9 provides a comparison of state-employed and private/church-employed chaplains. On the average, state-employed chaplains were paid about 50 percent more than private/church-employed chaplains.

As can be seen from Table 9, private/church-employed chaplains work substantially longer (ten hours more per week), spend more time in personal prayer/study, are much more likely to hold Bible/religious-education classes than government-employed chaplains. Perhaps this is part of the reason government-employed chaplains are "frequently looked upon as something less than authentic clergy, presumably unfit for the parish, interested in the securities of public employment." [198] Most of the 41 percent of government-employed chaplains who did not conduct Bible/religious-education classes had either classified themselves as liberal or had refused to identify themselves theologically on the 1973 survey. It may be that many of them do not really know what they believe. One chaplain noted on his survey next to the request for theological identification, "This should really put some respondees in a quandary." Apparently it did, since 23 percent of them could not or would not identify themselves theologically. It is not surprising that such chaplains display little interest in Bible classes and religious education.

Impact of Facilities for Ministry Within the Institution. In this area, the results of the 1973 survey were surprising: Chaplaincy programs do not appear to be significantly influenced by facilities (or their lack), except possibly group counseling in jails. The real determining factor in the scope of a chaplain's program is the chaplain's vision, imagination, ingenuity, and administrative ability. Nearly every kind of program can be held in any institution. It takes more effort to conduct programs in institutions with antiquated, inadequate facilities, but it can be done.[199]

Impact of Prior Parish Experience. It is a general fact that novices in the ministry make mistakes, although they at times try (successfully) programs more experienced ministers would not attempt. The rationale is to let the young minister make his mistakes and become a seasoned veteran before entering the chaplaincy.

Such rationale has several fallacies: First, it fails to allow for the fact that successful ministry in the pastorate will make it difficult for one to change from a ministry which God has blessed and in which he has done well into a new kind of ministry.[200] Second, this rationale fails to consider that this allows the chaplaincy to become a haven for dropouts from the pastorate.[201] Third, this rationale ignores the possibility that God will lead a man directly into the chaplaincy without other ministerial experience.

Table 10 compares inmate response to chaplains who entered the correctional chaplaincy without prior ministerial experience

TABLE 10

Comparison of Protestant Correctional Chaplains by Prior Ministerial Experience

	Protestant Chaplain Average	Average for Chaplains with no Prior Ministerial Experience
Percentage of Inmate Population Involved Weekly in:		
Worship/Preaching Services	32%	48%
Bible/Religious Education Classes	27%	34%
Individual Counseling	18%	24%

with response to the average chaplain. These data do not support the idea that pastoral experience makes one more effective as a chaplain.[202] Thus it may be that one way to improve the quality of men entering the correctional chaplaincy would be to recruit them directly from their theological schooling.[203]

A Comment

The preceding analysis has provided much insight into parameters that affect chaplain performance. However, the present state of knowledge about the praxis of the correctional chaplaincy is embryonic. Much more information is needed for this ministry to flourish. No significance should be attached to small numerical differences presented in the tables of this chapter.

6

The Chaplain

Two important questions are: What kind of persons are chaplains, and what kind of persons should be chaplains? This chapter answers these questions, providing data about Catholic as well as Protestant chaplains.

Characteristics Desired in a Chaplain [204]

What characteristics are desired in a chaplain? Six basic areas are examined: (1) spiritual characteristics, (2) biblical and theological training, (3) experience in the ministry, (4) recognition as a clergyman, (5) personality traits, and (6) limitations placed upon a chaplain's ministry by deficiencies in various areas.

Spiritual Characteristics

The chaplaincy is first and foremost a spiritual ministry. Whenever a chaplain's ministry becomes primarily social or psychological, that chaplain has abandoned his ministry and is not worthy to be called a chaplain. Consequently, the main characteristic desired in a chaplain is that he be a man of God.

Seven qualities mark the man of God. First, he must be a man called by God to the Christian ministry. The bane of Christianity has ever been those men who seek the Christian ministry as a profession without the call of God. Jesus told the disciples, "Ye have not chosen me, but I have chosen you, and ordained you, that ye should go and bring forth fruit, and that your fruit should remain . . ." (John 15:16). If a chaplain is not so chosen by Jesus Christ (i.e., called by God) there will be no permanent fruit in his ministry.[205]

Second, the man of God fellowships with God. Failure to spend time with God in prayer and in the Word of God will weaken the spiritual vitality of even a man called by God to the ministry. God will not allow any flesh to glory in His presence, whether for salvation ". . . lest any man should boast" (Ephesians 2:9), or for sanctification and Christian service (1 Corinthians 1:25–31). It is in a chaplain's personal devotions—*daily* devotions—that he prays for his own needs, to confess his sins, to know God better, to be filled with the Spirit, to know the mind of Christ, and to worship. He searches the Word of God to feed his own soul. No amount of intercessory prayer for others, or of study for messages and lessons for others, can be a substitute for the chaplain's personal devotions.

Third, the man of God is dedicated to the Lord and faithful to Him—that is, he is obedient to the will of God revealed in the Scriptures and by the Holy Spirit. Obedience is the simple, unequivocal test of a man's devotion to Jesus Christ (*see* Matthew 7:21–27; John 14:15). The Bible, the written Word of God, reveals the permanent, universal will of God and applies to all men of all times. In addition, the Holy Spirit reveals the will of God for an individual who is yielded (Romans 12:1,2) so that the dedicated man of God can speak of God's role in his choices as did the early Christian leaders (e.g., in Acts 15:28).

Fourth, the man of God is a man of spiritual maturity. The apostle Paul warns of the danger of an immature man in the ministry (1 Timothy 3:6).[206] Spiritual maturity requires both an extensive knowledge of God's truth and experience in its application.

Fifth, the man of God has a good personal testimony in his home and among his friends and business associates. Paul's criteria for Christian leadership include a man's relationship to his family (1 Timothy 3:4,5) and his reputation among unbelievers (1 Timothy 3:7).

Sixth, the man of God is continually growing spiritually. The goal of the Christian is to become like Jesus Christ in personality (Romans 8:29; Ephesians 4:13,15). The man of God, as a Christian and as a leader and example for other Christians (Philippians 3:17) grows toward this goal.

Seventh and last, the man of God does not rest upon past success in the ministry. Present enjoyment of the Lord and enthusiasm to do His will—and power in the ministry—come only from present obedience to and dependence upon the Lord Jesus. Every man of God is alert to the danger of losing his first love for Jesus and to the discipline of having his light removed (Revelation 2:4,5). Hebrews 12:5–11 and 1 Corinthians 11:30 illustrate similar aspects of God's discipline. The chaplain whose life shows these seven qualities that mark the man of God will satisfy the spiritual requirements for the ministry.

Biblical and Theological Training

Because the chaplain's primary responsibility is a spiritual ministry, he needs a thorough background in the Bible and in theology. The chaplain should be able to give a clear scriptural answer to most of the problems and objections that confront him. Because of the varied backgrounds of the constituency to whom he ministers, he needs a good understanding of theology, both an organized summary of biblical truth and an awareness of heresies past and current, so that he can present God's truth in a balanced and correct perspective, so that he can avoid the snares of adherents to the various sects, and so that he can focus his attention on the areas where an individual is likely to be confused as he learns the background of the individual.

It is inadequate to say that a chaplain should be a college graduate or a seminary graduate. *The items of significance are what a chaplain knows and how he is able to apply his knowledge, not what degrees he has earned.* Many Bible college graduates have received more credit hours of biblical studies than some seminary graduates. Moreover, the education received by students in some seminaries is destructive, bringing doubt upon the veracity and authority of the Word of God. On the other hand, the depth and breadth of training desired for a chaplain is usually beyond the academic capability of undergraduate education and must be found in seminary. Some men, however, can train themselves without the benefit of formal education. Charles Spurgeon is a classic example of such a minister for Christ.

Experience in the Ministry

Extensive experience in personal witnessing and counseling is invaluable because of the major role these play in the chaplain's ministry. Prior pastoral or related Christian ministries experience makes it easier for the chaplain to relate to pastors and other Christian leaders and to deal with them as coworkers in the ministry. However, prior pastoral experience is not essential for success in the chaplaincy.

Recognition as a Clergyman

A man's calling to the ministry comes from God, but the true man of God will be recognized by others as a man called by God to the ministry. Thus ordination and denominational endorsement are advantageous because they represent recognition of one's call to the ministry by the Christians with whom he ministers and serves. Neither ordination nor denominational endorsement should be viewed as essential. Some men of God have not been ordained. For example, Dwight L. Moody was a great minister for Jesus Christ, but was never ordained. Likewise today, F. F. Bruce, whose writings in the cause of conservative, biblical Christianty have had a great impact, is not an ordained minister. Some men will not be able to secure denominational endorsement. There are a growing number of Christians and churches outside the denominations in this nation. Men of God serving such churches frequently may not be able to secure a denominational endorsement or one from other church organizations such as the Independent Fundamental Churches of America because their ministry has not been within such groups. In addition, a biblically oriented, conservative, evangelical young minister in a denomination whose hierarchy is composed mainly of liberal ministers may find denominational endorsement hard to secure, particularly with what seems to be a trend to increasing universalism in many denominations. John Wesley was not the last sound Christian minister to be forced out of a denomination by a decadent ecclesiastical hierarchy. It has often happened since.

Personality Traits

A man who wants to become a chaplain must have a compassion for people yet be able to express his compassion without becoming too emotionally involved in the lives of those to whom he ministers. If he becomes too emotionally involved, he will soon be destroyed, because of the many terrible problems in the lives of his constituency. He needs patience, stability, and steadfastness, yet also the ability to make quick decisions in emergencies. The chaplain needs to be objective: to admit his mistakes when they occur, to view those to whom he ministers in a balanced way, to appreciate the position of the institution's authorities, to see through the con artist in the institution who attempts to use him, and to be able to receive criticism about himself or his ministry constructively.

He must have a great deal of mental and emotional stamina, especially when he has to deal with the urgency of counseling the suicidal, the excited, frightened, angry, or bitter person.

Limitations Caused by Deficiencies in the Chaplain

Chaplains are not supermen. No chaplain will have all the characteristics desired in a chaplain. What limitations are placed upon a chaplain's ministry when he is deficient in various areas?

The chaplain who does not qualify as a man of God has no ministry. He may function as a chaplain in the institution, but he has no spiritual ministry and does not deserve the title.

The chaplain who lacks adequate biblical and theological knowledge will find himself frustrated and thwarted by problems beyond his ability to overcome, because he does not have the "sword of the Spirit" (Ephesians 6:17) at his disposal. Such a chaplain will find himself frequently imprisoned by Bunyan's Giant Despair,[207] or else he will concentrate only on those few inmates to whom he can minister comfortably.

Ordination and denominational endorsement will open the doors to the institutional officials for a chaplain. If he is a man of God, the doors to these officials will open to him in time anyway.

After a man enters the chaplaincy, it will be his competency in counseling, not his formal training, that will determine the response of inmates to his counseling programs. Unfortunately, lack of formal training in counseling may close some doors (e.g., APCCA certification) because of current professional prejudices, even when one is an effective counselor.

It is hard for a man of God to have serious deficiencies in personality traits because the fruit of the Spirit of God (Galatians 5:22,23) overcome limitations in temperament by equipping him to deal with people effectively (e.g., joy and peace provide an inner security that removes any need to exploit those to whom he ministers; love and long-suffering and faithfulness provide stability and compassion; gentleness and goodness provide consideration in dealing with others; meekness and temperance, i.e., self-control, keep the chaplain from operating in anger). If the fruit of the Spirit do not characterize a chaplain's life, it is unlikely that he is a man of God. And if he is not, he has no ministry.

Supervision and Evaluation

A chaplain must be able to minister under supervision and accept evaluation of his work or else he is not likely to have the balance and growth that characterize wholesome ministry.[208]

Characteristics of Present Chaplains

Although about 5 percent of inmates in our nation's correctional institutions are female and about half of the inmates are nonwhite, 95 percent or so of the nation's chaplains are white males, as any gathering of chaplains demonstrates visibly.[209]

The average age for chaplains is in the middle forties, with chaplains serving juvenile institutions and Protestant jail chaplains averaging about five years younger.[210] The average chaplain has been in the correctional ministry for seven to eight years.[211] Most chaplains had from six to fifteen years of ministerial experience prior to becoming correctional chaplains. The distribution of ministerial experience prior to entering the chaplaincy is shown in Chart 2.

Only 4 percent of Protestant chaplains indicated they had been

CHART 2

Distribution of Ministerial Experience
Prior to Becoming a Correctional Chaplain

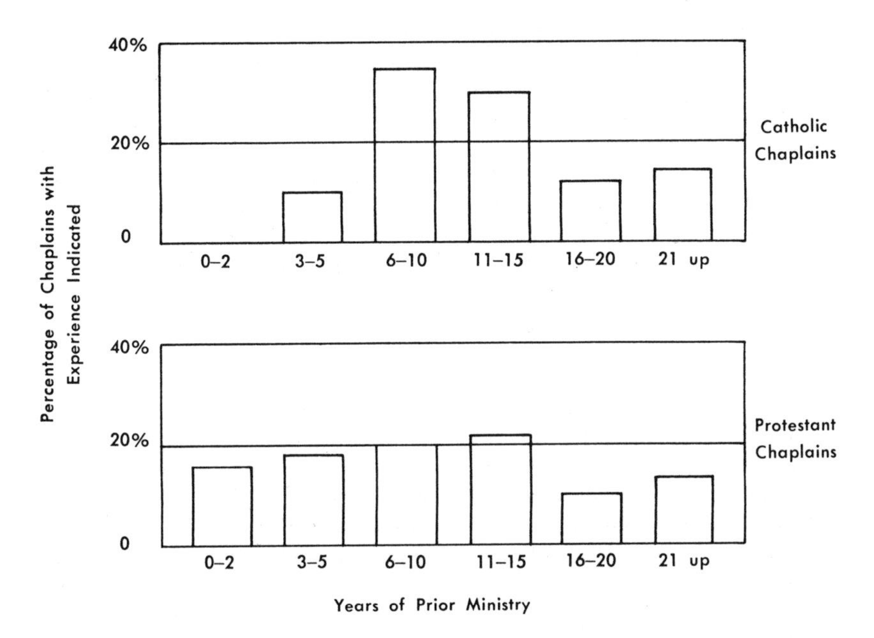

military chaplains, but those comprised about a third of those with twenty years or more of ministerial experience prior to entering the correctional chaplaincy. About the same proportion (3 percent) of Catholic correctional chaplains had served as military chaplains. A high percentage of Catholic chaplains had served formerly as missionaries (18 percent) compared with Protestant chaplains (only 3 percent had been missionaries). The vast majority of Protestant chaplains enter the correctional chaplaincy from the pastorate. A similar majority enter the Catholic chaplaincy from positions as assistant pastors or teachers (usually at the high-school level). Table 11 summarizes the reasons which chaplains gave for entering the chaplaincy.

Comparison of Table 11 with Chart 2 brings several items of interest to light. First, the control exercised by the Roman Catholic hierarchy shows itself in that no priests with less than two

TABLE 11

Reasons Chaplains Entered the Correctional Chaplaincy

Catholic Chaplains	
Told to or assigned by religious superior	40%
Asked to serve by state, Protestant chaplain, or inmates	10%
Tired of academic world, parish administrative hassle, etc.	7%
Desire to serve the poor and delinquents	13%
The opportunity presented itself	7%
Interest grew from contact with correctional institutions	10%
Miscellaneous (many friends were and are inmates, missionary returning found this an attracting ministry, CPE showed one he had something to offer, recognized the need for competent people in this field)	13%
Total	100%
Protestant Chaplains	
Requested to enter by denomination, chaplaincy organization, or correctional institution	22%
Interest grew from contact with the correctional ministry (including one chaplain who had a criminal past)	18%
Awareness of divine leading and inmates' need	20%
Desire to see lives changed and the challenge of the correctional chaplaincy	11%
Needed a job or more money, or the opportunity just presented itself	7%
Looking for a change, disillusioned with pastorate, divorced	9%
Felt ability to relate, interested in problem people, found satisfaction in correctional CPE	13%
Total	100%

years of ministerial experience are assigned to the correctional chaplaincy. The majority of Catholic priests told to enter the chaplaincy by their religious superiors had from six to fifteen years of ministerial experience before starting correctional work.

Earlier it was noted that some feel that many Protestant ministers enter the correctional chaplaincy because of problems in the pastorate. Table 11 substantiates this premise: 16 percent openly stated that they entered the correctional chaplaincy because they were disillusioned with the pastorate, were seeking more money, and so on. Most such men entered the chaplaincy with six to fifteen years of ministerial experience. Protestant chaplains with pastoral experience averaged 2.9 pastorates each, spending slightly over three years at each church. This does not speak highly of the stability of men who enter the correctional chaplaincy or of their abilities to establish long-term relationships with congregations. In addition, Chart 2 suggests that another 16 to 20 percent enter the chaplaincy after "retiring" from some other aspect of ministry. Thus, at least a third of Protestants in the correctional chaplaincy are other than the brightest and best of the ministerial crop in their prime.

Table 12 shows the educational background of full-time correctional chaplains. It appears that Catholic chaplains have more advanced academic training than do Protestant chaplains, although more Protestant chaplains have CPE. No single school was the trainer of unusually large numbers of correctional chaplains.

Economic backgrounds of chaplains as defined by the primary occupation of their fathers are indicated in Table 13. One occupation is striking by its absence: There are no career military men among the fathers of correctional chaplains. A higher percentage of Catholic correctional chaplains than Protestant chaplains come from homes where the father was a professional man. It is surpris-

TABLE 12

Education of Correctional Chaplains [212]

	Correctional Chaplains	
	Catholic	Protestant
1. Highest Academic Level Reported:		
a. Undergraduate study/BA or BS degree	3%	7%
b. Master's degree (MA, MS, or MRE)	13%	2%
c. Standard seminary training: 2 to 4 years for Catholics; BD or MDiv for Protestants	71%	78%
(Portion of these also possessing master's degree)	(⅓)	(⅙)
d. Advanced seminary training: ThM	—	9%
e. Doctoral degree (ThD or PhD)	13%	4%
2. Percentage having CPE	37%	64%
(Amount of CPE taken by most in quarters)	4–6	4–6

TABLE 13

Family Backgrounds of Correctional Chaplains

	Correctional Chaplains	
Father's Primary Occupation	Catholic	Protestant
Total Professional	53%	25%
Clergy or Catholic Lay Leader	4%	9%
Scientist/Engineer	18%	4%
Executive	9%	2%
Medicine/Attorney	14%	–
Teacher/Professor	–	4%
Accountant, Bookkeeper, Government Worker	4%	6%
Newsman	4%	–
Farmer	4%	25%
Businessman	4%	12%
Salesman	–	9%
Skilled Labor	39%	22%
Unskilled Labor	–	7%
Total	100%	100%

ing that less than 10 percent of Protestant chaplains are sons of clergymen.

Table 13 also shows that very few chaplains come from what might be called lower-class economic backgrounds. Two factors seem to account for this: First, clergy are primarily middle class —from middle-class backgrounds, earning middle-class incomes, and usually serving mainly the middle class. Second, those reli-

TABLE 14

Family Size of Correctional Chaplains [213]

	Catholic Chaplains	Protestant Chaplains	
Number of:	Brothers & Sisters	Brothers & Sisters	Children
0	13%	9%	7%
1	16%	23%	9%
2	23%	14%	39%
3 or more	48%	54%	46%

gious groups in America most likely to have clergy from lower-class economic backgrounds (e.g., Pentecostal and non-Caucasian groups) have limited representation among correctional chaplains (only about 10 percent).

Table 14 shows the family sizes of correctional chaplains.

Chaplaincy Requirements

Earlier in this chapter the characteristics desired in a chaplain were presented. The perspective was that of an Evangelical committed to orthodox, historic Christianity. Now it is appropriate to consider the requirements that employers of chaplains have established. The appropriateness of these requirements is discussed in the next chapter.

Government Employers of Chaplaincy

The federal and most state prison systems employ chaplains. Some jails also employ chaplains. While the precise requirements will vary from one employer to another, in general the government employer follows the requirements recommended by the ACA's *Manual of Correctional Standards.* These are that a chaplain possess: (1) college and theological degrees, (2) ordination and ecclesiastical endorsement, (3) parish experience, (4) a minimum of one year of CPE, and (5) the right personality.[214] In addition, a chaplain serving a correctional institution must have the approval of the institution's administration (sheriff, warden, superintendent, commissioner). Some penal system chaplains must also be nominated by a representative personnel committee, either local or state or National Council of Churches.[215]

Vickers' 1971 survey illustrates the variation in requirements among employers of prison chaplains: [216]

	Reported by:
No educational requirements	13% of the chaplains
Only college required	4% of the chaplains
College and seminary required	31% of the chaplains
College, seminary, and CPE required	52% of the chaplains
Denominational endorsement required	Over 85% of the chaplains

It is not known what changes in requirements may result if the government chaplaincy positions evolve primarily into a role of religious program coordinator.

Private/Church Employers of Chaplains

While some private and church employers of chaplains place the same requirements upon chaplains as do government employers, most have a more flexible attitude toward formal education and do not require CPE. For example, in 1973 only 10 percent of privately employed chaplains reported having CPE, in contrast to 72 percent of government-employed chaplains. Since many of the church organizations employing chaplains are conservative theologically, many of them accept Bible-college training as adequate theological education for a chaplain, as do many faith mission boards for their missionaries. Likewise, since a number of private chaplaincy organizations were founded by men without seminary training, they place more emphasis upon "God's call" of the chaplain to that ministry than upon his formal education (or lack of it). This emphasis may explain, in part, why privately employed chaplains spend 50 percent more time in personal prayer/study than do government-employed chaplains. This flexible attitude toward formal education is illustrated by the Good News Mission, one of the largest private employers of correctional chaplains in the country. The educational distribution of its chaplaincy staff in 1976 was: less than college degree, 12 percent; college degree, 19 percent; standard seminary training, 19 percent; advanced theological degrees such as ThM or ThD, 50 percent. In many cases, privately employed chaplains with limited formal education are either former offenders or former law enforcement personnel (state troopers, FBI agents, etc.) whom God has called to minister in jails and prisons.

The Chaplain and the Churches [217]

The local church is that unit of the Body of Christ through which His life is exercised in human society. It was to the church at Jerusalem that the Risen Christ kept adding those who were being saved (Acts 2:47). It was of the Church, both local and universal, that it is said, "Christ also loved the Church, and gave Himself for it" (*see* Ephesians 5:25). It was unto the fellowship of His Son Jesus Christ our Lord that God called the Corinthians in the local church (1 Corinthians 1:9). As a man and as a Christian, the chaplain has the God-laid responsibility of *membership in a local church.* There are many good reasons for this:

Reasons for Himself. Like any other Christian, he needs the opportunity of fellowship, instruction, and service in a local congregation. He needs a pastor. As a believer, he has been placed by God under the leadership of the congregation: "Obey your rulers and recognise their authority. They keep constant watch over your welfare, and they have great responsibility. Try to make their work a pleasure and not a painful burden—that would be no advantage to you" (Hebrews 13:17 PHILLIPS). In his own area of competence, the chaplain will know more than his pastor, but God put one over him who must answer for him as a member of the flock. In his pastor he has a source of spiritual help and insight that may well go beyond his own.

The normal healthy society of a local church can provide the counterbalance to the artificial, enforced "community behind bars" of the chaplain's daily work.

The emotional and spiritual drain upon the resources of the chaplain as he ministers to the empty, twisted, perverted men of his daily rounds, can be restored by the sympathies and stimulation of his church friends. The chaplain needs these warm spiritual contacts.

Reasons for His Family. The nature of the chaplain's duties may call for absences from home. It is specially comforting to him then to remember that the church family back home remembers him in prayer and, in particular, that its members are in contact with his wife and children. The hands of the church friends are available in emergency; the spiritual life of his loved ones is being ministered to by loyal Christians; the children are learning God's Word in Sunday school and are growing socially in a healthful environment. These personal benefits are his as a church member, and he values them.

Reasons for His Church. As a member of a local church the chaplain has a wide-open opportunity to magnify his office. While the Word of God directs Christians to minister to prisoners, very few individuals obey this divine command—partly through the indifference of ignorance. With one in their midst to inform and arouse them to their duty and privilege, they will be more likely to undertake such ministry.

Further, since the chaplain has direct knowledge of the consequences of breaking the civil and moral laws, he is in a position to teach and advise the youth of his church in the areas of his specialty. Some, hopefully learning from him, will avoid deportment that leads to conflict with the law.

A portion of the funds for the church-supported chaplaincy comes from the local church. It seems only right then that the chaplain should take his place humbly as a member, where his presence and advice may influence the annual church budget, and where his own tithes and offerings help support the whole program of the Lord's work. His passions find expression in both tears and coin.

Reasons for His Charges. The chaplain is aware that the basic problem of his inmates is sin. Sin in some form has been their downfall. His labor with them has been to show them God's solution in Christ; and now, for their continuing support, he can recommend to them membership in a local church. Here their association will be with other sinners whose soul-condition has been unmasked, and who are organic cells of the living Body of Christ. Of course, only as being in a local congregation himself can a chaplain so direct his charges without being open to a charge of hypocrisy.

The Chaplain's Fellowship. The chaplaincy, almost by definition, cuts across denominational structures and church hierarchies. The chaplain, as every believer, should learn well the implications of John's conditional sentences (*see* 1 John 1:7): "If we walk in the light as He is in the light, we have fellowship with one another, and the blood of Jesus His Son cleanses us from all sin." Here fellowship and atonement are made the concomitant results of "walking in the light." God Himself is the standard of truth and holiness, and to that standard we are called. Both fellowship with believers and cleansing from sin are conditional: they are equal benefits of deportment within the light of God. That is to say, this word of Scripture brings fellowship up to the level of atonement. Here is all the authority the chaplain needs for his association with cobelievers, no matter what their name or sign.

The Issue of Separation

If the chaplain is not fully assured of this liberty he has in Christ he may be injured by those who charge that he cannot say *S(h)ibboleth* (Judges 12:6)—that he is "unseparated" from contaminating associations. He may be persuaded to disassociation, as Peter and Barnabas were at Antioch (Galatians 2:12,13). It would be well for him to observe that Christ in him is that which differentiates him from those who are not Christ's.

Moses understood this principle. When pleading for Jehovah's continued presence in Israel (for his tabernacle had been removed from the center of the encampment), Moses argued, "If thy presence go not with me, carry us not up hence. For wherein shall it be known here that I and thy people have found grace in thy sight? is it not in that thou goest with us? so shall we be separated, I and thy people, from all the people that are upon the face of the earth" (Exodus 33:15,16). God's presence in his people made the difference. In the Greek Old Testament (LXX) the word *separated* is rather *glorified.* Here is separation by glorification. The *separation was not so much a pulling apart from other peoples as it was an elevation of God's people.* The presence of God among His own is that which distinguishes them from all others. The glory of Christ in the chaplain will distinguish him, and that Presence will elevate him above his critics. Sensitivity in this realm is unworthy of his calling; he need not fear the feet of clay. Having been sent forth as a free man in Christ, he is to be in bondage to no man; rather he is to stand fast in the liberty wherewith Christ has made him free. His ministry to bound men should make him value the more the liberty that God has given him.

The Issue of Ecumenism

The converse of separation is ecumenism, and the solution to both is the same: the presence of Christ in the chaplain and his dedication to the lordship of Christ. As noted earlier, in Christ the chaplain is in a fellowship that includes every other believer in Christ—both the weak in faith and the strong (Romans 14:1; 15:1). He is a representative of the entire Christian community, and at times may even be called upon to coordinate the religious programs of sects and even non-Christian religions, *but under no circumstances is his testimony to be watered down by yoking up with unbelievers* (2 Corinthians 6:14–18). To be in the world but not of it calls for discernment. To waive the enticements that may be offered by both "worldly" and "religious" organizations calls for obedience to his Lord. He cannot be in alliance with unrighteousness, with paganism or perverted Christianity, or with humanistic religion. His calling is higher and unique. To break the bands that Satan has forged upon his charges, he must keep his gospel pure, his deportment unquestioned, and his soul filled by the Holy Spirit. Neither separatism nor ecumenism need overly concern the chaplain who is assured of his spiritual anchorage. The minister who does not have the personal freedom from God to minister in the midst of ecumenism will be very limited as a correctional chaplain.

Creating Helpful Attitudes

The correctional chaplain must here overcome a twofold problem—one with his charges and the other with the churches.

The now-freed prisoner upon entering a church may expect the same interest in his welfare that his chaplain showed. Through this man of God, Christ reached out to him and took hold of his problems, helped untangle the strands of his life, endeavored to unite him again with his family or with sincere individuals who would help him. It is natural for him to expect the same helping hands in a church. But unless the church is prepared in advance, such helpful understanding may be slow coming. On either side, the chaplain can prepare attitudes.

The ex-inmate must learn that in any local church there are people of varying levels of spiritual growth. He will not find perfection in the Christians he meets. *His chaplain must teach him to make allowances for some hardhearted attitudes he will find even among church members.* If in the institution his basic needs were provided by others, on the outside he must work for them himself. Society in general may be slow to forget the reasons for his incarceration, and hence slow to grant him full acceptance.

And in the church, the chaplain can prepare the way by reasserting that all have sinned and were under God's condemnation. The kinds of sins committed did not affect the result for anyone—God's judgment. And as we have been forgiven, so must we forgive. This new man in Christ, with his sins now forgiven and his legal debt to society paid, is none other than a brother in Christ. The Philemon Epistle must again be read and fully accepted in the present churches. Once more Onesimus must be received by the very society he formerly injured, and received not just as a "spiritual brother" but as a brother beloved both in the flesh and in the Lord. Real humility is required here for the Church to be obedient to her Lord. Forgiven sinners can give no less.

In the practical outworking, it may be necessary to form a committee or a buddy system to give explicit care to former offenders. Such a group would assist in finding work, in ministering to the ex-inmate's family, in helping to form friendships with godly men. Investment in such a man may well pay off in the redeemed man's testimony—the very work which may keep another from falling into the devil's snare.

Such attitude adjusting by the chaplain, working in the Spirit, will increase the value of his ministry and his eternal reward.

The Chaplain's Personal Well-Being [218]

A chaplain must care for himself if his ministry to others is to be wholesome. As Jesus put it in His summary of our responsibilities to others: "Love thy neighbor *as thyself*" (*see* Matthew 22:39). A chaplain's personal well-being is vulnerable to assault in five basic areas: spiritual, mental, social (including family), physical, and professional. Dangers and their prevention in each of these areas are considered.

Spiritual Dangers and Their Prevention

The spiritual dangers which confront the chaplain are common to most Christian workers. First and foremost is the danger that the chaplain will fail to include adequate time in his schedule for prayer. Without prayer, men faint (Luke 18:1). Without prayer, men lack wisdom from God (James 1:5). Without adequate prayer, men worry unnecessarily (Philippians 4:6,7; 1 Peter 5:7). Without prayer, a chaplain's ministry will lack power.[219] This danger can be avoided only by constant reassessment of one's use of time, and a dogged determination to keep prayer in its proper priority.

A second danger is neglect of Bible study. The chaplain has a dual need for Bible study: to have a word from God for his parishioners and—even more important—to feed his own soul. The Word of God equips the man of God for his service of God (2 Timothy 3:16,17). Appropriation of God's Word comes only through *extensive meditation and personal application* of it (*see* Psalms 1:2; Matthew 4:4). As with prayer, the chaplain must *make* time in his schedule for Bible study.

A third danger is a propensity to walk by sight, not by faith (2 Corinthians 5:7). It is easy for the chaplain to become so engulfed in doing his ministry and facing its many problems that he fails to remember that God is both sovereign and faithful to those whom He calls (1 Thessalonians 5:24). A careful study of 2 Corinthians 2:14 through 6:10 is an excellent reminder of God's faithfulness in calling, directing, and empowering His servants so that they may daily "walk by faith, not by sight."

A fourth danger is an unwillingness to deal with sin as it enters one's life. Daily confession of sin (*see* 1 John 1:9) is needed by the chaplain to enable him to minister effectively to others who need spiritual cleansing. A threefold confession is needed: of the principle of sin, of particular sin, and of personal sins.[220] Failure to face, confess, and deal with sin in his life will wreck a chaplain's ministry and destroy his joy as a Christian.

A strong personal devotional life will prevent most of these problems. Unfortunately, many Evangelicals seem to think of the devotional life only in terms of a routine schedule of daily "devotions" of prayer and Bible reading. A much bolder and broader concept than that is needed. *The devotional life includes all that helps the chaplain to know God better and love Him more.* Thus the full devotional life contains not only the chaplain's personal prayer and Bible study, but also his reading of devotional literature such as Ruth Paxson's *Life on the Highest Plain,* of biographies of God's servants, and of practical mystics such as Brother Lawrence (*The Practice of the Presence of God*) and Frank Laubach (*Christ Liveth in Me*).

It takes planning to develop a full devotional life. The chaplain needs to be sure that his schedule includes ample time for personal prayer and the study of God's Word. The chaplain should cultivate the habit or practice of conscious awareness of Christ's presence at all times. The chaplain should try to read at least a book every month or two on the devotional life, spiritual living, and prayer. Books in this line [221] include such as Andrew Murray's *With Christ in the School of Prayer,* Howard Guiness's *Sacrifice,* and Watchman Nee's *The Normal Christian Life.* The chaplain should also read at least one biography about God's servants every month or two. Not only will this enrich his appreciation for God's varied methods of working in and through men, it will also provide him an abundant source of illustrations for his sermons and Bible lessons. Charles Spurgeon, that prince of preachers, is reported to have read a biography a week.[222] It has been this writer's practice to split his biographical reading between books on God's servants in general and those concentrating on a few men of special interest to him (Martin Luther, Charles Spurgeon, and Hudson Taylor), reading a number of biographies on each. Finally, the chaplain should include in his schedule retreats, Bible conferences, etc., for a concentrated spiritual refreshment.

Development of a full personal devotional life will not be achieved easily. It will require the steps above. But it will be worth it. The increased satisfaction and joy alone from the chaplain's personal relationship to the Lord will be more than worth the effort, to say nothing of his increased effectiveness as a minister.

Mental Dangers and Their Prevention

The thought life of the chaplain faces four main dangers. First, the heavy demands upon the chaplain's time may put him under such pressure that his thoughts become tangled because of the rush in which he finds himself. At this point, it is necessary to "rest a while" (*see* Mark 6:31). The chaplain *should not expect the pace of his ministry to be leisurely.* There are too many inmates who need to be snatched from the fire (*see* Jude 23) for the chaplain to dawdle. He needs to "redeem the time because the days are evil" (*see* Ephesians 5:16), but his life should not be frantic.

Second, the chaplain may identify too closely with the inmates to whom he ministers, losing objectivity and becoming too emotionally involved with them.

A third danger is pride. Because so many depend upon the chaplain for help, he may easily become filled with proud thoughts. This has occurred when the chaplain becomes hypercritical of others and is slow to recognize his own weaknesses. Paul gave a good prescription for this ailment: "Brethren, if a man be overtaken in a fault, . . . restore such an one in the spirit of meekness; considering thyself, lest thou also be tempted" (Galatians 6:1).

Fourth, it is easy for a chaplain to develop a defeated attitude. Many to whom the chaplain ministers will reject him, his help, and his message. Many whom he counsels will continue to live defeated, discouraged, dismal lives. This in itself is not an indication that the chaplain has misunderstood his calling or is ineffectual, but it still hurts when these things press themselves upon the chaplain's attention. When a chaplain is overcome by a defeated outlook, his ministry will become both ineffectual and limited.

The chaplain can counter this trend in his thought life by (1) remembering that God's men and their message have often been rejected—even Jesus, as when the rich young ruler He loved turned away (Mark 10:17 ff.); (2) remembering that his sufficiency for his ministry does not lie in himself but in God (*see* 2 Corinthians 2:16; 3:5,6); (3) recalling to mind those whom he has helped (if there are none, then the chaplain is in the wrong business); (4) looking at his ministry honestly and confessing his sins so that he may continue in the future cleansed from the wrong of his past; and (5) giving thanks and praising God even for the time of discouragement because it reemphasizes the greatness of a God who can minister through such an inadequate person as himself.

Social Dangers and Their Prevention

The first area of potential neglect is the chaplain's family. A chaplain may easily fail to provide spiritual leadership in his home, neglect the relaxation, entertainment, and amusement needs of his family, and not spend adequate time with his wife and children. The seriousness of this can be seen by the apostle Paul's warning that to fail to provide for one's family is worse than heresy (1 Timothy 5:8).

Ministers often go to one of two extremes about their society: neglect or conformity. Some ministers do not keep up with current events and have no political involvement—not even voting. They lack understanding of current slang, music, art. In contrast, Paul knew the Greek games (*see* 1 Corinthians 9:24–27), was cognizant of the language and thought of the philosophers (Acts 17:22–31), and could quote from Cretan literature (Titus 1:12). He sought to be all things to all men in order that he might save some (1 Corinthians 9:20–22). Some chaplains go to the other extreme, willingly conforming to the thought-pattern of this society (in disobedience to Romans 12:2) and put material gain and security ahead of serving God. The chaplain should be otherwise: content with such things as he has (Hebrews 13:5,6) and seeking God's kingdom first (Matthew 6:33).

Physical Dangers and Their Prevention

Many chaplains fail to consider their physical needs adequately. Failure to do so will not only make one's ministry more difficult (because the body affects the mind and emotions), it also dishonors God, since we are commanded to dedicate our bodies to Him (Romans 12:1). The apostle Paul recognized both the importance of proper care for the body (implied for example in 1 Thessalonians 5:23) and its secondary importance to the spiritual (cf. 1 Corinthians 9:27; 1 Timothy 4:8).

Three areas where a chaplain is likely to abuse or neglect his body are exercise, diet, and rest. If a chaplain gives proper attention to these and has regular physical checkups, he is likely to maintain the vigor and stamina required for an effective ministry.

Professional Dangers and Their Prevention

The primary professional danger is that the chaplain will fail to grow and develop. The chaplain or minister who does not strive to improve his skills as a biblical exegete, preacher, counselor, administrator, etc., is going to stagnate professionally. Such improvement may be acquired through reading, attendance at seminars or courses, and tutoring (formally or informally) by one competent in the field. It is important that the correctional chaplain also keep abreast of developments within the criminal justice system. In addition to reviewing some of the publications in this field and attending appropriate seminars and conferences, the chaplain may want to become involved in the National Criminal Justice Reference Service, which provides free abstracts on materials of interest to the subscriber.[223]

The chaplain should take as active a role as possible in his denomination and local clergy groups. This will help to improve both denominational and church interest in the correctional ministry and support for it.

Chaplain participation in professional associations such as the ACA, AEIC, APCCA will depend upon his interest and ability. Passive membership in one or more of these will contribute little to the chaplain's professional growth.

It is important that the chaplain develop some specific objectives for his professional growth. One might even call these his career plan. Otherwise he is unlikely to develop his full potential for ministry.

7

Current Problems and Issues of the Correctional Chaplaincy

Problems and controversy are normal. As Job put it, ". . . man is born unto trouble" (Job 5:7). If progress is to be made in this ministry, then the problems must be faced, solutions identified and implemented. Likewise, issues and controversies need to be addressed. To ignore them will cause the correctional chaplaincy to languish. To suppress open discussion of them, even if those with opposing views become vehement, is to create a situation in which bitterness will fester and later erupt in calamitous hostility. It is far better to seek resolution of the issues, perhaps synthesizing opposing views.

Current Problems

The majority of the problems extant in the correctional chaplaincy are deficiencies, as contrasted with excesses or abuses. Eight major problems are discussed in this section. Some of these overlap and are interrelated.

Lack of Promotion and Public Relations for the Correctional Chaplaincy

There is a great need for more correctional chaplains. One reason there has been so comparably little support for the correctional chaplaincy has been a lack of promotion for the chaplaincy and inadequate public relations for it. During the three decades since the Second World War, only a dozen or so books in English have dealt extensively with the correctional chaplaincy or ministry to prisoners; an average of about one article per year on chaplains or religion in correctional institutions has appeared in the professional correctional literature (journals such as *American Journal of Correction, Canadian Journal of Corrections, Federal Probation*); and only a few articles per year appear in *all* the religious periodicals of the country (Catholic as well as Protestant) combined—and most of these articles are a page or less in length. The distribution of newsletters and journals of the chaplaincy associations is so limited that they have almost no impact on promotion of the ministry behind bars.

The Church can be awakened and challenged to support the ministry behind bars. This can be illustrated by those organizations which have taken seriously the task of promoting the correctional chaplaincy. For example, the Good News Mission began in 1961 as a part-time jail ministry for one person and now supports a staff of thirty ministering to offenders—all financed by church contributions.

Most chaplains, especially government-employed chaplains, spend almost no time in promoting the correctional chaplaincy or public relations for it.[224] Likewise, most denominational liaison personnel for the correctional chaplaincy are submerged in a chaplaincy department whose primary interests are hospital and military chaplains. Consequently, the Church slumbers on, largely uncognizant of its responsibility and opportunity to minister to prisoners.

Effective public relations and promotion of the correctional ministry requires three simple steps: First, that those involved in the correctional ministry *seek every opportunity* to present this ministry to local congregations and to challenge (and rechallenge and *re*challenge) them with this ministry. If each chaplain were to set himself a goal of speaking to at least ten new churches a year about the correctional ministry, within a few years the support needed for the correctional ministry would be available. Second, the correctional ministry needs to be publicized by literature, radio, and TV. At present, the most extensive promotional literature of this sort are the newsletters and magazines published by the private church organizations ministering extensively among prisoners. Third, the Church needs a way to funnel its resources (people and funds) into this ministry. Church-supported chaplains and the organizations employing them provide such an avenue. More such organizations are needed. Denominations need to develop them for their people and not just have an office to serve primarily as a liaison with government employers of chaplains.

Lack of Study and Research Related to the Correctional Chaplaincy

In part this lack has been indicated by the earlier reference to the limited publications related to the correctional ministry. Volume 32 on *Philosophy and Religion* of the *Comprehensive Dissertation Index 1861–1972* lists only one doctoral dissertation on the correctional chaplaincy, and it deals only with counseling in a correctional environment.[225] The present book represents the first widespread dissemination of the data about chaplains from the extensive surveys of 1971 and 1973 (*see* Appendix B for a description of these).

Advancement of a profession depends upon a corpus of basic knowledge about it. Serious study of the profession or form of ministry is essential so that successive generations may build upon a sure foundation of established fact, and advance. It should not be surprising, therefore, if many secular, correctional professionals dismiss chaplains and religion as an insignificant factor in corrections, because chaplains have failed to study their profession.[226]

Extensive study is desperately needed in the following (among many other) areas:

· *A Comprehensive History of the Correctional Chaplaincy, Especially in the United States.*[227]

· *A Comprehensive Description of Religious Beliefs and Practices of the Incarcerated.*

· *Comprehensive Studies on Inmate Converts and the Impact on Behavior of Religion Behind Bars.*

- *A Study of "Indigenous" Religious Movements Behind Bars.*
- *A Comprehensive Study of Religious Volunteers in Corrections.*

Lack of Correctional Chaplaincy Training

Until training for the correctional chaplaincy becomes a part of the standard ministerial preparation in Bible colleges and seminaries, it is unlikely that adequate numbers of superior ministers will enter the chaplaincy. The Good News Mission course on the correctional chaplaincy was developed in 1972 to provide training not then available in Bible colleges and seminaries. This book was designed to help Bible colleges and seminaries incorporate such a course into their curriculums.

Chaplains also feel a need for more training. About three-fourths of prison chaplains in 1971 expressed a need for seminars to help strengthen their work.[228] Each year since this writer became a member of the APCCA, the idea of a chaplaincy training institute has been brought up. But nothing has yet come of it. There are papers and workshop sessions conducted by the APCCA at its national and regional meetings, each a few days in length. Some denominations and chaplaincy organizations have retreats for their chaplains. There are the standard CPE programs, but theological institutions have not yet developed formal programs of advanced training for correctional chaplains.

Lack of Musical and Religious Educational Materials Designed Especially for Inmates

Music has great power to motivate and to mold ideas. One of the factors which helped to establish the Lutheran Church so strongly in Germany was that Luther not only gave the German people the Bible in their own language "so that God might speak *directly* to them in His Word" but also gave them a hymnbook in their own language "that they might *directly* answer Him in their songs." [229] There is a great need to develop a book of hymns and spiritual songs for, by, and about prisoners.

Likewise, there is a need for religious educational materials oriented toward prisoners. Even when the Sunday-school material

—or other religious educational material—is not oriented toward a denominational emphasis, the reading and educational level and the illustrations and applications used often limit its usefulness. Needed are nondated lesson series of Bible studies oriented toward prisoners that take into account their educational backgrounds and living situations.[230]

A few publications exist (e.g., the *Crack in the Wall,* religious newspaper for, by, and about inmates) and communicate very effectively. More are needed.

Limited Use of Music and Audiovisual Resources by Chaplains

Correctional chaplains make very little use of audiovisual materials and spend very little time with music programs in their institutions. It may be that chaplains were not trained to use such aids during their ministerial training and did not master the use of them in the parish because the music and education programs were taken care of by either associate pastors or lay persons. Whatever the cause, chaplains should not neglect these potent means of communication.

Inappropriate Standards for Chaplains

Some of the standards widely applied to correctional chaplains do not bear a demonstrable relationship to proficiency and therefore are considered inappropriate. However, it is important to realize that even these standards are a great improvement over the lack of standards in the past, when political connections were the primary prerequisite for appointment as a correctional chaplain.

Two levels of standards exist for correctional chaplains: (1) requirements to enter the chaplaincy and (2) standards for leadership or demonstration of professional competence as a chaplain. Inappropriate standards exist in both areas.

Requirements to enter the chaplaincy were presented earlier. Several of these widely required of tax-financed chaplains seem inappropriate because they do not demonstrate a correlation to chaplaincy proficiency—namely: CPE, prior pastoral experience, and seminary training. The impact of these parameters on chaplain praxis was presented in chapter 5, raising serious questions about the propriety of these standards.

There are three groups which can lay claim to leadership or competence in the chaplaincy: (1) chaplains certified by the AEIC, (2) chaplains certified by the APCCA, and (3) members of the APCCA College of Fellows (criteria for membership include "recognized leadership" as a "person of distinction in the correctional area"[231]). The requirements for certification by the AEIC and APCCA may be found in Appendix E. Table 15 provides a comparison of these three groups of chaplains with the average Protestant chaplain.

The appropriateness of present APCCA standards seems questionable, since APCCA-certified chaplains and members of the College of Fellows involved a smaller percentage of the inmate population in all aspects of their religious and counseling programs (except group counseling by the College of Fellows) *than the average Protestant chaplain.* A further indication that the APCCA standards do not demonstrably relate to proficiency is that these "leaders" lack the dedication to their work of true leadership, working on the average five to eight fewer hours per week than the average chaplain. In general, leaders put in longer hours than the average worker.[232]

The data about AEIC-certified chaplains are presented simply to *suggest* that some of the AEIC ideals about certification are on the right track. At the time of the survey collecting the data shown in this table (1973), the AEIC was only a year old, and these figures are the average for just five chaplains, all of whom were church-supported and serving jails. Because of this small sample size, it would not be wise to draw conclusions from the performance of AEIC chaplains. The data for APCCA-certified chaplains came from 43 percent of the chaplains certified at that time and from 46 percent of the members of the College of Fellows.

It seems proper to ask what has caused the APCCA to develop inappropriate standards. Several factors seem pertinent. First, the APCCA leadership has long been dominated by government-employed (tax-financed) chaplains (80 to 90 percent are such), who apparently do not have the same perspective as church-

TABLE 15

Comparison of Certified Chaplains and Chaplaincy Leaders
With the Average Protestant Chaplain

	AEIC Certified	Average Protestant Chaplain	APCCA Certified	APCCA College of Fellows
Average Age (years)	39	44	50	56
Average Experience (years) as a Correctional Chaplain	5.2	7.1	11.9	19.0
Chaplaincy Time Use (hours per week):				
Personal Prayer/Study	9.2	7.8	6.5	7.7
Bible/Religious-Education Classes	2.8	2.4	2.0	2.0
Group Counseling/Discussion	2.0	3.0	2.3	1.7
Individual Counseling	19.8	14.1	13.8	10.7
Informal Contact with Inmates	6.5	2.9	1.2	1.7
Personal Contact with Releasees, Inmate Families and Friends	7.5	2.1	1.8	0.5
Involvement in Rehabilitation Activities and Court/Parole, etc.	8.0	2.9	2.2	2.2
Percentage of the Inmate Population Involved Weekly in Chaplain Programs:				
Worship/Preaching Services	66%	34%	21%	10%
Bible/Religious-Education Classes	53%	24%	9%	10%
Bible/Religious Correspondence Courses	21%	8%	6%	5%
Group Counseling/Discussion	5%	12%	9%	20%
Individual Counseling	13%	18%	15%	10%
Number of Individual Counseling Sessions Conducted by the Chaplain Each Week	23	23	17	14

supported chaplains. Second, the APCCA is ecumenical in orientation, with a tacit bias toward liberalism by its emphasis upon CPE. Third, most of the leaders in the APCCA have been government-employed chaplains *for a long time* (e.g., members of the College of Fellows average nineteen years in the chaplaincy). The significance of this is made clear by the conclusion of the Anglican Church's extensive study of its prison chaplains:

> We believe that the arguments against an indefinite term [i.e., permanent civil service appointment] are strong, and that in particular there seems to be a period after about ten or eleven years of service when many men become less and less effective. He may not fully realize it, or may even, while realizing it, deliberately continue, as he is unwilling to return to parish life or because he fears a fall in stipend.[233]

It is perhaps pertinent to cite the characteristics that this study stated as desirable in a chaplain and to compare AEIC and APCCA leaders with such attributes:

> The Chaplain should be a man of prayer, of mature experience of life and of people in life, and of such clear and simple convictions that no one could ever mistake his calling.[234]

AEIC-certified chaplains spend more time in personal prayer and study than the average chaplain; not so the APCCA leaders. All AEIC chaplains have the clear convictions of conservative theology; not so some of the APCCA leaders. Some of them cannot or will not identify themselves theologically.

What can be done? Both the AEIC and APCCA can examine their standards continually and eliminate requirements which do not bear a demonstrable relationship to proficiency as a chaplain. At present, AEIC certification standards are oriented toward a chaplain's present performance, while APCCA certification standards are more oriented toward the chaplain's background, training, and credentials, with less emphasis upon what he has achieved or is achieving as a chaplain. This is reflected in the facts that APCCA certification need not be renewed periodically and that a large percentage of APCCA-certified chaplains (more than a third in 1973) are not chaplains in a strict sense but denominational officials, directors of chaplaincy programs, etc. It is likely that APCCA standards will continue to dominate government-financed chaplaincy programs, while AEIC standards seem more typical of church-supported chaplaincy programs. "Competition" between the AEIC and APCCA can spur both on to function better.[235]

Failure to Appreciate the Indigenous Church Behind Bars

The concept of the indigenous Church Behind Bars (discussed in Chapter 11) poses a threat to many chaplains. It could make them superfluous, particularly if they are not qualified spiritually for leadership in the congregation because of unsound doctrine or ungodly behavior. Thus it is not surprising that there has been a failure to appreciate the indigenous Church Behind Bars.

Poor Leadership

Most of the problems discussed above have resulted because of inadequate leadership in the correctional chaplaincy for the past few generations, particularly in the APCCA and its predecessor, the Prison Chaplains' Association. While APCCA leadership has manifested numerous deficiencies (and primarily for the reasons identified in the discussion of inappropriate standards), it must be credited with having developed standards where none existed before and providing a professional identity for chaplains during the long years the Church has so ignored prisoners. Yet because of its leadership failings, ". . . the chaplains are not seen as a major resource of the church for reaching" prisoners.[236]

The question now is, will the virile, dynamic spiritual leadership so desperately needed for the correctional chaplaincy arise? If it does not, the correctional chaplaincy will continue to languish. It seems unlikely that such leadership will arise from the APCCA as long as it maintains its ecumenical orientation toward government-financed chaplains. Such leadership possibly may arise from the AEIC (begun in 1972), Good News Mission, International Prison Ministry, or some other organization with a broad base of ministry and a thorough commitment to Evangelical

Christianity (or a combination of these). Development of such leadership will face several hurdles. First, it must stimulate the study and research so desperately needed for a corpus of basic knowledge about this ministry and from which to develop appropriate standards and requirements. Second, it must begin to be a source of programs and materials that are effective in the jail and prison ministry as well as providing a communication link for all who want help in this ministry. Third, it must somehow pull together the fragmented segments of Evangelical Christianity and if not unite them in the ministry to offenders at least develop a wholesome cooperation among most of them. And fourth, it must find adequate funds to do the job and do it right.

Current Issues

In this section, three issues are discussed: (1) government employment of chaplains, (2) a chaplain's responsibility toward other religions, and (3) the effect of CPE. Other aspects of each of these issues have been treated earlier in this book.

Government Employment of Chaplains

The vast majority of full-time correctional chaplains in this country are employed by the government. Of the chaplains responding to the Pace survey in 1973, 40 percent of jail chaplains, 86 percent of chaplains serving juvenile institutions, and 91 percent of prison chaplains were government employees.

Arguments for Government Employment of Chaplains. Three main arguments have been presented for the government employment of correctional chaplains: First, the correctional institution must maintain control over the programs within it, including the religious program, and this is easiest if the head of the religious program is paid by the correctional institution.

This argument has little or no substance. The demands of security dictate that a correctional institution exercise control over the programs conducted in it and over the persons who conduct such programs—but such control does not require that those who are involved in or who run programs in the correctional institution be *paid by* the institution. For example, many volunteers have active, vital, and *official* roles in the programs of many correctional institutions without being on their payrolls, yet the institutions exercise control over these volunteers. In the Virginia penal system, the state does not pay the chaplains who are provided by a religious organization, yet these chaplains are an official part of the staffs of the penal institutions and function under the control of the penal system authorities.[237] A similar situation exists with chaplains for many jails. In these cases, control over the chaplains and their program is as great as when a chaplain is employed by the correctional institution. Control of the chaplain's paycheck by the correctional institution has a potentially deleterious consequence. The chaplain may become a lackey of the institution, or at least be perceived as one by many inmates.[238]

Second, it has been argued that the correctional institution has a responsibility to provide religious services in the same manner as it is responsible to provide rehabilitation and recreational services. The courts have disagreed. Correctional institutions may not unnecessarily abridge religious practices, but an institution has no obligation to provide religious services.[239] The institution must treat all religions equally. If it pays ministers of one religion, it must pay ministers from all religions on a similar basis. If the institution makes available facilities (e.g., a meeting room) for one religious group, it must do the same for any religious group. And so on.[240]

The past willingness of correctional institutions to provide ministers and facilities for religious groups in the Judaeo-Christian tradition and to ignore all others has been the source of much litigation in the past decade, particularly from the Black Muslims. Now that the government has been forced to provide for minority religious groups in a similar way,[241] this may sound the death knell for government financing of chaplains, for two reasons. First, many "Christians" will balk at the idea of their tax monies paying the salaries of a Black Muslim minister, a Satanist, or other such, eliminating the popular support for the idea of government-paid chaplains. And second, prison administrators may prefer to avoid the litigation which various groups will bring in order to get "one of theirs" on the chaplaincy payroll.

The simplest solution to this touchy situation is for the correctional institution to make available facilities for religious activities to all and not to pay any clergymen for ministering to inmates, but to allow as much access to inmates by the clergy as possible. This would eliminate the basis for most litigation about religion behind bars.

The third and final argument is the only one of substance. It is a very practical argument, contending that the churches will not provide the chaplains needed if the government does not pay for them. This has been true. Over 90 percent of correctional units have chaplains where the government will pay the chaplain's salary, but only 10 to 20 percent of correctional units are served by chaplains where the government will not pay the chaplains' salaries.

The question is, Would this be true if the Church were seriously challenged to provide chaplains? To date, there has been relatively little challenge presented to the Church in this respect. But, in general, where the challenge has been presented, the Church has responded. In addition, there has been the natural reluctance of the Church to pay chaplains if the state would pay them. Therefore, it is uncertain whether or not this argument is indeed valid.

Arguments Against Government Employment of Chaplains. Several main arguments have been developed against the employment of chaplains by government agencies. First, the Church, not the state, should finance clergymen. This argument is most important for Evangelical Christians. It is based upon a fundamental spiritual principle. Christ commanded His Church to minister. God's people, not the unsaved (taxpayer), ought to finance spiritual ministries. This was the method of the apostle Paul. He did not expect financial support from those whom he was evangelizing (*see* 1 Thessalonians 2:9). In the minds of many Christians, government employment of chaplains violates the separation commanded by 2 Corinthians 6:14–18, specifically, "What part hath he that believeth with an infidel?" Wherever the state finances the clergy, there is a clear danger of developing an established church.

The second argument is that the government has no right to tax its citizens to finance clergymen of a religious faith contrary to their own. It is the sort of argument that has brought about the ban on much prayer and Bible reading in the nation's public schools. The use of tax monies to support ministers forces both those of the same faith and those of a different belief to support them and, in the mind of this author, violates the Establishment Clause of the First Amendment to the Constitution of the United States.[242] It seems likely that litigation on this issue will increase in the coming decade, particularly as clergy from sects such as Satan cults or the Church of the New Song seek government support as chaplains.

The argument that government employment is likely to turn a chaplain into a lackey for the institution is difficult to support statistically, but it is clear that some chaplains have become "company men" for their government employers.[243]

The fourth argument against government employment of chaplains is upheld empirically, i.e., that private or church-supported chaplains tend to be more productive than those supported by government. Government-employed chaplains work about ten hours less a week than other chaplains and involve only three-fourths as many inmates in their religious programs. This problem is believed to stem from the security of government employment. The privately employed chaplain has both to interest church and community in his work and to produce demonstrable results in order to secure and maintain financial support for his ministry to the incarcerated. He cannot afford to be content with a program of little impact. Not so his government-financed counterpart.

The final argument against government employment of chaplains is a practical one. If there were no government funds to support chaplains, there would be no fights or legal battles about which clergymen should receive such funds. This would simplify both the correctional ministry and the problems which administrators of correctional institutions must now face. Likewise chaplains would no longer have to face some problems that they now confront, such as being expected to act at a civil marriage service.[244]

A Practical Concern. What would happen to the correctional chaplains employed at present by government agencies if the government stopped employing chaplains? Many of them have invested much of their lives in this ministry. It would appear that three options would be available to them: (1) continue as chaplains, but with private/church financing, (2) move outside the field of corrections, e.g., return to the parish ministry, or (3) change into some other role within corrections.[245]

A Comment. A most appropriate use of government funds would be to finance research projects about religion behind bars. Most of the areas in which study is needed that were mentioned earlier would be appropriate for government funding.

The Chaplain and Other Religions

The chaplain's relationship to the programs of religious groups other than his own is complex. In some institutions he may be responsible not just to coordinate the programs and use of religious facilities but also to "promote" all the programs—at least to the extent of seeing that they are advertised within the institution. Because of the varied religious complexion of the correctional world, this may include not just promotion of programs for the Protestant groups and Catholics, but also promotion of activities for Satan-worship cults, Metropolitan Community Church (homosexually oriented), etc. This poses a severe problem for all who take seriously such passages as 2 Corinthians 6:14–16 and 2 John 9–11.

Most would agree that the chaplain should not be compelled to violate the normal dictates of his faith by being forced to marry persons his faith would not allow him to marry (e.g., divorced persons) or by being coerced to serve Communion to one whom his faith would not allow to take it (e.g., a Catholic chaplain serving the Eucharist to an obvious non-Catholic). Yet the same freedom of conscience is not allowed the chaplain, or chaplaincy candidate, in the matter of separation from coordination/promotion of religions radically different from his. Some chaplains may be sufficiently flexible in their beliefs to marry anyone, serve Communion to anyone, and coordinate/promote any religious program. For example, the Protestant chaplain of the Virginia state penitentiary promoted and participated in a "joint religious service of Christians and Muslims" on July 4, 1976, a service billed as "a step toward removing obstacles which have divided Christians and Muslims philosophically."[246] Other chaplains have beliefs that prevent them from doing this.

Since the founding of this country, the Christian religion has enjoyed a privileged status. The past decade has witnessed an erosion of that privilege behind bars as courts have ruled that non-Christian religions must receive equal protection and status with the Christian religion. While each inmate has the God-given right to believe as he will (and the responsibility to take the consequences of such belief), *no godly chaplain is going to add to inmate confusion by assisting the spread of error and false teachings among the inmate population.* Instead he will follow Paul's advice to Titus and attempt to stop the mouths of those subverting many (*see* Titus 1:11). Such action is likely to bring censure from the ecumenically oriented and possibly criticism from the administration of the institution, yet the chaplain is merely following the dictates of his conscience and faith in the same manner as one refusing to marry or serve Communion to unsuitable persons.

It is likely that the problem will become more pronounced if our society continues to become more secular, since the attitude that all religions are equally good (if one should choose to be religious) will continue to spread, and disfavor will land upon any who contend otherwise.

The Effect of CPE

The impact of CPE on a chaplain's praxis and its propriety as a requirement have been discussed already. This discussion focuses upon a different issue related to CPE. There is no question that chaplains should be effective counselors. The question is more than whether or not CPE is the *only* way to become an effective counselor. The issue is, Does not the emphasis given to CPE in government-financed chaplaincy programs place an improper theological imposition upon chaplains and chaplaincy candidates? Does it not place the government employers of chaplains in the role of discriminating theologically? This is the issue which will be discussed here.

It is helpful to begin with a few facts about CPE. First, the primary benefit of CPE is that it helps one to understand himself because, as Clinebell notes, it "provides a depth encounter with oneself." [247] Second, it provides the advantage of extensive supervised practice in counseling. But third, CPE tends to diffuse the minister's focus so that he loses his vision of what Dr. Clyde Narramore calls *"the counseling privilege that dwarfs all others,"* that privilege *"of soul winning"* (emphasis his).[248] This can be illustrated by the following:

> A young woman in her late twenties was having extensive personal problems: anxiety, often distraught, indulging in limited sexual immorality. She turned for help to the minister for counseling of the church which she had been attending. He was an evangelical, with seminary, CPE, and advanced training in psychology and counseling. He counseled the young woman for several months with little improvement in her situation. Then the Sunday-school teacher of the young woman led her to Christ and, in a very short time thereafter, the young woman's problems were resolved. She had become a new creature in Christ. *The minister for counseling had not once dealt with the young woman about her relationship to Christ nor presented the plan of salvation to her* during his dozen or so counseling sessions with her.[249]

Fourth, CPE tends to de-emphasize the importance of sound doctrine. From its inception, CPE has failed to emphasize theological content—that was Hammett's conclusion in his review of CPE's first half-century—and it has been characterized by liberalism.[250] This explains in part the loss of evangelistic zeal by CPE-trained chaplains because as Wayne Oates observed, "One cannot have one theology for evangelism and another for his counseling and pastoral care." [251] In fact, much hostility has been observed toward sound doctrine (i.e., evangelical theology) from numerous ministers with CPE training.[252] Finally, CPE may help ministers become better counselors, but it is not the only means by which to become an effective counselor (or chaplain), and conclusive evidence has yet to appear that CPE training is superior to other forms of training for counseling or pastoral care.

Back to the issue. Normally ordination and ecclesiastical endorsement are required of chaplains. What about a minister whose religious tradition does not include ordination or ecclesiastical endorsement? For example, a Plymouth Brethren. Would or could he be acceptable as a correctional chaplain without ordination? [253] Most government employers of chaplains would at least say yes, even if in practice they fail to follow such a policy.[254] Likewise, would or could a minister whose theological position or religious tradition were opposed to CPE be acceptable as a correctional chaplain to a government employer of chaplains? If the answer to this question is no, then it would appear that government employers of chaplains may be guilty of imposing a theological position upon their chaplains, because CPE is characterized by liberalism (openly admitted by its promoters [255] and statistically correlated with theological persuasion [256]) and has not demonstrated itself as essential to proficient performance as a chaplain. A private/church employer of chaplains may properly impose theological standards and requirements, but not so a government employer of chaplains. This is the issue. Does CPE impose a theological position?

8

Suggestions for Effective Ministry to Offenders

The need for Christian ministry to offenders is so great that every effort should be put forth to ensure that the ministry is as effective as possible. In order to minister effectively, it is helpful to have information about the general characteristics of offender population. It must be remembered that each inmate is an individual and cannot be adequately understood as a stereotype, but the following characteristics help the prospective chaplain or Christian worker to know what to expect.

Characteristics of Offender Populations

The general characteristics of offender populations can be illustrated by the following two quotations:

> It is clear that convicted felons characteristically come from severely disordered families and social backgrounds. Poverty; homes broken by parental death, desertion, divorce, and separation; parental criminality and alcoholism; and restricted opportunity are nearly always present.[257]

> The great majority had an early onset of delinquency associated with frequent school difficulties, frequent fights, a poor job history, poor marital adjustment, frequent wanderlust, a bad military record with recurrent troubles, excessive drinking and drug use, and recurrent trouble with the police.[258]

The following provide detail to support the above summary. It is easy to understand why so many inmates wear the tattoo "born to lose."

Bad Family Situations. About two-thirds of adult male felons experienced gross disruptions of their families during childhood through divorce, parental death, desertion, or incarceration.[259] About half of married male inmates and over 80 percent of female inmates were separated or had been divorced at least once.[260] About a third had run away from home at least once as a youngster, and about half were completely on their own by age eighteen.[261]

Alcohol and Drug Abuse. It is estimated that 30 to 60 percent of inmates have abused drugs [262] and 50 to 60 percent (or more) of inmates have serious alcohol problems.[263] Neither of these problems is amenable to easy solution.[264]

Education/Employment Problems. Only a third or so of inmates have completed high school [265] (about 20 percent of adults and a third of juveniles in correctional institutions are functionally illiterate [266]) and nearly half of jail inmates in 1972 had a prearrest income of less than $2,000 per year.[267] Many inmates have never held a job as long as a year.[268]

Persistent Antisocial Behavior. About 60 percent of those convicted had previously been convicted of other offenses.[269] Based on the study by Guze, within three years after release, about 60 percent of male felons will be rearrested, with two-thirds of that group being reimprisoned (the recidivism rates for female felons is about half that for males); within eight to nine years after release, over 80 percent of male felons will have been rearrested at least once (at least half of them more than once), and half of the felons will have been imprisoned again at least once.[270] It is possible to diagnose formally 60 to 80 percent of convicted felons as "sociopaths" and another 12 to 15 percent as having anxiety neuroses.[271]

Young and Antagonistic. Most adult inmates are young, about half are under thirty.[272] Inmates are more conscious of their rights, more polarized (particularly along racial and ethnic lines), and much more politically conscious than in the past.[273] The problem of antagonism is intensified by the fact that two-thirds of convicted felons have a propensity for fighting,[274] and the removal of more stable, better adjusted inmates from prison populations by a greater use of probation, parole, and alternatives to incarceration leaves a more volatile concentration of bitter, antagonistic inmates than in the past.

Juvenile Offenders. The characteristics of juvenile offenders follow the same pattern as set by their adult predecessors. About one-quarter of the male and two-thirds of the female juveniles in custody are guilty of offenses that only apply to juveniles (curfew violation, truancy, etc.).[275]

From the preceding description, it should be clear that inmates need hope because they have so much cause to be hopeless. About a quarter of prison inmates have no one who visits them, and more than 5 percent have no one with whom even to correspond.[276] The effective ministry will encourage them to have hope in the One who can give hope.

Developing Programs for Ministry

While this discussion of developing programs for ministry is oriented toward chaplains, its application to others who lead in ministry among offenders should be clear. Five topics are covered: (1) principles for establishing programs with the institution, (2) coping with physical facilities, (3) using volunteers, (4) ministering to the institution's staff and officials, and (5) security considerations.

Principles for Establishing Programs

Whether he ministers in a jail, prison, reformatory, or another kind of correctional institution, the chaplain will be required to establish programs in his institution. He normally will be responsible for the religious programs within the institution. He may have to be responsible for other programs as well.

The chaplain must be trusted by both inmates and officials. Without confidence and trust in him from both sides of the bars, the chaplain's ability to establish meaningful, enduring programs will be severely limited.

The *first principle* for establishing programs is to pray. God's blessings upon a program and the timing of its establishment must be sought prayerfully. The chaplain must ever be alert to the danger of missing God's best for his ministry by being too involved in merely good activities and programs.

A *second principle* is to be sure a real need exists.

A *third principle* is that planning be both thorough and long-range. The chaplain who has good success in establishing programs within his institution is one who has looked to the future and planned for it. He determined that a real need existed. Then he planned the program long before it was established. He began to lay the groundwork for the program by appropriate suggestions to officials. He determined the attitude of officials toward the possibility of such a program.

The chaplain needs to think through all aspects of the program: costs, facilities, personnel, changes in the activities of the institution, how he will phase out of the program, etc. Only by doing thorough planning before presenting a program to officials for acceptance can the chaplain avoid the pitfall of getting official commitment to a program idea that cannot be put into practice.

The chaplain must tread a thin line. Often he must put pressure on officials to establish any new programs. Correctional officials often prefer the old, familiar, easy way of doing their jobs—even when it fails to meet all needs of the offenders. However *the chaplain must never push officials into programs they do not desire.*

A *fourth principle* is to seek "perfect" candidates to initiate a program. Whenever a new program starts, it is important that no one goof in its early phases. Therefore, the chaplain should screen participants (volunteers and inmates) carefully.[277]

It is wise to allow the institution's personnel time to adjust to changes in their routine. This philosophy of moving slowly will pay off in the cooperation which the chaplain will receive from the institution staff.

A *final word.* Never attempt a program which cannot be carried through. The chaplain is wiser to leave a program untried if he is not able to carry it through to completion. It will take only one or two aborted programs to destroy the institution's confidence in him. He will gain a reputation as an unrealistic visionary and minimize his potential to minister.

Coping With Physical Facilities

The correctional chaplain often needs a fertile imagination in order to devise ways to overcome limitations caused by the physical facilities of the correctional institution, especially in jails. As an extreme example, one jail chaplain even used the kitchen sink to baptize an inmate—by immersion!

Most prisons and juvenile institutions provide special facilities for programs under the supervision of the chaplain. Table 16 shows the facilities reported by chaplains in 1973.

Institutions without chapels can use the dining hall, a classroom, or a multipurpose room for worship services. However, many jails do not even have these facilities. In some situations, the inmates interested in the worship service can be moved into a single cellblock or tier. Often the jail will be so overcrowded as to preclude such prisoner movement. In this case, the worship service must be repeated at each cellblock or tier. A peculiar problem then arises, because the inmates interested in the worship service are not separated from those not interested.

TABLE 16

Facilities Reported by Chaplains in 1973

Type of Institution	Jail	Juvenile Institution	Prison
Facility			
Office for Chaplain	45%	92%	99%
Chaplain's Clerk & Office Equipment	14%	75%	87%
Chapel or Worship Room	59%	67%	100%
Room for Counseling by Visiting Clergy *	68%	75%	57%
Room for Religious Instruction	36%	42%	68%
Religious Library	18%	17%	63%

* This refers to a room separate from the chaplain's office. In many jails, this space must be shared with attorneys, probation officers, and detectives who want to interview inmates.

The chaplain needs to use tact and courtesy in securing reasonable quiet for the service. A TV or radio (or several) may be playing. Other disturbances may exist as well (loud talking, shower running, toilet flushing, etc.). When these sounds are not eliminated voluntarily by inmate initiative, the chaplain may politely request quiet for the few minutes of the service. If the chaplain displays respect for the inmates and treats them with the same respect that a minister would employ when visiting in a home, such requests will almost always receive compliance. The chaplain should alert the institution staff as to the times of worship services in order to minimize disturbances such as announcements over a PA system and guard movements through the area. When a disturbance occurs, the chaplain should pause and wait for it to cease if it is of a transitory nature (e.g., a guard passing through). If the disturbance is more enduring (e.g., a radio which an inmate refuses to turn off), the chaplain should ignore the disturbance and proceed.

The basic requirement for a class or group session is simply a place where interested participants may gather. It is preferable, but not essential, to have seating arranged. Most inmates have learned how to sit on floors. It will not hurt the teacher to do so too if needed.[278] Space for audiovisual equipment (and convenient electrical power sources) is desirable. Almost any kind of space can satisfy these requirements: a room set aside for classes, an unused cellblock or tier, even a blocked-off corridor (i.e., with doors closed at either end of it), a dining hall, library, office, or a laundry room. In any space normally used for other purposes than the chaplain's office, the possibility of pilfering exists. At times, it may be necessary to conduct classes or group sessions in an occupied cellblock or tier. In such cases, the cooperation of nonparticipating inmates should be sought in the same way as discussed above.

The two essential ingredients for a place to counsel are reasonable privacy and freedom from disturbance. The more pleasant the surroundings, the easier it will be for the counselee to open himself. The ideal is a private office or counseling room. However, the correctional chaplain may have to do much of his counseling in less desirable locations: an empty isolation cell, the laundry room, a storage room or closet, an infrequently used section of a corridor or stairwell, an empty dining hall, etc. Even the chaplain who has an office in the institution may want to counsel in other areas at times because of the problems of scheduling inmates to be moved to the area of his office, or because an inmate has requested counseling when he encountered the chaplain somewhere in the institution away from the chaplain's office.

When a room of adequate size is available, film showing can be done in the normal manner. When films are shown inside a cellblock or tier, problems may exist. Blankets may have to be used to block the light from windows. A cellblock wall or a sheet may have to serve as the screen. It may be necessary for inmates to sit on the floor when those of several cellblocks or tiers are brought together for viewing the film.

Analysis of the 1973 survey of chaplains revealed that chaplaincy programs are not significantly influenced by facilities (or their lack), except possibly group counseling in jails. Consequently, the main limitation on the scope of religious programs within a correctional institution is the lack of imagination and initiative of their leaders. Extensive programs are possible even in antiquated, inadequate facilities, as illustrated by Sheriff Bill Selph's Henrico County (Virginia) Jail in 1975. The jail has extensive programs: Sunday worship services, several Bible classes and Christian films each week, individual counseling, a library (housed in a former shower stall), education classes (with the highest ratio of GEDs (high school equivalency) earned per inmate of any jail in Virginia), etc. To accomplish this has required imaginative use of facilities—classes and film showings held in inmate living areas, conversion of the former punishment cell into a classroom, chaplain's office, etc. The kind of things done in the Henrico County Jail can be done elsewhere also.[279] Lack of facilities is not a valid excuse for not having programs.

Using Volunteers

Before the mid 1960s, religious workers were about the only volunteers within the criminal justice system. Since then the use of volunteers has increased immensely. Volunteerism has become a contemporary fad which is likely to be perpetuated because of the government-financed bureaucracy which has been developed to support (and control?) volunteerism.[280] The growth in volunteers has greatly benefited the Christian ministry behind bars. It has caused institutions to be more open to volunteer programs. It has relieved Christian workers of many of the secular tasks they had performed previously (education, library, job assistance, etc.), allowing them to devote more time in ministering to spiritual needs. Also, the increased use of volunteers within the criminal justice system has increased community interest in helping offenders.

It is important that volunteer programs be conducted properly. Bad volunteer experiences cannot only hurt people (volunteer, offender, or both), but can also create a very bad attitude in the institution toward volunteer programs and seriously damage a program's reputation in the community. These things can limit a ministry to prisoners.

Within the past few years an abundance of helpful literature on using volunteers within the criminal justice system has been developed. Of great help for those using volunteer programs behind bars are Marie Buckley's *Breaking Into Prison: A Citizen's Guide to Volunteer Action* (Beacon Press, 1974) and *Guidelines and Standards for the Use of Volunteers in Correctional Programs* (LEAA Technical Assistance Division, 1972).

This section briefly discusses the administration of volunteer programs, common problems, and a few examples of successful volunteer programs in jails and prisons.

Administration of Volunteer Programs. Any volunteer program should be thoroughly planned. What is its objective(s)? How will it accomplish them? When will it start? What type of volunteers, training, supervision, and support for them will be needed? A clear definition of duties, the line of authority (or chain of command), etc., is also essential.

Before beginning a program, it is important to prepare the institution for it. This requires much more than simply acquiring administrative approval. Bad reactions from institutional staff have hampered many volunteer programs.[281] It is vital, therefore, that the institution staff be oriented to the volunteer program and have its objective(s) and their relationship to it (and potential benefit from it) clearly explained.

Any volunteer program should be implemented slowly and carefully, using initially only the cream of the crop (in terms of both volunteers and offenders). Then after the bugs have been worked out of the program, it can be expanded.

In an effective volunteer program, it will be necessary for volunteers to be: recruited, screened, trained, oriented, supervised, appreciated and recognized (if they are to be retained), and, when necessary, fired.[282]

It must be remembered that volunteer programs are not free. It generally takes at least an hour of the program leader's time per month for each volunteer—or an hour of leadership time for every ten to fifteen man-hours of volunteer effort—for proper supervision of volunteers, plus time for recruitment, screening, and training. At present, chaplains average only a couple of hours per week training/supervising an average of fifteen to twenty volunteers, suggesting that many volunteer programs under chaplain supervision receive inadequate attention from the chaplain for proper administration.

Common Problems in Volunteer Programs. Most volunteer program problems are simply failures to plan the program thoroughly, to prepare the institution for the program, to screen/train/supervise/recognize volunteers, or to give adequate leadership attention to the program to maintain it. These failures manifest themselves in bad relationships between volunteers and institution staff, a high turnover rate in volunteers, and unstable programs.[283] Religious volunteer programs have an additional potential for problems: the religious incompatibility of volunteers. Often it is wiser not to mix volunteers who have strong feelings or beliefs that differ (e.g., mixing volunteers who are anticharismatic with those who are procharismatic can create problems). Normally the chaplain will have several programs for volunteers under his supervision, so he can put volunteers of one kind in one program and volunteers of another kind in a different program. This is not Machiavellian; rather, it merely applies the principle of being "wise as serpents, and harmless as doves" (Matthew 10:16).

Programs that Succeed

Here are some examples of successful volunteer programs under chaplain supervision:

Sunday Worship Services. Some programs rotate responsibility for the services among a group of churches. Some draw upon a team or teams of volunteers from various churches. Members of the team may come every week or have a rotation plan among the team members. It is very helpful if at least some week-to-week continuity of volunteers conducting the services can be maintained, either by staggered rotation or a cadre of volunteers who are present every week.

Bible Classes. Whether taught in a classroom or at the cellblock/tier, it is best to have a teaching team of two or three. The team approach allows more opportunity to deal personally with the inmates after the class, answering questions, counseling, and praying with them.

Christian Film Showings. Normally a film-showing team of two or three volunteers is preferred, as with a Bible-class teaching team.

Friendly Visitation/Literature Distribution. In this volunteers may circulate through the inmate living spaces or simply be present at a religious activity and give out Christian literature and offer their friendship.

One-on-One Counseling. The formal goals may vary from the goal of "inspirational friendship" for man-to-man (M-2) and woman-to-woman (W-2) aspects of the Job Therapy approach [284] to the goal of Christian discipleship for the one-on-one counseling programs of the Good News Mission.[285] Typically the counselor meets with the offender for an hour or so once a week and is encouraged to continue the relationship for at least the first six months that the offender is back in the community.

Yokefellow/Lay Group Counseling. These are small groups, meeting weekly (normally with eight to twelve participants), that are led by lay volunteers. They share their experiences and, hopefully, grow into more mature persons. Normally the sessions last between an hour and two hours.

Administrative Help. There are many varied opportunities for help within the institution. These range from organizing and maintaining the chaplain's literature stock and secretarial/receptionist types of work to helping to plan the schedule for use of the chapel and religious classroom. Often the volunteers helping in these things will be inmates whose job it is to serve as clerks for chaplains.[286]

Social Programs. There is a great range of social programs which may be found under chaplaincy supervision in various institutions: Alcoholics Anonymous meetings, Jaycee chapters, libraries, education programs (both tutors and teachers, from basic literature through college and vocational training programs), recreation activities, etc. In some, the presence of the chaplain is simply a formality, serving as the institutional staff sponsor. In other programs, he provides active leadership.

Outside the Institution. The use of volunteers outside the institution by organizations ministering to prisoners is even more varied than it is within the institutions. This may be illustrated by the kinds of volunteer activities outside the institution in the ministry of the Good News Mission. These include all kinds of office work (receptionist, typist, secretary, clerical duties), maintenance (equipment of all sorts, building, and grounds) and construction activities, technical (printing, radio technician, layout design, artwork, etc.), Bible correspondence course grading, inmate correspondence, assistance in public relations, follow-up of releasees and inmate families, job assistance, material help (clothes, food, money, furniture, etc.) in times of need.

These are *some* of the ways in which volunteers have been used successfully in the Christian ministry among offenders.

Ministering to the Institution's Staff and Officials

A chaplain's ministry is incomplete if he restricts his attention to the inmates. His total ministry involves both inmates and those who have contact with them.[287]

Who are the officials to whom a chaplain has the opportunity to minister? The most obvious are the institution's staff who have immediate contact with prisoners: in a jail, the jailors, matrons, bailiffs, and in some cases a teacher, doctor, and social workers; in a prison, the guards, matrons, administrative staff, teachers and instructors, psychologists, doctors, and others involved in various aspects of rehabilitation. The chaplain also has opportunities to minister to sheriffs, wardens, superintendents, marshalls, police officers, members of the court from judges down to secretaries, probation officers, parole board members, attorneys, and a multitude of other officials within the criminal justice system.

As a chaplain shows genuine interest in these as persons and in the work which they do, the Lord will open opportunities to share Christ with them.

Always his ministry should be performed with tact and courtesy, but God holds the chaplain responsible for these opportunities as surely as for the inmates in his charge (*see* Ezekiel 33:6 ff.).

Security Considerations

Security is the prime consideration of all jails and prisons. They are charged to keep their prisoners, most of whom do not wish to be there and some of whom will do almost anything to escape. In addition, the administration of the institution is concerned about the safety of its staff, the inmates, and everyone else who may enter the institution. Security is usually breached because of a lack of understanding by untrained personnel. For example, at one prison camp, the chaplain was surprised at how many men came out to the service one night and how much they wanted to sing—and with what gusto and volume. The singing was used to cover the sound of knocking a hole in the prison wall.

Because the chaplains perform most of their ministry inside the institution, they have a tendency to become complacent and may violate such fundamental security principles as "if the door has a lock, lock it." The most common abuse of inner security by chaplains and religious workers is serving as an inappropriate communication link between prisoners in different parts of the institution or between prisoners and those on the outside. Once one breaks a rule of inner security, he both loses some respect of inmates and provides inmates with a means of pressuring him to do their will.

Escape-minded prisoners will observe when the normal security procedures are violated and will create similar situations in hope that such violations will be repeated. Chaplains in particular should not allow situations to develop on their behalf which foster breaches in procedures, because doing so endangers institution staff. Some chaplains and Christian workers react badly to operating under observation by closed-circuit TV monitoring, two-way PA systems, or in the presence of a correctional officer. Anyone who does not have the freedom to minister comfortably in spite of these probably does not belong in a jail or prison religious program. Actually, such observation can expand one's opportunity for ministry—as it did on my second visit to the Hanover County (Virginia) Jail:

> The jail had not been served by a chaplain previously, so they were not quite clear how to treat me. After my first visit, the jail administration had received word that I (the new chaplain) would be taken hostage in an escape attempt on my next visit. Therefore, the jail assigned a correctional officer to stay with me the entire time of my ministry that day in the jail. This "shadow" did not hinder my ministry in any way—*and he had to listen to four sermons that day* as I preached at four different cellblocks. This occasion gave me a unique opportunity to share God's Word with this officer. In this case, the captor was a part of the "captive audience."

Some prisoners require more stringent security than others—at times for their own protection, at times for the security of the institution or other prisoners. Often some prisoners have to be kept separate from other prisoners (as when one inmate may be planning to testify against another inmate at his trial). At times, ministry to a prisoner will have to be conducted in the disciplinary cell when a prisoner has been confined for some infraction of the institution's regulations. Pastoral visits to inmates in disciplinary confinement have often been most fruitful in establishing relationships that God has used in turning men to Christ.

The chaplain should be certain that he understands what is contraband for his institution and should have a printed list to advise his volunteers. Contraband, quite simply, is anything not allowed by the administration. What *is* allowed varies widely from one institution to another. Some, for example, permit inmates to have razors and blades; others do not. Some allow inmates to have chewing gum; others don't. In any case where there is doubt about the propriety of an item, it should be cleared with the proper person in the institution administration.

The following security guidelines, developed for Good News Mission volunteers ministering in jails, provide a convenient summary of security considerations for volunteers.

1. Most inmates are average people. Some are very dangerous. (One cannot always tell the difference just by talking with them.)
2. *Do not give anything to inmates* except religious literature without explicit permission from the chaplain.
3. *Do not take anything from an inmate* without explicit permission from the chaplain.
4. *Do not contact anyone outside the jail* for (or about) an inmate without explicit permission from the chaplain.
5. Follow all rules (jail's and chaplain's) diligently.
6. If in doubt, ask the chaplain.

As a closing comment: It is well to remember that ministry in a correctional institution can be dangerous. There is always the possibility that a chaplain or Christian worker will be taken hostage, hurt, or even killed. It is natural for one to feel uneasy and somewhat afraid during his first visits in a jail or prison. If these feelings persist, however, and the potential danger of this ministry creates an abiding sense of fear in the person, it is probably a good indication that the Lord does not want that person in a jail or prison ministry. One indication that God has called one to this ministry is indeed his very freedom from such fear.

Follow-up

It is the desire of every good chaplain to see everyone to whom he ministers both receive Christ as Saviour and grow into wholesome spiritual maturity. The chaplain's ministry can be divided into two phases as it pertains to those to whom he ministers:

reaching and discipling. "Follow-up" describes the discipling process, both while the inmate is still in the institution where the chaplain serves and when he leaves it.

When an inmate has been reached for Christ, the role of the chaplain changes from that of evangelist to that of pastor. In order to develop wholesome maturity, the convert needs: (1) spiritual knowledge, (2) a daily devotional life, (3) a Christian lifestyle, (4) fellowship with other believers, and (5) participation in service to Jesus Christ. Follow-up helps these needs to be met. Converted inmates who have become solid, mature Christians have been the object of much follow-up effort.

Follow-up must be planned. This section discusses (1) follow-up within the institution after conversion, (2) follow-up of the inmate after he has been transferred to another institution (particularly applicable to jail chaplains, whose converts often are moved to prisons after their sentencing), (3) follow-up of the convert after his release, and (4) follow-up with the inmate's family.

Follow-up Within the Institution

When an inmate makes a profession of faith while in the institution, the chaplain should arrange a counseling session with him as soon thereafter as possible (if not the next day, certainly before a week has passed). The purposes of this session are (1) to make sure the inmate understood his commitment to Christ (i.e., to be sure that he was in fact regenerated—or, if already a Christian, that he has repented and has now rededicated himself to Christ) and answer questions which may have come to his mind, (2) to provide the inmate with the tools which he needs for spiritual growth—a Bible, appropriate tract(s), first lesson in a Bible-study program, etc., (3) to explain to the new convert what is needed for Christian growth, and (4) to inform the inmate about the religious programs of the institution that can help him mature spiritually.

The second step is for the chaplain to enroll this new Christian in a new convert's class. This class should cover such basic topics as: what the Bible is and how to use it, how to become a Christian, prayer, witnessing, and how to know God's will for one's life as well as the cardinal doctrines of the Christian faith. Third, the chaplain should assist and encourage the new convert to develop friendships with mature, stable Christians in the institution. Fourth, the chaplain should keep a steady flow of tracts, Christian books, tapes, etc., to the inmate, being careful not to overwhelm him but continuously providing him with appropriate materials for his point of spiritual development. Fifth, the chaplain may set up a "spiritual buddy" for the inmate on the outside, either a correspondent or one who will visit the inmate in a one-on-one counseling program. Finally, the chaplain may have a special program of discipleship training for Christian inmates desiring intensive spiritual development.

The above is *in addition* to the routine worship and preaching services, regular Bible classes and Christian films, and counseling. The chaplain should schedule periodic interviews with every Christian to help that person assess his needs and to understand clearly how God wants to use his life (i.e., his areas of Christian service).

Follow-up at Another Institution

Many inmates will go through several institutions during their time of incarceration. The inmate may be held in several different jails while being tried upon a variety of charges once he has been apprehended. Then he may go to the receiving unit or diagnostic center of the state prison system before being sent to the unit where he will serve his time. Even then, he may be transferred to another unit (as his security classification changes, because of threats upon his life, for needed medical treatment, etc.). A good chaplain is concerned about the spiritual growth of his "son in the faith" through such meanderings.

The most immediate thought on follow-up is to refer the inmate to the chaplain and religious programs of the institution to which he has gone. Unfortunately, such referral can be harmful if the chaplain is not evangelical. For example:

> Dave, a recent convert, was sent to the prison from the jail. Dave's wife had left him during his confinement at the jail. Concerned about doing the right thing when he received a letter from his wife stating her desire for divorce, Dave sought

> the chaplain's counsel. As they talked, Dave asked what the Bible said about his situation. The chaplain replied, "You can forget the Bible. It doesn't have anything to say about today's situations." During his stay in that prison, Dave made little progress spiritually.

The question of religious referral is intricate. One does not want to discourage an inmate from taking full advantage of every avenue of goodness in his evil environment. Yet, at the same time, the Scripture warns of the danger of false teachers (e.g., 2 Peter 2) and commands spiritual leaders to stand firmly against corrupted doctrine (e.g., Titus 1:9–11), and even prohibits association with those who abandon the doctrine of Christ (2 John 9–11).[288]

The solution to this problem is threefold: First, the chaplain should seek to train every convert to be aware of the problem of false teachers and to be wary of all who do not fully accept the Bible's authority. The more grounding the convert can be given in basic biblical doctrine, the less likely he is to be tripped up spiritually either by a liberal's rejection of God's Word or by a cultist's distortion of it. Second, the chaplain can seek to discover the names of mature evangelical inmates at each institution whose chaplain or program he cannot recommend. Then the chaplain can refer his converts to these as "elder brothers" in Christ. Finally, where there are institutions without a strong evangelical witness, the chaplain can encourage the evangelical community around the institution to begin a ministry within it.

Inmates transferred to institutions where the chaplain is not evangelical should be encouraged to participate in the religious program because of the need of their united witness before the unregenerate majority.[289] However, they should be warned not to be misled doctrinally and encouraged to find spiritual feeding in Bible study, prayer, and fellowship with others who love Jesus and accept God's Word. They should pray for the chaplain that he might become the man God wants him to be.

If the chaplain at the institution is a good one, it is appropriate to send him a letter about the convert and request that he continue to follow him up.

In addition, letters of encouragement and Christian literature can be of great help to a lonely inmate with only a few fellow believers at his unit.

Releasee Follow-up

There are four basic steps for follow-up with the inmate convert who is released. He should know that he has access to the chaplain or Christian worker. He should feel free to call him up if needed (even if it's in the middle of the night). The chaplain or Christian worker should inculcate such an attitude. The chaplain should maintain contact with the releasee (letter, phone, personal visit), especially during his early days of freedom. The prime objective of the chaplain's follow-up program for the releasee should be to get him actively involved in a local church and then to entrust his future discipleship to the leadership of that church.[290] If the convert will live in a distant area upon release, the chaplain can do little more than contact a minister or friend in that area and urge him to try to help the releasee.[291]

Follow-up With the Inmate's Family

This begins by encouraging the convert to tell his family of his conversion—and, where appropriate, aiding his communication with them along this line. Then, the family should know that the chaplain is available to counsel by mail or phone or in person [292] and to help them become involved in a sound evangelical church. The chaplain can provide the inmate's family with the same kinds of Christian literature for growth as he has provided for their loved one behind bars. In particular, many families find great benefit from taking the same Bible correspondence courses as their inmate relatives.[293] If the family lives reasonably near the institution, the chaplain may arrange for ladies to visit the inmate's wife in order to become supportive friends.

A Needed Perspective

The one who is called to minister to prisoners needs an *infinite capacity for disappointment.* Often he will fail to measure up to the needs of the moment. Perhaps because of tiredness or preoccupation with something else, he will not heed or adequately respond to an inmate seeking his help. Satan will use guilt feelings about such failures to discourage and destroy. Let every worker remember that God is not bound by our inadequacies and that he wastes nothing, not even our mistakes and failures, but weaves them into His pattern for human history, even bringing good from our evil.[294]

The Christian worker in the jail or prison will be disappointed in the limited commitment of inmates to Christ and the falling away even of those who had been close to the Lord. The apostle Paul knew this heartache. Second Timothy 4 contains examples: Demas, a former missionary with Paul, forsook him, loving this present world (verse 10); all abandoned Paul at his first hearing (verse 16). At times, such will be the experience of the one serving Christ behind bars. But God will strengthen him, as He did Paul (2 Timothy 4:17), and the promise of fruit in due season will prove itself true (*see* Galatians 6:9).

9

Communicating the Gospel

Communication of the Gospel of Jesus Christ involves (1) an *approach* to gain a hearing, (2) a *presentation* of the message, and (3) an appropriate *response* from the hearer. Too often communication is misconstrued as only a presentation. This chapter is organized about these three aspects of communication.

Approaching Inmates

This section addresses the means by which a chaplain gains a hearing for himself and for the message of his program. These are classified into two groups: essential elements and some techniques. The essential elements pertain to the attitude or atmosphere that exudes from the chaplain and his program. The techniques are a brief, partial description of methods by which inmates may be approached or attracted to the chaplain's ministry. While some inmates will come to the chaplain or his program completely on their own, for the majority of inmates it is necessary for Christians to take the initiative in establishing the relationship which makes communication possible.

Essential Elements

Prayer that God the Holy Spirit will guide and provide the wisdom and strength needed to approach every inmate must pervade the chaplain's ministry. Friendliness coupled with patient perseverance can open even hostile inmates to the Gospel. It is mandatory that the chaplain and his workers be sincere. A chaplain can ruin his ministry if he pretends interest where he has none. It is far better for him to admit honestly that he is not interested in the inmate or his story than to pretend interest. Inmates are expert at detecting "con jobs."

The chaplain should not cause inmates to feel that they cannot honestly and *openly* express their thoughts to him, whether doubts, opposition, or confession of sinfulness. Otherwise, inmates will present only a facade of themselves to the chaplain.

Care must be exercised in making commitments. Failure to keep his promises will bring a reputation as an empty talker and destroy the chaplain's ministry. Inmates are disappointed enough by themselves and the system to risk turning to another who they feel may disappoint them.

Most inmates need an attentive ear. Constructive listening by one who will not put up with lies or nonsense but who will pay serious attention to what an inmate says will not only help the inmate relieve his inner tensions but will also do much to make him receptive to the Gospel.

The chaplain must be concerned about right. As one chaplain said of the chaplain's role in correctional reform, he must "fight for justice at every level." A chaplain should serve as conscience for the institution, challenging unreasonable rules and improper inmate treatment. As he does so, inmates will become more interested in him and his ministry.[295] He needs discretion in how he goes about it.[296] It is not his role to run to the administration with every prisoner complaint.

Some Techniques

Converted inmates have a great potential to interest their fellow prisoners in the Gospel and the chaplain's ministry. This potential should be utilized wherever possible. It is important for the chaplain to go to all places in the institution where inmates work and live: kitchen, laundry, shops (if any), the yard, hall corridors with the cleaning crews, cell areas, etc. Informal, friendly contacts with inmates where they work and live help to establish rapport and demonstrate the chaplain's interest in the inmates as individuals.

Participation in social and recreation programs by the chaplain and his volunteers can establish relationships that will open men to Christ.[297] Care must be taken, however, to ensure that too much time is not consumed by such activities. The potential of such is illustrated by the change in Al's life.

> Al, a 45-year-old junkie and often-convicted offender, was an avid chess player. But no one in his cellblock knew how to play. He was also antireligious. The chaplain began to play chess with Al, one game a week (about twenty minutes), deliberately avoiding any mention of religion because of Al's attitude. After a month, Al said at the close of a game, "OK, Chaplain, preach me a sermon. I'll listen." For the next month, Al and the chaplain played their game of chess and followed it with a fifteen- to twenty-minute talk about Christ and the Word of God. The chaplain listened attentively as Al poured out his bitterness. About this time Al gave his life to Jesus, and the talks after the chess games became discipleship sessions. Then Al began to participate in both the counseling and Bible-study programs of the jail.

Incentives or enticements? A number of methods can be used to increase inmate attendance at and participation in the chaplain's programs: refreshments at the services and meetings, women in the program, awards (e.g., a study Bible) for participation, etc. Even when not associated with a particular service or program (e.g., distribution of Mothers' Day cards by the chaplain to those inmates who desire them), such methods will increase the openness of inmates to the chaplain's ministry. The question is, At what point do these stop being incentives and become enticements? It is not bad that some inmates come simply because of the attraction. Some who so came have been caught by the Lord, as will others be in the future. The attraction becomes wrong when its use begins to distract seriously from the primary purpose of the program.

Comments

No single method of approach will be effective with all inmates. Thus a variety of approaches should be used. No single person is able to establish rapport with all inmates. Therefore, the chaplain should involve a number of helpers in his ministry. The chaplain should not be offended or upset if some of his volunteers are able to approach some inmates who are closed to the chaplain's ministry. Some laymen can have more rapport with inmates than the chaplain does. No jealousy will arise if the chaplain remembers that "there are diversities of gifts, but the same Spirit" (1 Corinthians 12:4) and that God uses the gifts of all of His workers. Each is responsible for the proper use of his gifts (1 Peter 4:10). The chaplain and his volunteers labor, but it is God who brings results (1 Corinthians 3:7). Let the chaplain rejoice in the abilities, energies, and resources of all. As Jesus said, "Who then is a faithful and wise servant, whom his lord hath made ruler over his household, to give them meat in due season? Blessed is that servant, whom his lord when he cometh shall find so doing" (Matthew 24:44–45).

Presentation of the Message

After a hearing for the Gospel has been obtained, the message must be presented. This section examines (1) study and preparation of messages and lessons, (2) establishment of a point of contact, (3) presentation factors, and (4) communication aids.

Study and Preparation

There is not space here to present a thorough discussion of hermeneutics, exegesis, or homiletics. The reader must turn to the standard texts on these matters.[298] However, a few suggestions about the preparation of messages and lessons for inmates may benefit some readers.

The chaplain or volunteer who seeks to prepare an effective message must (1) have the *proper relationship* to God (*see* 1 Corinthians 2:9–14), (2) approach the Bible with the *proper attitude* (i.e., truly believe it is God's Word as stated in 2 Timothy 3:16–17), and (3) submerge his study and preparation in prayer, trusting God, the Holy Spirit, to guide his thinking.

A seven-step procedure has been found very helpful by many who minister to inmates after a passage for study has been selected prayerfully.

1. Become familiar with the passage. Read it a number of times, possibly in several different translations to get several different perspectives on the passage. Meditate on it. Memorize key parts and phrases.
2. Determine the setting and context of the passage. Who is speaking? To whom? When? Where? Why?
3. What does the passage actually say? What are its main points? One should be alert for figures of speech. The bearing on the passage of the customs and lifestyles of the day should be considered (e.g., the shoe ceremony in Ruth 4:7).
4. Relate the passage to its larger context: the chapter it is in, the Book of the Bible it is in and its place in the Book's theme or argument, its relation to other passages of the Scripture on the same subject.
5. Ask, What does God want *me* to learn from this passage? Until a person has allowed God to work in his own life through a passage, it is unlikely that God will anoint his lesson or message for others with power. Unfortunately this matter of personal application is often neglected by preachers and religious teachers.
6. Check out the difficulties and problems of the passage. Someone might ask a question. It is important to be at least aware of these, even if one has no satisfactory answer. It does not hurt the chaplain or Christian worker to admit honestly, "I've thought about this problem and studied it, but still have not been able to resolve it for myself." For example, this author has not yet found a truly satisfying answer for Jesus' harsh initial treatment of the woman of Canaan (Matthew 15:22 ff.) nor to comprehend fully why Jesus advised His followers to arm themselves (Luke 22:36).

7. Ask, What does God want *me* to tell *others* from this passage? This will determine the main emphasis of the message or Bible lesson.

If the main points of the message or lesson are taken directly from the wording of the Scripture (a phrase or key word), then the inmate will tend to recall the main points of the message/lesson each time that he reads that portion of Scripture. For each main point, it has been found helpful to explain it, then illustrate it, and apply it. This pattern (Explanation/Illustration/Application) can be used with each main point in turn.

The Point of Contact

Effective preaching and teaching must begin at a point of contact between the preacher or teacher and his audience. Otherwise little communication occurs. For example, the apostle Paul's sermon at the Areopagus began with a reference to the altar in the Areopagus with the inscription "To an unknown God" (*see* Acts 17:23).[299] Billy Graham usually begins his sermons with a reference to some recent event or events reported in the public news media; this provides a point of contact with the general American audiences which he addresses.

The name of an inmate often allows an effective point of contact for preaching or teaching. Particularly is this true of lessons or messages that have to be delivered at the cellblock or tier where inmates are housed and whose format is informal with opportunities for inmate dialogue. An inmate named Joseph offers the opportunity to present the story of Joseph from the Book of Genesis and with it to explain the wisdom of God in providing deliverance for His people through Joseph (Genesis 37–50). Then, the parallel with God's provision for redemption through Christ can be drawn. The story of Joseph brings an additional point of contact with many inmates. Joseph was imprisoned unjustly. Many inmates claim, and often believe, that they are incarcerated unjustly. God was able to work in Joseph's life in spite of his incarceration. This can provide a point of contact to encourage the inmate to believe that God can work in his life as well, even though he is in jail or in prison.

The stories of other Josephs in the Bible offer similar possibilities for lessons and sermons: Joseph, the husband of Mary (Matthew 1–2; Luke 1–2); the Joseph considered as a replacement for Judas (Acts 1:23); and Joseph (known also as Joses) whom the apostles called Barnabas (Acts 4:36). Most inmates have an innate curiosity about the significance of their names and of the history of others with the same name. This same curiosity usually extends as well to the names of their close associates in the jail or prison. The names of persons in Church history offer similar opportunities for points of contact in one's preaching and teaching ministry.

Most prisoners listen with interest to messages and lessons which are drawn from biblical passages that are concerned with imprisonment.[300] These provide a natural and strong point of contact with the incarcerated. Likewise, any message or lesson that involves the legal process (e.g., the parable of the unjust judge which Jesus told in Luke 18) has a natural point of contact that will ensure inmate interest.

Experiences of the inmate population in the recent past also provide excellent points of contact. An inmate's unexpected release, the sentence a man received and his reaction to it, an attempted suicide, an escape or escape attempt, new paint on the walls, the food, the problems of inmate living—all provide points of contact for a wide variety of sermon and lesson topics. The wise preacher or teacher will use these to gain inmates' attention for his messages.

Discretion and good taste are essential in using such points of contact. Obviously, only those things which are public knowledge in the institution should be used. No personal experiences of inmates should be used unless these are already known to the inmate population. Likewise, the chaplain or layman is wise to avoid those items which could become a source of serious agitation. An example of such is the striking or beating of a prisoner by a guard.

The sermon or lesson that begins with any of the points of contact mentioned above can be either impromptu or planned.[301]

The preacher or teacher must always keep in mind the example of Philip, who found the Ethiopian eunuch reading in the prophet

Isaiah and preached to him Jesus Christ (Acts 8). Whatever the point of contact, whether message or lesson, spontaneous or planned, the end result must lead to Jesus Christ.

Presentation Factors

Effective preaching and teaching must not only begin at a point of contact, it must also be tailored to the intellectual capabilities of the audience, to the level of their biblical background and religious experience, and to their general life experiences.

The American correctional system contains prisoners who cover the spectrum from imbecile to genius, whose education goes to the PhD level and beyond, as well as those who have essentially no formal education. The average intelligence of inmates is somewhat lower than the national average.[302] Their educational and literacy levels were noted in Chapter 8. These are below those for the population in general. Thus the preacher or teacher of the incarcerated must keep his vocabulary basic, his allusions simple, and must not expect his audience to have a broad background of general knowledge.

The biblical and religious background of inmates is also limited. It is true that many study the Bible and take religious instruction in jail and prison. It is true that a few inmates have an extensive knowledge of the Word of God (even though many of them have not tried to apply their knowledge to their daily living). But in general, jail and prison inmates are ignorant of the Bible and have had very little experience in or with churches since becoming teenage. It is best to assume when preaching to or teaching a group of prisoners that inmates know nothing of the Word of God. Thus even common names like those of David, Paul, or John have to be identified. No special or technical theological or biblical terms, such as *regeneration, reconciliation, Judah, Pharisee, apostle,* should be used without explanation. Most inmates have confused comprehension of such basic religious events as Good Friday and Easter and are usually ignorant of church polity, denominational distinctions, etc. Frequently, the inmate is unable even to name the church or its pastor where he "attended" when he was free.

Messages should concentrate on spiritual basics: the nature of

God, salvation, faith, grace, the Person and work of Jesus Christ, elements of discipleship, Christian ethics, use of God's Word, witnessing, etc. Message structure should be simple and include repetition of major truths.

Essentially all prisons but less than 60 percent of the nation's jails have a separate place (chapel, multipurpose room, classroom, dining hall, etc.) for religious services. Therefore, many inmates will be preached to or taught at their cellblocks and in their dormitories if the Gospel of Jesus Christ is to be presented to them. In this environment, noise predominates: the banging of steel doors is frequent, several radios and televisions may be playing within hearing, inmates may be shouting at one another, an intercom or PA system may make announcements at unpredictable intervals. Guards and other persons may use the passageway in which the preacher or teacher is standing. Medicine may be delivered to a prisoner in the middle of a sermon or lesson. An inmate may be brought to or taken from the cellblock. In a dormitory, several may be moving around while the lesson is being presented. Others may be involved in a card game.

Communication Aids

The effectiveness of the chaplain's or the Christian worker's preaching and teaching ministry can be enhanced by the use of communication aids such as films, tapes, records, and literature. Unfortunately, many chaplains fail to use audiovisual aids extensively. Many also have a nonchalant attitude toward the use of Christian literature, often being content merely to have a tract rack near the chapel entrance.

As a communication aid, Christian literature has three basic purposes: (1) to establish rapport by demonstrating interest in the inmate, (2) to attract to Christianity, and (3) to educate. Whenever the chaplain or Christian worker offers Christian literature to an inmate (whether a tract, book, newspaper, or Bible), it can be an opportunity to demonstrate personal interest in that inmate.

When possible, a library of Christian books and literature should be established in a place to which as many inmates as possible have access. In addition, chaplains and Christian workers should make a habit of leaving literature with *all* inmates who do not refuse it. The inmate who shows no interest at the time often will read everything within reach because of boredom. The Spirit of God can use even knowledge gained in this way. However, the chaplain must be alert to the danger of putting too much literature in the hands of the uninterested. More than once in jails and prisons, Bibles and other religious books have been burned or flushed down the toilet (and created plumbing problems).

It is possible to use too much literature with an interested inmate. It is easy to saturate a prisoner with so much literature that his interest in Christ is quenched. A little salt can bring out the flavor of a piece of meat. Too much salt can make the same piece of meat inedible. It is desired to see the inmate progress spiritually at a maximum rate, but caution in the overuse of literature is needed.

The chaplain should not restrict his use of literature to prisoners. There are ample opportunities to give literature to members of the institution's staff. These opportunities should be taken advantage of.

It should be obvious that a strong Christian ministry in a jail or prison will require a substantial amount of varied Christian literature. The Directory of Appendix D will help both chaplains and Christian workers find some of the literature resources which they need—especially sources of Bible correspondence courses.[303] Both chaplains and Christian workers should help inmates in pursuing such study of God's Word.

The variety of audiovisual aids is great: tapes and records of messages, music, testimony; simple charts and maps; slides and filmstrips; films; models and examples of various biblical items; etc. A number of basic Christian concepts are more easily grasped when illustrated on a chart or blackboard by simple line drawings.[304] Such illustrations can also be put on paper sheets and used with small groups of inmates.

The communication effectiveness of films makes it particularly unfortunate that chaplains do not use films more in their ministry. An excellent assortment of Christian films is available.

Budgetary considerations may restrict the chaplain or Christian worker from simply ordering films through a religious film distributor. Some films are available free for use with prisoners.[305] Others may be obtained through local Christian businessmen's organizations, military chaplains (when military personnel are held in the institution), public libraries, or local film distributors —often at a very nominal charge if not free.

Inmate Response: Preaching/Teaching for Decisions[306]

This section deals with the desired response to all godly preaching and teaching: decisions for Jesus Christ.

A "decision" is a settling or terminating by giving judgment on a matter, a resolution arrived at after consideration, a judicial determination of a question. The words *determination* and *resolution* enlarge the meaning of decision. *Determination* implies adherence with fixed purpose to a course of action settled on; *resolution* implies constancy and courage, especially in the face of danger or difficulty. For our purpose, *a decision is a determined, resolute, and specific commitment of one's life to Jesus Christ.*

The basic idea in decision is "cutting off from" in order to "isolate unto." One cuts himself from self, sin, the world, and all with a sense of finality. He shuts and locks the door behind him and throws away the key. As the song says: "No turning back, no turning back!" Mated to this is the positive attachment to Jesus Christ for His total invasion of oneself.

Three elements are involved in the act of decision: first, the renouncing of all dependence upon one's own efforts to save himself; second, the placing of full trust in Jesus Christ as Savior and Lord; and, third, the surrendering completely of all of oneself to Jesus Christ as His purchased possession for time and eternity.

This decision is the most important step to be taken by a human being. With it, the miraculous transformation begins: "If any man be in Christ, he is a new creature" (2 Corinthians 5:17).

Necessity of Urging Decision

Several factors show the necessity of urging decisions from those to whom we preach or teach:

Purpose of Preaching/Teaching. Preaching/teaching the Word of God should not be aimless, but directed to the purpose that the sinner might be saved. Too often the gibe of Bishop Whately is true: "He aimed at nothing, and hit it."

A leading layman said, "Once I would come to church with great expectancy of seeing sinners moved to Jesus Christ by the plain preaching of the Gospel with its drawing invitation extended. Now, we dutifully sit through bland 'Bible studies' with no invitation of hope to sinners and no challenge to Christians."

The opposite should be true.

According to the Book of Acts, the disciples of Jesus Christ, as they were filled with the Holy Spirit, preached and taught with such direct, convincing, personal appeal that whole cities were stirred; and in less than fifty years they had, in the terms of their adversaries, "turned the world upside down"! (Acts 17:6)

The great evangelist J. Wilbur Chapman said that "a sermon is preached in order that a decision may be influenced, a crisis reached and passed, and such a manifold change in life as leads one out of great moral darkness into spiritual light. . . . The man presents the Word with definite desire for the conversion of hearer and with so persistent an appeal that the most indifferent cannot easily resist its power."

The sermon or lesson *must be planned for the objective* of leading the hearer to commit his life to Christ Jesus. "Persuasion, rather than instruction, is the great end of preaching," asserted Bishop Matthew Simpson in his lectures on preaching.

Implications From Christ's Commands About Discipleship. The command of Jesus Christ to His own is "Go and make disciples. . . ." This demands preaching and teaching for decisions. The Lord Himself extended His gracious invitation for decision when He said, "Come unto me, all ye that labor and are heavy laden, and I will give you rest. Take my yoke upon you, and learn of me . . ." (Matthew 11:28,29).

Jesus demands decisive action from those who hear Him: "If any man will come after me, let him take up his cross, die daily, and follow me" (*see* Luke 9:23; 14:27).

Because the fields are overripe and the harvesters few, the Lord commanded, "Pray ye therefore the Lord of the harvest, that he will send forth labourers into his harvest" (Matthew 9:37,38). Harvesters cut the grain and bring in the sheaves: the object of the preacher is to harvest souls to Jesus Christ. The goal is not social work, social reform or getting men and women to give up some sin or other, but to turn them to Jesus. "He that winneth souls is wise" (Proverbs 11:30).

Jesus compares the work he calls His disciples to do with fishing: "Come ye after me, and I will make you to become fishers of men" (Mark 1:17). Whether by hook for the single or with the net for the many, the object is to catch men.

Examples of God's Servants in the Bible. The Lord's command to urge men to decision for Him was obeyed by His servants.

When Moses came down from the mount to the corrupting Israelites, he cried, "Who is on the Lord's side? let him come unto me" (Exodus 32:26). At the end of his valedictory, Moses detailed the blessings and cursings for obedience or disobedience, and concluded with the demand for decision by the Israelites, "I call heaven and earth to record this day against you, that I have set before you life and death, blessing and cursing: therefore choose life, that both thou and thy seed may live" (Deuteronomy 30:19).

Just before his death, Joshua exhorted the people, ". . . choose you this day whom ye will serve; . . . but as for me and my house, we will serve the Lord" (Joshua 24:15).

The challenge of Elijah was a call to decide: "How long halt ye between two opinions? if the Lord be God, follow him: but if Baal, then follow him" (1 Kings 18:21).

The disciples preached and cities were stirred. Paul wrote, "Now then we are ambassadors for Christ, as though God did beseech you by us: we pray you in Christ's stead, be ye reconciled to God" (2 Corinthians 5:20).

Examples of God's Servants in Church History. John Wesley instructed preachers who followed him to be so emphatic in making known the demands of Jesus Christ that the hearers would either "Be glad or mad."

Dwight Moody [307] spoke of the tragic loss that led him to give an invitation after every message. On Sunday night October 8, 1871, he gave a talk on the text "What then shall I do with Jesus which is called Christ?" and with all his power of entreaty, presented Jesus Christ as Savior and Redeemer with these concluding words: "I wish you would take this text home with you and turn it over in your minds during the week, and next Sabbath we will come to Calvary and the cross, and we will decide what to do with Jesus of Nazareth." That night fire swept Chicago and laid it in ashes. "What a mistake!" he said later. "I have never dared to give an audience a week or a day to think of their salvation since. If they were lost, they might rise up in judgment against me. I remember Mr. Sankey's singing, and how his voice rang when he came to that pleading verse:

> Today the Saviour calls,
> For refuge fly!
> The storm of Justice falls,
> And death is nigh!

"I have never seen that congregation since. I have hard work to keep back the tears today. I have looked over this audience, and not a single one is here that I preached to that night . . . I will never see those people again until I meet them in another world.

"But I want to tell of one lesson I learned that night, which I have never forgotten, and that is, when I preach, to press Christ upon the people then and there, and try to bring them to a decision on the spot! I would rather have that right hand cut off than to give an audience now a week to decide what to do with Jesus.

"I have asked God many times to forgive me for telling people that night to take a week to think it over; and if He spares my life, I will never do it again."

Moody felt that too few tried to reap the obvious harvest of souls. He accounted for the overwhelming numbers of people who publicly committed themselves to Christ in meetings he held in Britain by saying: "Under God I came along and gave all those sinners the public opportunity that the great preachers did not. We reaped where Spurgeon, Parker, Temple and all had sowed."

Hearers Need the Opportunity to Decide. What is forgotten often in discussions of preaching/teaching for decision is the fact that *hearers* need *the opportunity to decide.*

Dr. George Crane's formula is true: "Impression without expression induces depression."

According to Dr. Ernest Dichter, the famed expert on consumer motivation, "The inner tension toward completion, known as 'closure,' is the psychological basis of the need to finish, to round off, to smooth out, to sum things up. . . . Basic within all men is the tendency to organize their world into a simple and complete meaningful entity. . . . This tension to closure . . . is a source of motivational energy, and makes him an active participant."

Frustrations develop from the irresolutions and the indecisions of life. The most basic of all needs for closure comes from the sense of sin and emptiness and purposelessness of life. Without Jesus Christ all is wrong and out of shape. To tell a man about Jesus is not enough; he must be told how to "close" with Him.

Any salesman knows that all he says and does must conclude in a sale. The retailer is "not running a museum, but a salesroom." Hundreds of books are published on selling, and they all underline the necessity of closing the sale. The salesman is to try to get the prospect to buy the product; that's the only reason he called on him. He is patient and persevering because he knows that only about 3 percent of the prospects buy the first time they are asked, which means that 97 percent of the prospects who will buy want to be asked more than once! By the seventh time asked, 90 percent of them buy. Professor George Burton Hotchkiss points out that "the complete psychological process in a sale is not only getting attention, creating desire, and convincing, but the bringing to decision and action."

The hunger of every human being is to know God. Unexpressed and undefined, the thirst is still there. When the famed preacher Phillips Brooks met blind and deaf Helen Keller, he immediately told her through her teacher, Anne Sullivan, about Jesus Christ. After she heard, Miss Keller cried out, "All my life I wondered about God. Now I know His name—Jesus!"

It is a cruel jest or an exercise in futility to tell of the glories of Christ and eternal life without making it possible for the hearer to turn to Jesus. The hearer must be pointed to the Door.

The famished are not relieved by seeing the profuse display of the bread and meat, no matter how beautiful. They must *eat!* The Nazi guards added to the misery of starving prisoners behind barbed wire by eating sumptuous meals where the doomed could see them.

The invitation of the Word is, "Taste, and see that the Lord is good" (*see* Psalms 34:8; 1 Peter 2:3).

Man's Inclination to Procrastinate. Procrastination and indecision are natural to mankind. The common excuse is "tomorrow." Most human beings will go to any length to avoid making decisions.

Under the seducing spell of the present, men too easily forget the future. Nevertheless, "Swift to its close ebbs out life's little day." Even the longest earthly life will cease. No man knows when the Lord will require his life of him. Who can set the time of death's call? The time to prepare is now, while it is day.

Scriptural Warnings and Exhortations. Repeatedly the Scriptures emphasize the urgency of the moment of truth, the time of decision.

In beseeching the Corinthians to "receive not the grace in vain," Paul quoted from the warnings of the Old Testament:

> For he saith, I have heard thee in a time accepted, and in the day of salvation have I succoured thee: behold, now is the accepted time; behold, now is the day of salvation.
>
> 2 Corinthians 6:2

Ample opportunity for salvation is provided by Christ Jesus; yet there is prodigal neglect. One day there will be the fearful realization, "The harvest is past, the summer is ended, and we are not saved" (Jeremiah 8:20). Jesus warned: "Be ye also ready, for ye know neither the day nor the hour wherein the Son of man cometh." How horrible it will be to be unready and find the door shut and hear the Bridegroom say "I know you not!" (*see* Matthew 25:1–13).

Those who would work for the salvation of souls are reminded by Jesus that the day of opportunity for service will close at the setting of the sun of grace: ". . . the night cometh, when no man can work" (John 9:4).

Too many are like the Corinthian deputy governor, Gallio, who "cared for none of those things" (Acts 18:17). He fatally overestimated earth and underestimated heaven with what could be labeled the great insanity—materialistic worldliness.

The Lord rebuked the man who was fully occupied with riches and possessions:

> Take heed, and beware of covetousness [i.e., the love of money]: for a man's life consisteth not in the abundance of things which he possesseth . . . . this night thy soul shall be required of thee: then whose shall those things be, which thou hast provided?
>
> Luke 12:15,20

Some are fickle like Agrippa with his "Almost thou persuadest me to be a Christian" (Acts 26:28). Almost is no better than not at all. To hear of Christ Jesus and be almost saved is still to be lost. John Turnbull remarked that *almost* modifies *persuadest,* not *Christian.* There is no such thing as an "almost" Christian. It is the persuasion that is almost. None would accuse Paul of failing; in this instance, it is the dissolute king whose pleasures, sins, and lusts block the persuasion of the devoted disciple. *But how often the one who presents Jesus Christ fails in the persuasion by neglecting specific challenge like the pinning down of David by Nathan:* "Thou art the man"! (2 Samuel 12:7).

The cares of living mount so high that a man fools himself by what he thinks is a reasonable excuse: The matter of deciding to receive Jesus Christ is too important to be inserted between life's lesser concerns, so a better time then must be set apart for consideration. Festus used this argument with Paul, who had "reasoned of righteousness, temperance, and judgment to come" and spoken to the governor of faith in Christ. "Felix trembled and answered, Go thy way for this time; when I have a convenient season, I will call for thee" (Acts 24:24,25). The tragedy in this procrastination is the foolish ignoring of the fact that the more convenient season rarely comes, and that difficulties increase with the years. "To day if ye will hear his voice, harden not your hearts . . ." (Hebrews 3:15). The messenger must be constantly aware of the shortness of time and opportunity.

The Invitation to Decision

"Extending an invitation is the greatest agony in the ministry," acknowledged the Reverend John R. Bisagno. "We live and die a thousand deaths in the ten or twenty minutes in which the invitation is extended. When souls stand between life and death, we must be dependent upon the Holy Spirit and most sensitive to His leadership."

Although extending an invitation may be "the greatest agony," this is the object of the message.

Dr. Charles L. Goodell said, "The value of a sermon is not in its form but in its effect. . . . What is a great sermon? . . . The sermon which leads a man to forsake his sins, to give up his indifference, to yield to Jesus Christ and follow Him to newness of life—that, by every standard of holy judgment, is a great sermon, no matter what critics may say about it."

Never to be ignored for a moment is the fact that the messenger is acting in Christ's stead: "As my Father hath sent me, even so send I you" (John 20:21). The Lord Jesus came "to seek and to save that which was lost" (Luke 19:10).

Because it is the work of God, those who would serve Him must be filled with the Holy Spirit: "But ye shall receive power, after that the Holy Ghost is come upon you: and ye shall be witnesses unto me . . ." (Acts 1:8). The promise of God is the granting of His Spirit to them who *obey* or submit unto Him (Acts 5:32) and *ask*. Jesus said, "If ye then, being evil, know how to give good gifts unto your children: how much more shall your heavenly Father give the Holy Spirit to them that ask him?" (Luke 11:13).

Confidence in the effectualness of God's Word is essential. The Lord God pronounced that His Word should not return unto Him void, but it shall accomplish that which He pleases, and it shall prosper in the thing whereunto He sent it (Isaiah 55:9–11).

The messenger must have deep conviction of the stark truth

that men without Jesus Christ have the wrath of God abiding upon them now, cannot see life, and are eternally lost. The more one studies what the Bible says about the destiny of the lost, the deeper his conviction.

Percy Crawford taught that fishers of men should meditate on the truths concerning the lost until they take hold of the heart.

Jesus Christ knew men were perishing and lost, and He loved us enough to take the sinners' penalty at the price of His shed blood. He sends those who found Him to reach others at all cost!

The messenger of the Gospel should be daily cleansed within and without. Paul testified: "And herein do I exercise myself, to have always a conscience void of offence toward God, and toward men" (Acts 24:16).

If there is a time and occasion when a Christian must be fully surrendered to God, it is at the moment of persuading men to decision.

Dr. Howard Gray of the Mayo Clinic stated that he was "far more conscious of the care to be exerted and delicacy employed in leading a person to Jesus Christ than in the most difficult surgery. In the latter the health of the body is at stake; in the former the issues are eternal."

But surely as the instruments of the Almighty God with His power, wisdom, and Spirit, His servants dare not avoid bringing men to decision, or even hesitate.

Only the Holy Spirit can teach a man how to lead others to decision. There are no rules or laws—just suggestions. The following suggestions pertain to *manner* of appeal:

> *Be bold and invite with authority.* The disciples prayed that "with all boldness they may speak thy word" (Acts 4:29). With no apology, invite the sinner to come to the Lord. With the authority of heaven, demand repentance, decision, and action.
>
> *Be plain and specific.* Tell exactly what you want the people to do and why.
>
> *Be urgent.* Time is running out. Rehearse the necessity of *now.*

Be quick and smooth in the transition to the appeal. Avoid any distractions.

Be positive. You *know* what Jesus can and will do for all who come unto God by Him.

Be dignified and honorable, with no trickery or gimmicks. Let the Spirit of God move hearts. Be conscious that you are the ambassador for Christ Jesus.

Be prayerful and dependent on the Holy Spirit. Don't let pride enter in. Let the government be upon Christ's shoulders.

Be enthusiastic. There is joy in heaven over one sinner that repents (Luke 15:7). You are inviting men to meet Christ.

Be as long and frequent as is necessary. The Holy Spirit must lead. Keep in mind the long-suffering of the Lord. Salesmen know that as many as nine out of ten people will not say yes until after the seventh appeal. In most instances in public meetings, few if any respond before the *third* verse of an invitation hymn.

Be wide in the appeal. Include: first, the sinner who needs to receive Jesus Christ as his Savior; second, the backslider who must know he is welcomed by the Lord; and, third, the uncertain who need assurance. On some occasions, those who are burdened and troubled in soul can be invited.

The Purpose of the Servant of the Lord

The apostle John gave the reason not only for his writing the Gospel but, by implication, the reason for the labor of every servant of Jesus Christ: ". . . these are written, that ye might believe that Jesus is the Christ, the Son of God; and that believing ye might have life through his name" (John 20:31).

Let us determine "by all means to save some" (*see* 1 Corinthians 9:22).

10

Counseling Offenders

Counseling is an important aspect of Christian ministry, especially in jails and prisons, because inmates must live in an atmosphere permeated by tension, fear, hostility, and frustration, and are at the same time deprived of much of the encouragement and support normally provided by family and friends that help one to cope with the problems and pressures of life.[308] This section does not purport to teach one how to counsel. Such instruction would be impossible in so brief a space. Moreover, an abundance of materials exist on this subject. Instead, this discussion of counseling is designed to provide a perspective on counseling which this author feels is much needed, to make a few suggestions that should prove helpful in counseling offenders, and to identify both counseling techniques common within correctional institutions and resources that can assist the reader in his counseling.

A Perspective on Counseling

Almost every form of Christian ministry in jails and prisons involves counseling at some level. It may be establishment of a friendly, supportive relationship between a volunteer who visits an inmate for an hour each week as a one-on-one counselor. Or it may be the preacher who "counsels" an inmate who responded to an invitation to commit his life to Jesus at the close of a preaching service. But, in general, *counseling* is used more restrictively, implying that the counselee has come to the counselor seeking help in dealing with a significant personal problem. From here on, *counseling* is used in this restrictive sense.

Our society has placed a great emphasis upon counseling, resulting in (and partially resulting *from*) the phenomenal growth during the past two generations in the number of persons employed in the fields of psychology and sociology. Likewise, since the 1920s, counseling has been emphasized as a major aspect of pastoral ministry, often labeled "pastoral counseling" or "pastoral care." [309] Thus, many in our society have a vested interest in counseling and, at least some of them, react badly to adverse comments about counseling, irrespective of the truth of such comments.[310]

Such a great emphasis has been placed upon counseling that some chaplains spend far more time in counseling than in any other activity. For example, Protestant correctional chaplains with CPE spend over 45 percent of their workweek in counseling.[311] This emphasis seems typical of ministers with CPE.[312] Although "during recent years, counseling has been the chief locus of concern for pastoral theology and pastoral psychology" [313] in many seminaries, the conclusion of Clebsch and Jaekle is that "counseling holds little promise of becoming the center around which pastoral care as a role of the ministerial generalist can be polarized." [314]

In addition to an undue emphasis upon counseling by many, it appears that not one of the various approaches to psychological counseling has been able to demonstrate success statistically in helping counselees solve their problems.[315] In particular, this has been true in the counseling of offenders,[316] as illustrated by the following:

> In a large-scale test of the effectiveness of psychological counselors over a period of years, with matched samples of treated and non-treated boys, it was found that despite the strong belief of the counselors that they were effective, there was essentially no difference in terminal adjustment or in delinquency or, subsequently, in criminal behavior between the two groups.[317]

Likewise, pastoral counseling has yet to demonstrate itself effective when subjected to rigorous statistical analysis of results among its counselees and suitable control groups. This should be expected, since most pastoral counseling differs little from secular counseling because "non-churchly agencies have devised the theoretical psychologies that pastors employed in their work." [318] Even a limited examination of literature on pastoral counseling reveals that many writers:

1. do not possess an evangelical view of the Bible or of the spiritual requirements placed by the Bible upon everyone called of God to the Christian ministry;
2. give little attention to the work of the Holy Spirit within the counselee;
3. do not discuss in a significant way the role of prayer in the counseling process; and
4. fail to address the therapeutic impact of obedience to biblical injunctions such as found in James 5:14,15.[319]

Therefore, it has been encouraging to witness the growing interest in biblically based approaches to counseling such as the nouthetic counseling advocated by Dr. Adams.[320] (*Nouthetic* was coined by Adams to describe his approach to counseling. It is from the Greek word for *confronting.*) It is hoped that such counseling approaches will be developed fully by evangelical scholars so that an approach to counseling will result which:

1. is thoroughly consistent with the Bible,
2. contains an adequate theory of personality to explain all known psychological and physiological phenomena, and
3. proves itself effective in solving counselee problems, even when examined by rigorous methods of statistical analysis.

The present consensus seems to be that the key to effective counseling is the counselor himself. Thus, in training of pastoral counselors, the question has evolved from What must I *do* to be of help to the person? to What must I *know?* to What must I *say?* to What must I *be?* [321] Truax and Clarkhuff isolated three primary factors that characterize effective counselors: (1) accurate empathy, (2) nonpossessive warmth, and (3) genuineness.[322] The question then becomes, How can a counselor develop these characteristics?[323]

For the Christian counselor, the answer lies in his relationship to God the Holy Spirit. The Holy Spirit is the Paraclete (παράκλητος), which means the one called to one's aid; thus, an advocate, exhorter, comforter—in brief, a counselor. In effective Christian counseling, the Holy Spirit works both in the counselee and in the counselor. The Spirit can enlighten the counselee to see his condition clearly and how to deal with his problem. In the counselor, the Holy Spirit can provide insight and understanding about the counselee and his situation; but more importantly, the Holy Spirit can produce in the counselor those personal characteristics which will make him an effective counselor. Primarily, these characteristics are the product of what the New Testament in Galatians 5:22–23 calls the "fruit of the Spirit": love, joy, peace, longsuffering, gentleness, goodness, faith (or faithfulness), meekness, and temperance (or self-control). *Any* Christian manifesting the fruit of the Spirit has the characteristics of an effective counselor.

The fruit of the Spirit appear in the life of *every* Christian who meets four simple conditions:

1. an unconditional commitment to Jesus (of the sort commanded in Luke 9:23 and 14:27) is required;
2. one must be saturated with the Word of God (see Colossians 3:16 in context);
3. sin in one's life must be confessed and forsaken (as in 1 John 1:9); and
4. one must be filled with the Spirit through obedience to God's will (*see* Ephesians 5:18 ff.):

When these conditions are met, God's Spirit produces His fruit in the Christian's life and thus equips him to be an effective counselor.

The Christian should neither despise counseling nor disparage formal counseling and training.[324] Counseling is a vital, essential part of Christian ministry to offenders in jails and prisons. While counseling should not be exalted unduly, neither should it be neglected. Everyone who counsels extensively should seek to acquire as much counseling knowledge and skill as he can, but *at the same time the Christian must maintain his dependency upon God the Spirit for effectiveness in counseling,* because his effectiveness is far more dependent upon his relationship to God than upon his counseling approach and technique.

Counseling Suggestions

The following mental states are common among inmates and should be recognized and responded to appropriately by the counselor:

Depression/Disappointment. Life behind bars is hard. Often both present and future are bleak. Many have overwhelming problems.

Loneliness. Separation from family and loved ones makes incarceration desperately lonely. Ubiquitous *distrust* tends to isolate inmates from one another. If a Christian counselor proves himself to be a trustworthy friend with genuine concern for the inmate and his well-being, some of confinement's painful loneliness can be overcome.

Fear. Jails and prisons are saturated with fear. The future is uncertain: a long sentence, parole denial, permanent abandonment of the inmate by his wife and family, etc. Behind bars, the danger of physical abuse is always present: it is easy for one to be hurt, maimed, sexually assaulted, or killed. Paranoia is fostered by confinement, and many inmates are tormented by exaggerated fears.

Bitterness/Resentment. The brutality endured by inmates from their fellow inmates (and occasionally from institution staff), plus the often callous and inequitable treatment afforded by the criminal justice system, breeds much resentment and bitterness. The great problem of bitterness is that it restricts the working of God's grace in one's life (cf. the context of bitterness and its result in Acts 8:23; Ephesians 4:31; Hebrews 12:15). At times, the counselor will become the object for a vehement outpouring of inmate bitterness. Normally the counselor should not react to such as a personal criticism, but instead should view the outpouring as an opportunity for healthy catharsis.

Guilt. Unrelieved guilt is a severe problem for inmates. Not only are there the problems of the guilt associated with the inmate's crime (when he is guilty) and the hurt which he has brought to his family and loved ones by his actions, but the mountain of guilt may grow as the inmate is involved in the desperate struggle for survival within the institution. An effective counselor will help the inmate face his guilt, confess his wrong to God and experience God's forgiveness, make appropriate restitution,[325] and come to know the joy of freedom from the oppression of guilt.

Bad Feelings About Oneself/Poor Self-Image. Most inmates have a very poor opinion of themselves. They are convinced that they are losers. Self-acceptance is possible if an inmate comes to know the reality of God's acceptance of him through salvation in Jesus:

> Jim, in his fifties, was an alcoholic. He had not been able to accept himself because of atrocities he committed in the Second World War. During the twenty-seven years from 1945 to 1972, Jim used alcohol to hide from himself, going through half a dozen marriages, in and out of jails and prisons, even spending a prolonged period in the Menninger Hospital in Kansas for treatment of his alcoholism (a wealthy wife at the time invested over $10,000 in efforts to cure him). In 1972, Jim was born again in a jail. Because Jesus accepted him *in spite of his past,* Jim began to accept himself—and has not returned to the bottle.

Help From the Counselor. The counselor's acceptance of the inmate is often the first step in the process that can lead the inmate to a healthy self-acceptance. Most counselors find it difficult to accept certain kinds of inmates. Child-abusers and transvestites are difficult for many counselors to accept. Counselors should pray that God will provide grace to have the freedom to minister effectively to such inmates, or that God will prevent the counselor from having to deal with them.

The counselor should always remember that his relationship with the counselee can help the counselee far more than mere advice. To use a biblical phrase, "Love covers a multitude of sins" (1 Peter 4:8 NASV). Likewise the counselor needs realistic expectations of what is likely to be accomplished in a counseling session or series of sessions. Otherwise, he may become disappointed and the counselee may develop a sense of failure. The counselor should not overidentify with the inmate. The inmate is responsible for his life. The counselor cannot assume even part of that responsibility without hurting both himself and the inmate.[326]

It is appropriate for a Christian counselor to pray for God's guidance and help as he begins a counseling session.[327] This helps both counselor and counselee to be aware of God's role in the therapy. The Christian counselor should assure the counselee that he will pray for him—and encourage the counselee to pray for God's help with his problem. In many cases, it will be appropriate to discuss the counselee's prayer life. Such conversations will reveal much about his relationship to God. It is important that prayer never become simply a mechanical or routine formality in a counseling session, but that prayer always be an act of communication with the Living God.

Finally, the counselor who is an evangelical Christian *should expect God to work through his counseling* in a significant and powerful way to help those whom he counsels. Always his counseling should be immersed in prayer and conducted in dependence upon God the Holy Spirit for wisdom, insight, and that spiritual fruit which will make him an effective counselor.

Counseling Approaches Prevalent With Offenders

Nondirective (Rogerian) Counseling

During the 1940s and 1950s, the literature and seminary teaching of pastoral counseling was largely dominated (as was much of secular counseling) by the client-centered approach of Carl Rogers, with insight as its central goal.[328] Unfortunately, this caused many Protestant pastoral counselors "not to take guilt as seriously as its destructive effects warrant."[329] This kind of counseling is still widespread in correctional work because it is the approach in which many chaplains and secular counselors were trained. Reasons for revising—or abandoning—this approach (depending upon the point of view) may be found in Adams' *Competent to Counsel,* Clinebell's *Basic Types of Pastoral Counseling,* or Glasser's *Reality Therapy.*

Confrontational Counseling

Most confrontational counseling emphasizes the counselee's responsibility for his behavior and improvement. This is a significant change from the nondirective, client-centered approach in counseling. The growing emphasis upon confrontational counseling has brought a renewed appreciation for the counselee's guilt in misbehavior, as illustrated not long ago in Karl Menninger's book *Whatever Happened to Sin?.* The standard of behavior to which one is called to conform depends upon the kind of confrontational counseling: society's norms (reality therapy), conscience (integrity therapy), the Bible (nouthetic counseling), and peer group ideals (many encounter groups, especially those used in drug therapy that are patterned after the Synanon approach). The most common forms of confrontational counseling among inmates are reality therapy and encounter groups. Some evangelicals ministering to offenders employ nouthetic counseling.

Behavior Modification

This approach to therapy is based upon the assumption that at least some personality disorders and behavioral patterns "can be regarded as learned responses that have been built up into conditioned reflexes" [330] and, consequently, that one can be retrained to behave normally and acceptably. Basically, specific rewards (or punishments) are given for specific acts of behavior, and the counselee is conditioned to respond in the desired manner. Carried to extremes, behavioral modification results in "brainwashing." Mitford cites an experimental program at Marion Federal Prison to determine firsthand "how effective a weapon brainwashing might be for the U.S. Department of Justice's future use" on "agitators, suspected militants, writ-writers and other troublemakers." [331] William Sargent wrote a provocative application of such methods to religious experience in *The Battle for the Mind: A Physiology of Conversion and Brainwashing.* The propriety of using behavioral modification (especially its increasing use of drugs in what is euphemistically called "chemotherapy" and "aversion therapy"), even upon prisoners who voluntarily chose to participate in such programs, is a subject of continuing debate.[332] In fact, the *American Journal of Correction* stated "the next great controversy in the American Correctional System may center on the question of behavior modification programs for inmates."[333] This approach to therapy is more widespread in juvenile institutions than in those for adults.

Supportive and Crisis Counseling

Many employed as counselors by jails and prisons are engaged primarily in supportive and crisis counseling. They help inmates decide in which programs they should participate, suggest how to deal with the multitude of adjustment and living problems encountered by inmates, and provide a listening ear for inmates who are upset or who just need to talk with someone. Alcoholics Anonymous (AA) programs[334] fit into this category of counseling, as do Yokefellow groups[335] and the multitude of programs using one-on-one volunteer counselors.

Transactional Analysis

Some would include transactional analysis (abbreviated TA) under confrontational counseling because "it confronts the patient with the fact that he is responsible for what happens in the future no matter what has happened in the past."[336] However, the popularity and widespread use of TA in correctional institutions justifies a separate category for it. Originated by Eric Berne, TA provided insight for Berne's bestselling book, *Games People Play,* and was popularized by Thomas Harris's practical guide to its use, *I'm OK—You're OK.* Its greatest value seems to be its ability to describe personality functioning in language which the general public as well as the psychological specialists can understand. Some are beginning to incorporate Gestalt therapy into TA, and this may become common in correctional work.[337]

Counseling Resources

The annotated bibliography below presents a few materials that may be of interest and value to those who counsel offenders. The items are grouped into four categories: (1) biblically oriented counseling from an evangelical perspective, (2) pastoral counseling in general, (3) other general resources for counseling, and (4) counseling resources related to special problems common to offenders.

Biblically oriented counseling from an evangelical perspective

Adams, Jay E. *Competent to Counsel.* Presbyterian and Reformed Publishing Co., 1970.

Develops nouthetic counseling: a biblically oriented, authoritative approach to counseling. In this writer's opinion, the most helpful guide at present for evangelicals counseling offenders.

———. *The Christian Counselor's Manual.* Baker Book House, 1973.

A sequel and companion volume to *Competent to Counsel.*

Crabb, Lawrence J., Jr. *Basic Principles of Biblical Counselling.* Zondervan, 1975.

Provides a healthy perspective on biblically oriented counseling by one with a PhD in Clinical Psychology.

Narramore, Clyde M. *Encyclopedia of Psychological Problems: A Counseling Manual.* Zondervan, 1966.

A very useful handbook from an evangelical psychologist.

———. *The Psychology of Counseling.* Zondervan, 1960.

Has a helpful section on the use of Scripture in counseling.

Pastoral counseling in general

Clebsch, William A., and Jaekle, Charles R. *Pastoral Care in Historical Perspective.* Harper Torchbooks, 1967.

This volume lives up to its title and was described by Seward Hiltner as "the most important book on pastoral care to be published in several years."

Clinebell, Howard J., Jr. *Basic Types of Pastoral Counseling* (revised and enlarged). Abingdon Press, 1966.

A survey of the entire field of pastoral counseling. The book incorporates new thrusts and techniques of psychotherapy and counseling, including supportive and directive counseling. Very useful.

Dicks, Russell L. *Principles and Practices of Pastoral Care.* Fortress Press, 1963.

The introductory volume of the *Successful Pastoral Counseling Series* by its general editor. Nondirective approach.

Hiltner, Seward. *The Counselor in Counseling.* Abingdon, 1952.

Written from a nondirective orientation.

McNeil, John T. *A History of the Cure of Souls.* Harper Torchbooks, 1951.

One of the best historical records of pastoral counseling.

Oglesby, William B., Jr. *Referral in Pastoral Counseling.* Prentice-Hall, 1968.

Provides guidelines for the pastoral counselor in referring counselees to other professions and service organizations.

Other general resources for counseling

Bandura, A. *Principles of Behavior Modification.* Holt, Rinehart and Winston, 1969.

Drakeford, John W. *Integrity Therapy.* Broadman Press, 1967.

Dye, Allan and Hackney, Harold. *Gestalt Approaches to Counseling.* Houghton Mifflin, 1975.

Glasser, William. *Reality Therapy.* Harper & Row, 1965.

Harris, Thomas A. *I'm OK–You're OK.* Harper & Row, 1967.

A practical guide to transactional analysis.

Lieberman, David A. (ed.) *Learning and the Control of Behavior: Some Principles, Theories, and Applications of Classical and Operant Conditioning.* Holt, Rinehart and Winston, 1974.

Perls, F. *Gestalt Therapy Verbatim.* Real People Press, 1969.

Developed Gestalt therapy.

Wicks, Robert J. *Correctional Psychology: Themes and Problems in Correcting the Offender.* Cranfield Press, 1974.

A general basic text covering the field of psychological activities in correctional institutions.

Counseling resources related to special problems

Buffum, Peter C. *Homosexuality in Prisons.* NILE&CJ, 1972.

Excellent summary of homosexual problems in correctional institutions.

Burns, John and three other recovered alcoholics. *The Answer to Addiction.* Harper & Row, 1975.

A provocative, helpful (but not specifically Christian) explanation of why addiction is so great a problem and why the only answer is a spiritual one. Applies both to alcohol and drug addiction.

Clinebell, Howard J., Jr. *Understanding and Counseling the Alcoholic* (Revised). Abingdon Press, 1968.

A standard text for pastors on counseling alcoholics.

Drakeford, John. *Forbidden Love: A Homosexual Looks for Understanding and Help.* Word Books, 1971.

A case history of one "cured." Provides much insight into homosexual behavior.

Dunn, Jerry G. *God Is for the Alcoholic.* Moody Press, 1965.

The most helpful single book known to this author for anyone trying to help alcoholics and their families.

Lingeman, Richard R. *Drugs from A to Z: A Dictionary.* McGraw-Hill, 1969.

Excellent handbook with both formal and popular (and slang) names for drugs, plus descriptions of their effects.

11

The Church Behind Bars

The task of the Church of Jesus Christ is to evangelize all men and to make mature disciples of all who believe in Jesus. Artificially the pursuit of this objective at great distances is called *Foreign Missions,* while in the immediate vicinity it is called *Evangelism.* But the task is the same.

It is helpful to think of jails and prisons as a mission field because this makes it easier to see how to apply principles that will promote the accomplishment of the task which Jesus has given His Church. In many ways, the mission field behind bars is the most "foreign" of mission fields. Many of the principles developed for promoting the cause of Christ in the overseas mission field can be applied directly to the Church Behind Bars, which, like the church at Pergamos, is in Satan's stronghold (*see* Revelation 2:13).

This chapter explores the principles of missions that seem appropriate to the Church Behind Bars and discusses their application in jails and prisons. Obstacles to the development of an indigenous Church Behind Bars are considered, and suggestions are presented regarding the establishment of the Church Behind Bars. Attention is given to the important relation of the chaplain to the Church Behind Bars.

Appropriate Principles of Missions

During the past century the principle of the indigenous church has come to the forefront in missions theory and, at least partially, in practice.[338] A problem of missionary endeavor prior to that time was paternalism: the missionary (imported from afar) *always* was the spiritual leader and in control of the mission or church. God used Roland Allen to help the modern church see the error of its paternalism on the mission field and begin to appreciate both the theory and practice of the principles of the indigenous church. His 1912 book *Missionary Methods: St. Paul's or Ours?* forced the Christian Church to look very seriously at its approach to missions. This book and his 1927 work in a similar vein, *The Spontaneous Expansion of the Church—and the Causes Which Hinder it,* are as applicable to the mission field behind bars as to any mission field overseas.[339]

There are three key ideas that undergird the indigenous church principles. The first is that, in general, men are most easily and effectively won to Christ by their own kind. As Allen put it, the *aim* of missionaries and church leaders must become the evangelization of "each country by its own Christians."[340] Studies repeatedly demonstrate that "the most effective method of evangelism is person-to-person witness" and particularly from one the convert had known well.[341] As Allen stated:

> Only when the non-Christian population is face to face with a change in their neighbors, and an ordered church life of their neighbors which can be ascribed to no white [i.e., outside] influence, are they compelled to face the fact that they are in the presence of a spiritual force which is strange to them, in the presence of the Holy Ghost.[342]

The second key related to the indigenous church is that paternalism[343] breeds weakness. As Allen notes, "Where churches are helped most, there they are weak, lifeless, and helpless."[344]

The third key is the most difficult for chaplains and correctional administrators. It is that leadership for an indigenous church may come from within the church instead of being imported from outside (in the person of a missionary or *chaplain*). Allen saw that the apostolic practice was to "found churches every place where we make converts, churches equipped with all the divine grace and authority [i.e., leaders, ministers, self-determination] of Christian churches."[345] Allen summarized: "Spontaneous expansion must be free; it cannot be under our [i.e., missionaries'] control. If we want to see spontaneous expansion we must establish native [or relative to prisons, *inmate*] churches free from our [in this case, *chaplains'*]control."[346]

The history of foreign missions in this century has proved the validity and effectiveness of the indigenous church principle. It produces Christianity whose churches are self-determining (they guide themselves), self-supporting, and self-propagating. This has been illustrated by the Little Flock movement in China, the church in Ethiopia during the Second World War, and many others. This also has been true historically.[347]

Application of the Indigenous Church Principle Behind Bars

The first step in application of the indigenous church principle behind bars is *commitment* to that principle. This involves acknowledgement that the three keys mentioned above do work, confession that they have not been used in the past as they should have been, and willingness to change our ways in order to use them in the future. Without such commitment, there is no hope of applying the indigenous church principle behind bars.

There is little question of the validity of the first key to jails and prisons. Inmates listen more readily, and respond more, to offenders whose conversions have demonstrated their reality by godly living than they do to anyone else. Allen summarizes this principle:

> Spontaneous expansion begins with the individual effort of the individual Christian to assist his fellow, when common experience, common difficulties, common toil have first brought the two together. It is this equality and community of experience which makes one deliver his message in terms which the other can understand, and makes the hearer ap-

> proach the subject with sympathy and confidence—with sympathy because the common experience makes approach easy and natural, with confidence because the one is accustomed to understand what the other says, and expects to understand him now.[348]

The second key to the debilitating result of paternalism has begun to be appreciated much more in the past few decades. It does not help a person to do for him what he can and should do for himself. To do for the individual what he can and should do for himself is not only to make him weak, but also to keep him weak and immature. This is the almost inevitable result of coddling. This lesson has been hard to learn on the mission field. Too often the zeal of converts has been stifled by missionaries who come to do what the converts were doing: witnessing, teaching, etc. This stems from *"a very widespread conviction amongst our missionaries that new converts, so far from evangelizing others, need to be nursed themselves if they are not to fall away."* [349] (*Emphasis* Allen's.)

It may be even harder to learn for the Church Behind Bars. Chaplains and Christian workers should expect inmate converts to witness, to desire to learn God's Word, to grow spiritually, to use their gifts and abilities, *and should not coddle them.* When the inmate John in chapter 1 was threatened if he continued to read his Bible, he was not coddled. He was challenged to please Jesus. The command of Jesus is simple and applies to *every* believer: "Be thou faithful unto death" (Revelation 2:10).

One reason paternalism continues unabated is that it is addictive. The paternalistic one feels good because he is "helping" and is needed. The more he "helps," the more his "help" is needed. Furthermore, the nearly universal principle of human indulgence (briefly stated, I will not do for myself what someone else will do for me) causes adverse feelings and reactions when the "helped" one is forced to do for himself. Consequently, paternalism has not only a tendency to perpetuate itself but also to expand.

It is also true that the dependent condition of the confined discourages inmate initiative and maturity. However, inmate self-help programs such as Alcoholics Anonymous, Jaycee chapters, etc., do work. They help inmates mature and develop self-respect. A similar effect should be expected in the religious self-help program of an indigenous church.

The greatest difficulty in applying the indigenous principle behind bars lies with the third key—the idea that inmates can and often should be leaders of the Church Behind Bars. On the mission fields, recognition of the role of indigenous leadership has slowly evolved in this century, and even today there are significant questions about who should control programs of a number of churches—the indigenous leadership or the foreign missionaries. Obviously, this will also be a problem for the Church Behind Bars.

In thinking about an indigenous Church Behind Bars, three issues demand consideration: (1) the requirements for spiritual leadership, (2) the possibility of such leadership developing within a jail or prison, and (3) the likelihood of correctional administrators allowing inmates to have formal control of religious programs within the institutions.

The Bible places a premium on practical godliness as a prime requirement for spiritual leadership (1 Timothy 3:1–13; Titus 1:5–9). Today in America, primary emphasis is on academic training, that is college and seminary. Little emphasis is placed upon practical godliness. In fact, this author knows several chaplains of state prisons who abuse alcohol and indulge in sexual immorality, yet they remain chaplains at their institutions. No doubt their disgraceful lives not only offend Christian sensibilities but also turn many inmates even further away from Christ. Unfortunately, their institutions, their denominations, and the local councils of churches do not reprimand them. Likewise, there are a number of chaplains, mainly of liberal theological persuasion, who are unregenerated. This is not a new problem. More than two centuries ago, Gilbert Tennent preached his fiery sermon "The Danger of an Unconverted Ministry." [350] The roots of the problem go back to the earliest days of the Church. Jude wrote of it in the first century (verse 4), it intensified in the patristic church, and has continued to this day because, as George Williams noted, "the ministry became more of a career than a calling. The ministrant became much less an organ of the local church and spokesman of the community before God and much more of a professional cleric, appropriately trained and promoted, even from one parish to another." [351]

The Bible also places a premium on sound doctrine in spiritual leadership. This emphasis is found throughout Paul's pastoral epistles (for examples, see in context 1 Timothy 1:3; 4:6,13,16; 6:3; 2 Timothy 1:13; 2:15; 3:14–17; 4:3; Titus 1:9; 2:2). The contemporary ecumenical emphasis of accepting any cleric as a "spiritual leader" completely ignores the question of doctrinal soundness as a requirement. For example, the ecumenically oriented APCCA has included in its membership clergy from the Unitarian-Universalist church. From the early church to the present, unsound doctrine within Christendom has plagued the Church. It is illuminating to observe that the same basic heresies have been present from the beginning, as illustrated by the following quotation from Ignatius, who was martyred at the beginning of the second century:

> There are some vain talkers and deceivers, not Christians, but Christ-betrayers, bearing the name of Christ in deceit, and corrupting the Word of the Gospel; while they intermix the poison of their deceit with their persuasive talk, as if they mingled aconite with sweet wine, that so he who drinks, being deceived in his taste by the very sweetness of the draught, may incautiously meet with his death. One of the ancients gives us this advice, "Let no man be called good who mixes good with evil." For they speak of Christ, not that they may preach Christ, but that they may reject Christ; and they speak of the law, not that they may establish the law, but that they may proclaim things contrary to it. For they alienate Christ from the Father, and the law from Christ. They also calumniate His being born of the Virgin; they are ashamed of His cross; they deny His passion; and they do not believe in His resurrection. They introduce God as a being unknown; they suppose Christ to be unbegotten; and as to the Spirit, they do not admit that He exists. Some of them say that the Son is a mere man, and that the Father, Son, and Holy Spirit

> are but the same person, and that the creation is the work of God, not by Christ, but by some other strange power.[352]

Finally, the Bible places emphasis on God's initiative in raising up spiritual leaders. The Lord *gave* apostles, prophets, evangelists, and pastor-teachers to the Church (Ephesians 4:11). The Lord *put* the apostle Paul into the ministry (1 Timothy 1:12). The Lord *calls* men to the ministry. Too many have entered the clergy as one of the helping professions but are not called of God to the Christian ministry.

At this point, it is pertinent to consider Roland Allen's comparison of leadership training by Jesus with leadership training on the mission field:

> Christ trained His leaders by taking them with Him as He went about teaching and healing, doing the work which they, as missionaries, would do; we train in institutions. He trained a very few with whom He was in the closest personal relation; we train many who simply pass through our schools with a view to an examination and an appointment. Christ trained His leaders in the midst of their own people, so that the intimacy of their relation to their own people was not marred and they could move freely among them as one of themselves. We train our leaders in a hothouse, and their intimacy with their own people is so marred that they can never thereafter live as one of them, or share their thought.[353]

The Church has developed ways of accepting indigenous leadership on the mission field. Similar methods can be applied behind bars.

Next, it is appropriate to ask, Is such leadership likely to develop from inmate populations? Both experience and the instruction of Scripture (e.g., 1 Timothy 3:6; 5:22) teach that it takes time for spiritual leadership to develop and mature. Jesus spent about three years training the Twelve. During their first missionary journey, Paul and Barnabas appointed elders in churches who had been Christians only a few months (Acts 14:21–23). Thus the question becomes, Are significant numbers of inmates likely to be in their institutions the months and years needed for leadership to arise from the converts? For prisons, the answer is an unquestionable yes. Many will spend years in the same institution. For jails, the answer is no. Few inmates will spend longer than six to twelve months in jail; the nominal stay for inmates with serious charges is about three months.[354]

Finally, the question of prison administrators allowing inmates to formally control religious activities must be addressed. The answer to this question has already been decided, both by the courts and in current penal practice. The courts have ruled that First Amendment rights—freedom of religion, speech, and association—should be abridged only for serious reasons that relate directly to prison security or operations. Likewise, prisons allow a multiple of programs that to a large degree are inmate controlled, even where these have a staff or outside "sponsor" (AA meetings, Jaycees, etc.). In particular, the Black Muslims have pushed the very issue of establishing an "indigenous church" behind bars through the courts and have set the legal precedent for such. Thus, if an indigenous Church Behind Bars seeks to be established in a proper way, it should face no unsurmountable opposition from prison administrators.

Objections and Obstacles to Development of the Church Behind Bars

The first objection that has to be considered is the prison administrator's question, "Why an inmate-led church? We have a chaplain." The answer to this objection is manifold:

- Inmates have a constitutional right to their own church/worship approach.
- Even if a chaplain is an evangelical, spiritual minister, he can retard the spiritual progress of inmates by paternalism.
- Many chaplains are not evangelical, spiritual ministers and, consequently, cannot provide the ministry needed. Moreover, the denominational distribution of government-employed chaplains is (1) not representative of the national population, (2) not representative of inmate popu-

lations, and (3) not concentrated in those groups most effective in reaching inmates.[355]

Thus, the presence of a chaplain does not in itself remove the need for an indigenous Church Behind Bars.

The second objection that comes to mind is, How can the prison administration control this thing? Prison administration must be concerned about knowledge and control of all activities within the institution. Also, many prison administrators are wary of any activities that promote unity among sizeable segments of the inmate population because of the action potential possessed by a cohesive group within the institution. Such groups also reduce the institution's manipulative power over inmates. Again, the answer to this objection has several facets:

- An inmate-led church should be subject to the same regulations and procedures as other religious activities. Thus the fact that the church is indigenous makes it no more a problem for the prison administration than religious programs under the supervision of the chaplain or church groups from the outside.
- Already in many institutions there are inmate-led Bible classes, prayer meetings, etc. Some of these are operated informally in inmate living quarters or in recreation areas. Others are conducted formally in chapels, classrooms, and elsewhere.
- A biblically oriented indigenous church should not have any reason to conduct any of its activities in secret, and therefore members of the institution staff should be welcome at all meetings. Staff members who know Christ should be welcomed and accepted as brothers. Positions of leadership within the indigenous church should be open to any qualified person: inmate, guard, warden, chaplain, etc.

A third objection that might be raised is that the indigenous church concept is likely to produce within the prison the same proliferation of religious groups extant in American society, particularly since there are many oddballs among inmate populations. And if it occurs, how in the world can the prison administration accommodate all such religious groups?

This objection is valid at one point. It is likely that there will be a proliferation of religious groups behind bars. But, so what? Such has already occurred. A plethora of denominational and sectarian programs and activities exists already in major prisons. For example, the schedule of religious activities (1976) for the U.S. Penitentiary at Leavenworth, Kansas, during a week includes the following: Mormon service, Christian Science service, Jehovah's Witnesses service, Church of Christ Communion, Lutheran Communion, United Pentecostal Bible Study, Seventh Day Adventist service, Reorganized Latter Day Saints Bible study, Yokefellow meetings, Salvation Army services, plus general Protestant services, a variety of Catholic activities including a Cursillo group, and several varieties of Muslim meetings. Therefore:

- Increasing the present kaleidoscope of religious groups by the addition of indigenous inmate church groups will not appreciably increase the administrative burden on prison administrators.
- While the available spaces and times for services and activities have to be allocated among the various groups, the prison administration can just add the indigenous inmate church(es) to the list and continue to allocate in a fashion that does not show preference to one group over another.
- Prison administration should welcome a proliferation of inmate-led churches. The more constructive activities to which inmate energies can be devoted, the better the prison will operate. The more different inmate-led churches, the more inmates are likely to be involved.

A fourth objection is that inmates don't know how to lead a church. The answer here is simple:

- Inmates can learn to lead a church just as they have learned to lead Jaycee chapters, AA groups, etc. A suggested pattern for the organization of such is presented later in this chapter.

A fifth objection is that inmates will use the indigenous church to their own advantage. Consider:

- There should be no more advantages available to inmates by participation in an indigenous church than by participation in present religious activities or other inmate activities.

A final objection is that churches on the outside will not recognize the Church Behind Bars and may even object to its existence. There is little validity in this reasoning because:

- Such lack of recognition and objection—even if such should occur—does not set aside the First Amendment right of inmates to their own religious preference.
- Use of the organizational and activity suggestions presented in this chapter will help an indigenous church in a prison find acceptance and recognition, as will participation in the National Fellowship of Congregations Behind Bars.

There may be other objections, but the six above cover most that are likely to be raised. Each of these has been answered.

Suggestions for the Church Behind Bars

This discussion covers six areas: (1) congregational structure and organization, (2) doctrinal position, (3) activities, (4) leadership requirements, (5) relationships to other groups, and (6) resources to aid the indigenous church in its ministry.

Congregational Structure and Organization

Three basic forms of church polity exist: Episcopalian, Presbyterian, and Congregational.[356] In the first two, persons outside the immediate congregation exercise a significant degree of control over the congregation (whether bishop or presbytery). Restrictions upon correspondence among inmates (even religious correspondence) would make these two forms of church polity inappropriate for an indigenous church because they would effectively close some leadership positions to inmates.[357] Thus the congregational form of church organization (i.e., the one where all authority for the church's decisions and actions lies within that congregation) seems most appropriate for the Church Behind Bars.

A very simple organization will suffice. One such is illustrated below:

Board of elders—elected annually by the members of the congregation as their leaders.

From the board of elders and selected by them:

- A president for administrative leadership of the congregation and for liaison with the administration of the institution
- pastor-teachers for the regular preaching services, Bible classes, and spiritual guidance of the congregation
- secretary-treasurer for the obvious duties

Other officers as needed (e.g., ushers for worship services).

Two books are recommended relative to the structure and organization of the indigenous church in prison. One is Alexander Rattray Hay's *New Testament Order for Church and Missionary* (New Testament Missionary Union, 1947). This basic text on ecclesiology is very helpful. The other is Leslie Flynn's *19 Gifts of the Spirit* (Victor Books, 1974), an excellent discussion of the Christian's responsibility to discover and use his spiritual gifts.

Formal organization is not recommended until at least ten serious believers likely to be in the institution at least a year are interested in forming an indigenous congregation, and until there has been a substantial history (at least six months) of inmate-led ministry (Bible studies, prayer groups, witnessing efforts, etc.).[358]

Doctrinal Position

The doctrinal position of a congregation behind bars should be narrow enough to keep within the mainstream of historic, orthodox Christianity but broad enough to allow unity among *all* who know, love, and serve Jesus. A congregation may develop its own statement of doctrine, or it may turn to others who have already developed such a statement. For example, the National Association of Evangelicals developed a doctrinal statement to accomplish that purpose, and this could be used. So could the doctrinal statement of the AEIC, which is presented below for illustration:

> The AEIC doctrinal statement is not a comprehensive statement of truths held by evangelicals. Instead, it is an identification of some of the most important beliefs which characterize evangelicals in the tradition of historic, orthodox Christianity.
>
> We believe the Bible to be the inspired, the only infallible, authoritative Word of God.
>
> We believe that there is one God, eternally existent in three Persons: Father, Son, and Holy Spirit.
>
> We believe in the deity of the Lord Jesus Christ, in His virgin birth, in His sinless life, in His miracles, in His vicarious and atoning death through His shed blood, in His bodily resurrection, in His ascension, and in His personal return in power and glory.
>
> We believe that regeneration by the Holy Spirit is absolutely essential for the salvation of lost and sinful man.
>
> We believe in the present ministry of the Holy Spirit by whose indwelling the Christian is enabled to live a godly life.

Activities

Activities of the Church Behind Bars should move toward four objectives for its members: (1) growth in knowledge of God's truth and godly maturity, (2) increase of love for and among the brothers, (3) sharing the Gospel and love of Jesus with everyone, and (4) doing good to all. Accomplishment of these objectives requires:

- Times of worship. These should include singing of hymns and sharing of testimonies and blessings as well as prayer and attention to God's Word.
- Times of prayer and study together. In all of these activities, there should be a continual emphasis on the believers' responsibility to pray for one another, to share insights with one another, and to help one another.
- Personal witnessing of God's truth by all who know Jesus (individually or in pairs). Each prison congregation should strive diligently to evangelize the entire population and staff of its institution. A major weakness of Christianity in prison today is that too many inmates see their faith only as an individual, personal relationship to God and fail to see their responsibilities to the brethren and to the lost in that prison.

Leadership Requirements

It has already been indicated that the Bible places prime emphasis on personal godliness, sound doctrine, and God's call to the ministry for spiritual leadership. Therefore, it is recommended that no one be selected as an elder who (1) has been a believer behind bars less than a year, (2) has not led at least several others to a saving knowledge of Jesus, (3) does not have an extensive knowledge of God's Word, and (4) is not recognized by inmates as one seriously trying to live by God's Word. Moreover, leadership positions should be open for all who qualify within the institution: inmates, staff (including the chaplain), and volunteers.

The elders should elect their president and determine which of the elders will be the preachers and teachers. All elders should pray and allow God to guide their decisions.

Relationships to Other Groups

An evangelical indigenous church in a prison would be encouraged to be a part of the National Fellowship of Congregations Behind Bars, a branch of the AEIC which provides a forum for sharing among congregations and can provide advice when problems arise. It can also help released members integrate into churches in society.

It is recommended that inmates *not* pursue ordination behind bars. Elders should be commissioned by their congregations and dedicated to their tasks by the laying on of hands. They should have full authority to minister fully *within* their congregations (preach, teach, baptize, and administer communion).[359] There are groups within the Church whose leaders do all these things without ordination (e.g., Plymouth Brethren).

By not pursuing ordination for its leaders, the indigenous Church Behind Bars would minimize its conflicts with churches on the outside. When leaders of the Church Behind Bars are released from prison, their being called of God into the ministry should become quite clear to the Church outside, and ordination can be pursued at that time.

Resources

The Directory in Appendix D identifies a number of sources from which Christian literature and Bible courses may be obtained. The National Fellowship of Congregations Behind Bars was mentioned earlier.

The Chaplain and the Church Behind Bars

If a chaplain (or a missionary) believes in the principles of the indigenous church, once there are converts or believers among the population, he must ask the question, What is my role now? Recognizing that paternalism can hinder the spontaneous expansion of the church, *the chaplain (or missionary) must seek grace from God for the humility to serve as a brother among other brothers in the Church and not impose himself as a lord over the Church.*

Normally, the special biblical and theological training of the chaplain will make him a great asset to the Church Behind Bars, if he meets the requirements for leadership in the congregation. Some chaplains cannot satisfy the requirement of personal godliness. Some chaplains have never led a single inmate to a saving knowledge of Christ. And some chaplains do not possess sound doctrine. Chaplains who do not qualify for leadership in the Church Behind Bars may harass it. A chaplain selected for leadership in the Church Behind Bars will use his gifts and abilities as directed by the elders, in the same way as any other elder.

It will take great courage, self-assurance, and love for both the Lord and the brethren for a chaplain to be a brother among brothers, just as it does for the missionary in the field. But then Jesus said, "He that is greatest among you shall be your servant" (Matthew 23:11).

12

Organizing for Effective Ministry to Offenders

The task of ministering to offenders which Christ has given His Church is both difficult and demanding. It will be accomplished only with much dedicated effort guided and anointed by God's Spirit. Proper organization of the activities of God's people in this endeavor will bring forth the greatest results. This chapter presents suggestions about such organization.[360] Three basic topics are considered: (1) the agencies or organizations through which ministry to offenders is performed, (2) organization of programs of ministry, and (3) the role of professional associations in the correctional ministry.

Agencies and Organizations Ministering to Offenders

There are four basic kinds of agencies providing ministry to offenders. First, there is the government agency which employs chaplains (usually a correctional institution or a penal system).[361] Second, there are cross-denominational[362] religious organizations which employ correctional chaplains and/or provide other substantial ministry to offenders, either as their primary or exclusive area of ministry or as only a small part of much broader endeavors.[363] Third, some denominational agencies employ chaplains and provide ministry to offenders.[364] And fourth, individual congregations provide ministry to offenders.[365]

If the Church of Jesus Christ is to minister to prisoners as it should, then this ministry must increase substantially. How can this best be done, organizationally?

It is thought unlikely that the government agencies employing chaplains at present will significantly increase the number of chaplains in their employ. If anything, that number may decrease.[366] It is possible that some of the several hundred correctional institutions large enough to justify a full-time chaplain but not currently employing chaplains will begin to employ them in the future. Normally three steps lead up to an institution's decision to start employing chaplains.[367]

- A single individual or small group of individuals, usually clergy, become deeply interested in development of a chaplaincy program and serve as its instigator, promoter, and catalyst.
- The idea of a chaplaincy for the institution is promoted among as wide a spectrum of the religious and civic community as possible, and their interest in it is expressed to the administration of the institution by individuals, representatives of churches and civic groups, and religious associations such as councils of churches and ministerial alliances.
- The administration of the institution is approached and worked with to develop a chaplaincy program within its staff structure. Normally an administrator of a correctional institution (particularly a sheriff, since he is usually an elected official) will not consider the use of tax monies for a chaplain unless he has become convinced of considerable community support for (and substantial political influence behind) the idea of a government-employed chaplain for his institution.

Often the individual or group which has served as catalyst in developing the chaplaincy position will have the say in who is appointed as chaplain.

Before considering cross-denominational organizations ministering to prisoners, the potential for increasing ministries to offenders by single denominations and individual churches needs consideration. Both of these have *great potential for increased ministry* to offenders in the community (follow-up, halfway houses, etc.), as part of the total religious programs in correctional institutions (e.g., a weekly Bible class in the jail conducted by a particular local church), in ministry-support functions such as providing literature (including Bible correspondence courses), films, etc.,[368] and in providing chaplains for small institutions.[369]

Cross-denominational agencies are the organizations with the *greatest potential for increasing ministry* to offenders in medium-sized and large correctional institutions. Three facts support this statement. First, they are the largest source of ministry to offenders at present, other than government-supported chaplains. Their ministries have a major role in the programs of many state-supported chaplains who are using their Bible correspondence courses, special evangelistic services by them, involving them as regular participants in Bible-study and counseling programs,[370] etc. Second, growth in such organizations and their support during the past two decades has been substantial. Third, they are particularly suited for ministry to offenders because they are not confined within the limits of a single denomination. Effective ministry to prisoners must reach across denominational boundaries to inmates of varied backgrounds and work with releasees and inmate families in many churches.

In discussing expansion of the ministry to offenders, the question arises of whether to start new organizations or merely to increase the endeavors of existing ones. No simple answer can be given to this question. In many cases, the answer is obviously to expand the ministry of an existing organization. Such would be the case where an existing organization is already providing a limited ministry (e.g., a part-time chaplain for a jail with 200 inmates) and a more extensive ministry is needed (e.g., a full-time chaplain) in that jail. In other cases, it is not possible to provide a needed area of ministry by expanding existing organizations. For example, only two organizations in the country (Forgotten Man Mission and the Good News Mission) provide full-time jail chaplains for jails in a number of jurisdictions, and only one of these organizations, the Good News Mission, ministers in more than one state. Thus most persons interested in starting full-time jail chaplaincy programs will have to establish new organizations.

It is appropriate to identify characteristics of a cross-denominational organization that help it to be effective in ministering to offenders. This discussion is oriented toward ministry in a locality (a jail chaplaincy, halfway house, follow-up program for inmate families, etc.), and some of it may not be as applicable to an organization providing what could be called a "support" ministry (literature, evangelistic meetings in prisons, etc.). The ideal cross-denominational organization:

- *Is legally qualified for contributors to claim tax deductions for contributions.* Without such, many sources of financial support for the organization will be eliminated or restricted.[371] (It may be necessary for an organization with such IRS recognition to restrict its role in matters of correctional reform in order not to conflict with IRS restrictions on tax-exempt organizations' efforts to influence legislation.)
- *Is under the cognizance of a responsible local board with broad representation of the community.* The board may actually control the organization (as in a board of directors or a board of trustees) or the board may have only an advisory role. (It is helpful to balance the membership of the board among pastors, Christian businessmen, and members of the criminal justice system. Membership should have as broad denominational representation as possible and as much influence in the community as possible.[372] Boards with narrow representation and without some civic or political heavyweights are generally limited in their ability to help the ministry. The board should be an active, decision-making board and not passive. Passive boards severely limit their usefulness.)
- *Has a name suggestive of its ministry to offenders.*
- *Maintains an effective public relations program.* The Church and community quickly forget about the needs of offenders unless they are repeatedly brought to their attention. The public relations program can include presenta-

tions to churches and civic groups, newspaper articles and radio/TV programs, publication of a newsletter or magazine, conducting seminars, and tours of the correctional institution for ministers, etc.

- *Has a clear understanding of its purpose and objectives.*
- *Is open to new ideas* and different ways of operating and keeps its organizational structure as simple and as objective-oriented as possible.
- *Is faithful to the Word of God.*

Cross-denominational agencies ministering to prisoners normally draw their financial support from individuals, businesses, congregations, denominational agencies, and foundations.[373] A brief discussion of each funding source follows.

A substantial portion of support for cross-denominational agencies comes from individual Christians. Most of these contribute small or modest amounts. A few contribute substantially. This source of support can respond quickly to appeals for funds but is often unstable and unpredictable. Many organizations have found the *faith promise* approach helpful in seeking support from individuals.[374]

Present laws allow a business to contribute a small percentage of its income to charitable organizations and to claim a tax deduction for the contribution. Since all businessmen are concerned about crime problems, the organization ministering to prisoners has a natural opening. The support from the business community is stable and dependable, if sought as a continuing (e.g., monthly) contribution, in contrast to a single donation. Businessmen of the agency's board are the ones most likely to develop contributions from businesses.

Church financial support can be sought either at the level of the local congregation or through some agency of the denomination. Seeking financial support from a congregation for a ministry in its area is likely to bring forth volunteers and prayers as well as funds. Either kind of church support normally requires long periods of time (and much effort) to develop, since congregations and denominations normally operate on a yearly budget cycle.

Church support is usually a very stable form of support and will continue year after year.

To date, foundation funding of religious ministry to offenders has been limited. Professional fund raisers usually have the greatest success in developing funds from foundations. Most foundations prefer to donate funds to start programs or finance property/equipment purchases rather than to finance normal operations of an organization.

Every cross-denominational agency ministering to offenders is caught in a dilemma with respect to how much time it should spend in fund raising and public relations, especially if it wishes to expand its outreach. It can spend so much time promoting its ministry that it has no time to minister. But without the funds, it has no resources with which to minister.

Program Organization

The term *program* in this discussion covers such a wide variety of activities that it is very nebulous. The program may be a weekly Bible class for inmates at a small local jail. It may be an extensive one-on-one counseling program in a large prison. It may be a Bible correspondence study program for inmates. It may be a Bible, Testament, Christian literature distribution program. It may be a follow-up program working with inmate families.

The purpose of organization at this level is to make sure the program is properly executed and to prevent frustration (and dropout) of volunter workers because of poor program management.

What Are We Here For?

Proper organization of a program begins with a clear definition and understanding of its purpose. This can be achieved by a written *statement of purpose* which covers (1) for whom the program is designed, (2) its goals and objectives, and (3) how these are to be achieved. A sample *statement of purpose* is presented below for a weekly Bible-class program for misdemeanants in a local jail:

The Bible class is for the misdemeanant inmates in the jail. The class will be held from 7:00 to 8:00 o'clock on Thursday evenings in the jail classroom and will be led by a teaching team of volunteers under the supervision of the chaplain. A maximum of ten misdemeanants may attend the class. Because the average stay of misdemeanants in the jail is relatively brief, the primary thrust of the class will be evangelism. The objective of this class is to see as many as possible regenerated. The plan of salvation will be clearly presented in each lesson, and time will be reserved at the end of the class period for counseling with inmates who wish to commit their lives to Christ. The lesson topic and lead teacher will be determined by the teaching team leader.

Who's In Charge?

The second step in program organization is a clear delineation of responsibilities: a "job description." Often the Sunday worship services at a correctional institution are rotated among a group of churches, each one responsible for the service once a month or once a quarter. In such cases it is not uncommon for some of the churches to have no one formally in charge of their group. Consequently, a church will sometimes have only a small number go to the jail for the service, and with a program not thoroughly prepared. Even if it is just for one service at the jail every three months, someone needs to be officially in charge and responsible for the program! This means a chaplain for an institution should have a number of people with whom he works in charge of various programs (the teaching team leader of a Bible class, the man for the Sunday services on the second Sunday of each month, etc.), just as a pastor works with the Sunday school superintendent, the head usher, etc., of his congregation. Most religious programs in jails and prisons are so loosely organized that at times they collapse simply because no one was in charge.[375]

The one in charge of a program needs a clear understanding of what his job is and what his helpers (if any) are to do. For example:

Bill was the team leader of the weekly film-showing program. He was responsible for picking up the film at the chaplain's office and returning it there after the showing, along with a report of inmate attendance and response. Joe, his assistant, was responsible for setting up the screen and operating the projector, both kept in the film-showing room. Bill would get a list of inmates to see the film (collected/made up by the chaplain) when he picked up the film and would give the list to the correctional officer in charge, so that the inmates could be brought to the film-showing area. Bill was responsible for comments at the close of the film, but he could assign that task to his assistant. Both were expected to be involved in counseling interested inmates after the film. Joe was responsible for notifying Bill if he could not attend. Bill would then pick a substitute from one of the three trained alternates (and would do the same in case of his own absence, allowing Joe to fill his role). If neither Joe nor Bill could be present, then the chaplain was to be notified so that he and one of the alternates could conduct the film showing. If for some reason the film showing had to be cancelled (e.g., a disturbance within the institution), the chaplain could simply call Bill and cancel for that showing.

Be Wise

In organizing the personnel for a program, three principles will make it work much more effectively. First, a *cadre* is essential. These volunteers are the core of the program. They are committed to it. They are trained and competent for their tasks. They provide the volunteer leadership of the program and the one(s) in charge will always be drawn from them. Second, the cadre should be *supplemented.* For example, when a church provides Sunday services, one or two men may form the cadre, but a dozen may come from the church to provide the service: a speaker, musician, choir, etc. Members of the cadre are familiar with the institution regulations and procedures, they can "shepherd" the group from the church so that the program is most effective.[376] Third, there should be *depth* in personnel. There should be backup for each position, i.e., an alternate for everyone involved in the program. If the program involves a weekly event, either the responsibility for the assignment should be limited in time to no more than three to four months before a break is taken, or some means of rotation [377] should be devised so that the program does not become a burden to the volunteer.

Some may claim these principles are visionary, asserting there will not be adequate Christian interest in programs to offenders for their application. Two reactions to such negative comments are appropriate: First, our programs will rise no higher than our ideals. Those content to limit their programs by low ideals may ignore these principles. Second, as volunteer programs continue to increase within the criminal justice systems, standards will evolve to improve the quality of content and execution. Great progress has been made in this area.[378] Consequently, *quality management and organization of religious programs will be required also.* The above principles simply help develop a quality program organizationally.

Who's Who?

Religious programs for offenders have often been negligent in identifying their workers. This poses no problem as long as the workers are few in number and the programs very limited or conducted only under the supervision of a chaplain. In order for religious programs to expand, the following identification procedures are helpful for those responsible for the programs and for the institution staff:

1. Religious volunteer ID cards at the entry point to the institution. The ID card should contain the following: the volunteer's name, address and phone number, social security number, date of birth, physical description (sex, height, weight, eye and hair color—and a picture if possible), job at the institution (e.g., Bible-class teacher), and the hours the volunteer is normally at the institution. A sample card is shown below. These cards can be maintained in a 3-by-5 file box at the entry point to the institution. Every one of the cadre and as many of the other religious volunteers as possible should have such an ID card on file at the institution. No one should be allowed into the institution for religious programs unless an ID for him is on file or he is personally

known and vouched for by one whose ID is in the file.[379] The comments section is useful for noting who can bring equipment (guitar, projector, etc.) into the institution.

Sample ID Card (actual size is 5″ x 3″):

Name ______________________
Address ______________________
____
Photo
Phone: (home) ______ (Bus.) ______
Soc. Sec. No. ______________
Description:
Date of Birth: ______________
Sex ______ Ht. ______ Wt. ______ Hair ______ Eyes ______
Volunteer Job(s) ______________________
____
Hours Authorized in Institution ______________________
____
Comments:

2. Religious volunteer background information. Before one is accepted as a volunteer for religious programs working with offenders (at least as a member of the cadre or regular volunteer), it is helpful to acquire background information about the prospective volunteer. Normally this is best done by an *application form* followed by a personal interview with the applicant. The following items have been found to be useful parts of such a form.

a. Personal information: name, address and phone (home and business), social security number, date of birth, sex, height, weight, eye and hair color, marital status, spouse's and children's names and dates of birth.

b. Employment data: present job and employer, other jobs and employers within the past five years.

c. Health data: general health situation, health problems, major illnesses, use of alcohol, drugs, or medication (past and present).

d. Legal data: arrest and incarceration record (reason and disposition), bonding record (bond refusals, if any, with dates and reasons).

e. Church data: [380] Church membership (where, since when), church participation (showing *weekly, monthly, occasionally, never*—for Sunday school, Sunday morning worship, Sunday evening worship, midweek activities, other), current jobs/offices in the church, attitude of pastor and church leaders towards the applicant's involvement in the ministry to offenders (strongly supports, interested, unconcerned, opposes, unknown).

f. Spiritual data: A narrative description of the applicant's conversion, how he led someone to the Lord, a summary of his experience in Christian work, an explanation of why he believes God wants him in the ministry to offenders, and what kinds of things he is interested in doing and willing to do.

g. References: It is normal to ask for a couple of character references and the name of one or two who can attest to the applicant's capability for the job in which he wishes to serve.

h. Information not acquired directly from the applicant. (Some prefer to have a separate form for this data.)

(1) Summary of comments from the references.

(2) Summary of comments from the applicant's pastor.

(3) Notes from the personal interview with the applicant.

(4) Record of applicant's/volunteer's progress: date(s) of training, acceptance as a volunteer, job assignment, termination; evaluation of progress, needs, etc.; miscellaneous notes about the volunteer.

3. Comprehensive Volunteer List. Each program needs a comprehensive list of the regular volunteers involved. Other-

wise, it will be difficult if not impossible to plan coverage for personnel who are ill, on vacation, etc., or make orderly modifications to the program when it has to be altered or expanded.

The Role of Professional Associations

For individuals and organizations ministering to offenders, participation in professional associations can serve several useful purposes. The associations related specifically to the correctional ministry (AEIC and APCCA) cannot only be a forum for communication of ideas, program, and standards for ministry to offenders, but can also serve as a channel for recruiting personnel or finding a suitable position. The general religious and ministerial associations (National Association of Evangelicals, local ministerial groups, etc.) can serve as vehicles by which to bring the correctional ministry to the attention of the Church.

Participation in the professional societies of the criminal justice system (ACA, National Sheriffs' Association, etc.) will not only keep one abreast of current activities and ideas in the criminology world but will also help officials to think of the chaplain and Christian worker as fellow professionals in dealing with offenders. Contacts with sheriffs, wardens, and superintendents at meetings of such groups can lay the groundwork for later ministry in their institutions.

Conclusion

The fear of the Lord is the beginning of knowledge and wisdom (Proverbs 1:7; 9:10). The fear of the Lord prevents abuse of the weak and oppression of others (Leviticus 19:14; 25:17). The fear of the Lord results in obedience, love, and service to God in all things (Deuteronomy 10:12).

To a large degree, the Church has disregarded biblical mandates to minister to prisoners and to call for reform of the criminal justice system so that righteousness, not oppression, would characterize it. Consequently, the Lord may ask, as He asked those who disregarded His commands in the days of Malachi, "Where is my fear? saith the Lord of hosts unto you, O priests, that despise my name" (Malachi 1:6). It is unbecoming to avoid the brunt of this question by ineffectual excuses. Long ago, a stern but ardent follower of Christ, Tertullian, observed, "In truth, it is nothing but willful disobedience which destroys the fear of God." [381] Chaplain, pastor, theologian, and layman must each examine himself on this issue, for all are priests in the household of God (cf. 1 Peter 2:5,9).

Upon chaplains lies responsibility for leadership in jails and prisons and for development of indigenous congregations behind bars; but chaplains also serve as prophets both to the Church, calling its attention to the needs of this ministry, and to the criminal justice system, serving as conscience for it.

It is pastors who must awaken their congregations and direct them to pray for, give to, and personally minister to offenders. To pastors will come praise or censure from the Lord as their congregations fulfill or neglect the commands of God in this area. It will avail little to plead that other demands for attention were heavy. Such preoccupation does not negate this responsibility.

Before the criminal justice system will heed cries from the Church for reform, theologians [382] must provide a comprehensive criminology that accounts for the facts about criminal behavior at least as well as do theories of secular sociologists. It is incumbent upon theologians to collect, analyze, organize, and publish adequate data so that a biblical view of man and the social benefit of conversion may not be dismissed casually by professionals within the criminal justice system. Likewise, theologians must develop ministerial training programs to prepare men for the chaplaincy.

The question is simpler for the layman: Am I doing what God wants from me in the ministry to prisoners?

If upon examination one finds that he has despised God's name by disregard of his duty, the biblical response calls for repentance, confession, and action.[383] Repentance is a change of mind from disregard of to assent to God's command. Confession is open acknowledgment of fault coupled with petition for God's forgiveness and cleansing. Action flows from obedience to God's command.

This book has set forth biblical imperatives for ministry to offenders and identified the ministry that is needed. The present ministry to prisoners was described and information provided both to make it more effective and to help it to expand. This book has gone forth with the author's prayer that our Lord will use it to promote ministry to prisoners so that many more may come to Christ and grow to maturity in Him.

> Blessed is the man that feareth the Lord, that delighteth greatly in his commandments.
>
> Psalms 112:1

> For as the heaven is high above the earth, so great is his mercy toward them that fear him.

As far as the east is from the west, so far hath he removed our transgressions from us.

Like as a father pitieth his children, so the Lord pitieth them that fear him.

For he knoweth our frame; he remembereth that we are dust.

Psalms 103:11–14

Appendix A

Scripture Passages Related to Prisoners

Rev. Frank E. Scholte, a chaplain of the Good News Mission serving the Henrico County Jail (Virginia), assisted in the development of this Appendix.

Because many inmates have a keen interest in what the Bible says about prisoners, these passages are identified as an aid for those who preach to inmates and teach them. The context of the verses referenced should be examined carefully since often only the core verse(s) of a passage are listed.

Passage	*Comment*
Genesis 39:19–41:14	Joseph's imprisonment upon a false charge (attempted rape) and his prison experiences.
42:15–20	Joseph imprisons his brother.
45:4–8	Joseph's attitude toward his unjust imprisonment.
Numbers 21:1	Arad takes some Israelites prisoner.
Judges 16:21,25	Samson's imprisonment.
1 Kings 22:27	Micaiah imprisoned for telling the truth.
2 Kings 17:4	King Hoshea imprisoned.
25:27–30	King Jehoiachin in prison.

Passage	*Comment*
2 Chronicles 16:10	Hanani imprisoned for his prophecy.
18:26	Micaiah imprisoned for telling the truth.
Job 3:18	Prisoners rest together in death.
Psalms 69:33; 79:11; 102:20	God gives attention to prisoners.
142:7	A prayer for release from prison.
146:7	God releases prisoners.
Ecclesiastes 4:14	Even a prisoner can become king.
Isaiah 10:4	God's people are beneath prisoners without Him.
14:17	Lucifer does not open prison doors.
20:4	Prisoners of the Assyrians.
24:22	Eschatological imprisonment of the kings of the earth.
42:7	The Messiah to deliver prisoners from the prison.
42:22	The imprisoned state of rebellious Israel.
49:9	Prisoners told to go forth in the day of salvation.
53:8	A prophecy of Christ's imprisonment.
61:1	The ministry of God's Anointed to captives (fulfillment in Luke 4:18).
Jeremiah 29:26	Shemaiah to put self-made prophets into prison.
32:1–3	Jeremiah imprisoned during Nebuchadrezzar's siege of Jerusalem.
32:8,12	Jeremiah did business while in prison.
33:1	The Word of the Lord came to Jeremiah in prison.
36:5	Jeremiah under house arrest.
36:26	Jeremiah miraculously preserved from arrest.
37:4,15–38:13	Jeremiah beaten and imprisoned (even in the mire of the dungeon) after the Chaldean army broke off its siege of Jerusalem.

Passage	*Comment*
Jeremiah 38:28	Jeremiah's imprisonment continues until the fall of Jerusalem.
40:1–4	Jeremiah's brief confinement by the Babylonians.
52:11	King Zedekiah blinded and imprisoned until his death.
52:31–34	King Jehoiachin's imprisonment.
Lamentations 3:34	God does not willingly crush prisoners.
3:53–55	Jeremiah's prison prayer.
Daniel 3:1–28	Three Hebrews in the fiery furnace.
6:16–24	Daniel in the lion's den.
Zechariah 9:11–12	God's deliverance for prisoners.
Matthew 4:12	John the Baptist put into prison.
5:25–26	Advice to avoid prison by out-of-court settlement.
11:2	John the Baptist sends a question to Jesus from prison.
14:3,10	John the Baptist loses his head in prison.
18:30	A debtor put into prison.
25:36,39,44	Jesus blesses those who visit prisoners and curses those who do not.
27:15–21	Release of the prisoner Barabbas.
Mark 1:14; 6:17,27	John the Baptist in prison and his death.
15:6	Release of the prisoner Barabbas.
Luke 3:20	John the Baptist in prison.
4:18	Ministry of the Messiah to captives.
12:58–59	Advice on how to avoid prison.
21:12	Imprisonment of Jesus' disciples predicted.
22:33	Peter's willingness to go to prison for Christ's sake.
23:19,25	Barabbas, his crime and release.
Acts 4:3	Imprisonment of Peter and John.
5:18–23	Imprisonment of the Apostles and their miraculous release.

Passage	*Comment*
Acts 5:40	Apostles beaten for preaching and released.
7:54–60	Stoning of Stephen.
8:3; 9:2,14,21	Saul's imprisonment of Christians.
12:1,2	James killed by Herod.
12:4–17	Peter's imprisonment and miraculous release.
12:18,19	Guards executed for a prisoner's escape.
14:19	Paul stoned and left for dead.
16:22–39	Beating, imprisonment of Paul and Silas, plus an earthquake, result in salvation of the Philippian jailer.
17:6–9	Jason's bond provides freedom for Paul and the missionary team.
20:22–24; 21:11	Paul's advance knowledge of his imprisonment in Jerusalem.
21:30–35	Paul beaten by a mob in Jerusalem and rescued by Roman guards.
22:4	Paul's reference to his putting Christians into prisons.
22:24–29	Paul almost beaten while a prisoner.
23:1–10	Paul's hearing before a rowdy court.
23:11	God's assurance to the prisoner Paul.
23:18	A guard heeds a prisoner's request.
23:23–35	Paul transferred to another prison because of a threat on his life.
Chapter 24	Paul's hearing before Felix.
Chapter 25	Paul's hearing before Festus and his appeal to Caesar.
Chapter 26	Paul's hearing before Agrippa.
27:1–28:15	Paul's trip to Rome in custody.
28:16	Paul's house arrest in Rome.
28:17–20	Paul's description of his imprisonment.
2 Corinthians 11:23	Paul refers to his imprisonments.
Ephesians 3:1; 4:1	Paul, the prisoner of Christ.
6:20	Paul, an ambassador in bonds.

Passage	*Comment*
Philippians 1:11–18	Paul's imprisonment advances the gospel.
Colossians 4:10	Aristarchus, Paul's fellow prisoner.
2 Timothy 1:8	Paul, the prisoner of Christ.
1:16,17	Onesiphorus ministers to Paul the prisoner.
2:9	God's Word is not bound because the preacher is in prison.
4:16,17	Paul abandoned by friends at his trial.
Philemon 1,9	Paul, the prisoner of Christ.
10	Onesimus was saved in prison.
23	Epaphras, Paul's fellow prisoner.
Hebrews 13:3	Remember prisoners.
1 Peter 3:19	Christ preached to spirits in prison.
2 Peter 2:4	Fallen angels in chains.
Jude 6	Fallen angels in chains.
Revelation 2:10	Satan will cast some into prison.
2:13	Antipas martyred.
20:7	Satan is released from his prison.

Appendix B

Correctional Chaplaincy Surveys

A survey of chaplains made in 1967 reports findings from eighteen Protestant chaplains in federal prisons. Its results are summarized in E. M. Clarke, "Expectations and Role Performances of Chaplains in Federal Penal Institutions," *Journal of Pastoral Care,* 24:135–139, June 1970.

Two extensive surveys of correctional chaplains exist and are described below. Results from these surveys have been used extensively throughout this book. The data from the two studies, done independently of one another, agree on all points covered by both.

1971 Survey

This survey was performed by Hylon Vickers as part of the requirements for an MA degree from Sam Houston State University, Huntsville, Texas. The results are contained in Vickers' unpublished master's thesis, "The Place of Religion and a Religious Program in Adult Corrections" (1971).

This survey was oriented to the ministry of chaplains in state and federal prisons and has no responses from chaplains serving local jails or juvenile institutions. About two hundred full-time and one hundred part-time chaplains participated in this survey. The survey included questions about the chaplain and his background, his role in the institution, information about the institution and personnel practices.

1973 Survey

This survey was conducted by Dale K. Pace as part of the requirements for a ThD degree from Luther Rice Seminary, Jacksonville, Florida. The results are contained in his unpublished doctoral dissertation, "Contemporary Praxis of the Correctional Chaplaincy" (1974).

The scope of this study (actually it included two surveys) encompassed quantitative description of activities under chaplain supervision, chaplain time use, the degree of inmate participation in programs under chaplain supervision, chaplain attitudes about correctional reform and advice for new chaplains, background information about chaplains and their training/experience, and data about correctional institutions. More than 250 chaplains responded, providing a balanced representation of chaplains by denominational affiliation, location of their ministries, and types of institutions served (jails, juvenile institutions, state and federal prisons).

Some results from this study were reported: about leadership of Protestant chaplains in Dale K. Pace, *Correctional Chaplains: Shepherds or Hirelings?* (an essay published by the AEIC, 1974); about Catholic chaplains in Dale K. Pace, "Catholic Praxis of the Correctional Chaplaincy," *The Chap-Lett*, vol. 21, no. 1, July–August 1974; and about Protestant chaplains in Dale K. Pace, "Problems of the Correctional Chaplaincy," *The Chap-Lett*, vol. 22, no. 1, June–July 1975.

Appendix C

Thoughts on the Effects of Conversion

Many evangelicals ministering to offenders have used the slogan "Rehabilitation through Regeneration." Yet many of those "converted" behind bars continue in or revert to illegal and immoral behavior. Why is this?

First, there is the problem of false professions of faith, i.e., professions which do not bring regeneration. Many inmates have gotten "jail house religion" without being *born again.* A Southern prison chaplain expressed the essence of this problem when he said, "My converts come back [to the prison], the Lord's don't." Certainly everyone ministering to inmates needs to take care not to rush an inmate into a profession of faith before the Holy Spirit has brought conviction of sin, before there is repentance and faith on the part of the individual, before there is a willingness to commit his life to the leadership of Jesus Christ. Otherwise, regeneration is unlikely to occur.

However, the fact of false professions does not explain *all* the failures of converts. The situation is more complex than that. This brings up the second consideration: What actually happens to one who is converted? What changes are promised by the Bible for *everyone* who is converted?

The Bible presents man as a trinity: spirit, soul, and body (1 Thessalonians 5:23).[384] At times, the Bible uses *spirit* and *soul* interchangeably for the immaterial part of man (e.g., Matthew 10:28, Hebrews 12:23), but at other times the Scripture indicates a distinction between the soul and the spirit (e.g., Hebrews 4:12). Always, however, man is presented as a whole, a unity.[385]

The spirit of man is his key to eternity. A dead spirit leads man to eternal death in hell—and *all* men are dead spiritually until regeneration. A living spirit leads man to eternal life with the living God.

The soul of man is his personality: his intellect, his emotions, his will. (The English word *psychology* is derived from the Greek word for soul, ψυχή). Some men are fortunate enough to have souls (i.e., personalities) that are not so marred by their fallen nature as the souls of other men, just as some men have healthier and stronger bodies than other men. Because of this, a lost (unsaved) man with a "good" soul can appear to be a much nicer person than a saved man with a more severely crippled soul.

At regeneration/conversion—the new birth—the dead spirit of a lost man is made alive and he becomes saved. Although the spirit, soul, and body of man are inextricably united and each affects the other two, conversion (i.e., a man's dead spirit becoming alive) does not automatically and immediately remove defects in a man's soul any more than it does for his body. Men do not expect a physical cripple to walk simply because he has been born again, yet many expect one with a crippled personality to become suddenly whole and well-adjusted just because he has been converted.[386]

The living spirit in the Christian will tend to produce many wholesome changes in a convert's personality (and in his body), but the changes may come slowly, and some problems may continue for a long time. What is being described here is God's usual way of working in the life of a convert. It goes without saying that God can heal anyone's personality or bodily ills completely—and instantaneously if He so chooses.

Most inmates have crippled personalities: for some, the result of drug and alcohol abuse; for others, the consequence of being given over by God to a reprobate (i.e., malfunctioning) mind because they refused to know God (*see* Romans 1:28). After conversion, many offenders will still have crippled personalities, just as many of them will continue to suffer physical problems (damaged livers from alcoholism, etc.).[387] Consequently, it should not be surprising if regenerated offenders do not all immediately become model citizens and church members.

It is important for Christians ministering to offenders to understand what to expect to occur in the lives of converted offenders for two reasons: First, unrealistic expectations on the worker's part will lead to frustration, disappointment, discouragement, and possibly even unnecessary feelings of guilt. Second, the worker can lead the convert to have unrealistic expectations of what will happen in his life. When these are not fulfilled, the convert may give up spiritually (thinking that he is still lost or simply incompetent) or else become bitter, feeling that God has cheated him. Either will cause him to stumble (cf. Matthew 18:6–7).

The characteristics clearly stated by the Bible to apply to *all* who believe in Jesus and are converted are:

> Regeneration (John 3:3; Ephesians 2:5).
>
> Incorporation into the Body of Christ (1 Corinthians 12:13; Ephesians 2:11–22).
>
> Indwelling of God's Spirit and His witness of sonship when the convert is dependent upon God as his father (Romans 8:9–16; 1 Corinthians 6:19,20).
>
> Response to God's Word (John 8:47; 10:4,14,27; 14:23,24; 18:36).
>
> Chastisement/discipline (Hebrews 12:5–11).
>
> Love (the whole Epistle of 1 John).

These realities can and should be expected from every convert. No single feeling or emotional experience is common to all conversions. Some are joyous. Others feel relieved as a burden of guilt is lifted. Others have no strong emotion at the time of conversion.

Appendix D

Directory of Organizations and Periodicals Directly Related to Jail and Prison Ministry *

The listing below contains only periodicals and organizations that are extensively involved in jail and prison ministry. In general, the areas of an organization's ministry are indicated. These are: providing (1) literature, (2) Bible correspondence courses, and (3) films or tapes. Two kinds of ministry are indicated: provision of chaplaincy services or merely conducting services. Where appropriate, geographic limitations are presented. Prison, jail, and juvenile government agencies which provide for chaplaincy services from government funds are not included in this directory, nor are the denominational liaison offices for the correctional chaplaincy. Many denominations also offer Bible correspondence courses for prisoners, and these, in general, are not listed in this directory.

The directory does not purport to be complete. However, it provides some guidance about the organizations currently involved in correctional ministry. An extensive directory of 490 secular and religious organizations involved in penal activities and reform may be found in Mary L. Bundy and Kenneth R. Harmon (ed.) *National Prison Directory—Organizational Profiles of Prison Reform Groups in the United States* (Urban Information Interpreters, Inc., P. O. Box AH, College Park, Maryland, 1975).

* The organizations in this directory were based upon a listing of resources for jail and prison ministry in the July, 1976 issue of the *Journal of the Association of Evangelical Institutional Chaplains.*

American Bible Society
P. O. Box 5656
Grand Central Station
New York, New York 10017

Provides Bibles and Scripture portions for chaplains to use with prisoners.

American Catholic Correctional Chaplains' Association (ACCCA)
c/o Chaplain O'Brien
P. O. Box 32
Huntsville, Texas 77340

Formerly published *The Chap-Lett.*

American Correctional Association (ACA)
L-208 Hartwick Office Building
4321 Hartwick Road
College Park, Maryland 20740
Phone (301) 864-1070

A professional society with affiliated societies covering the gamut of professions in corrections. Publishes the *American Journal of Correction.* Information about affiliates such as the National Jail Association, National Sheriffs' Association, International Halfway House Association, etc., may be obtained from the ACA.

American Indian Missions, Inc.
P. O. Box 2800
Rapid City, South Dakota 57701
Phone (605) 343-0554

Will provide an 850-word-vocabulary New Testament for inmates and Christian literature of interest to American Indians.

American Protestant Correctional Chaplains' Association (APCCA)
c/o Rev. Adlai Lucas
Secretary-Treasurer
South Carolina Dept. of Corrections
P. O. Box 11159
Columbia, South Carolina 29211

An ecumenically oriented society for chaplains. Publishes a journal/newsletter.

Assemblies of God
Prison Division
1445 Boonville Avenue
Springfield, Missouri 65802

Provides correspondence courses and handles the supply of *The Way* edition of The Living Bible for inmates.

Association for Clinical Pastoral Education
241–245 West Main Street
Kutztown, Pennsylvania 19530

Many correctional chaplains belong to this society. Publishes the *Journal of Pastoral Care.*

Association of Evangelical Institutional Chaplains (AEIC)
1036 South Highland Street
Arlington, Virginia 22204
Phone (703) 979-2200

A society for evangelical lay and clergy persons concerned about ministry to offenders. Publishes a journal and sponsors the National Fellowship of Congregations Behind Bars.

Bible Believers Cassettes, Inc.
130 North Spring Street
Springdale, Arkansas 72764
Phone (501) 751-7000

Provides a free loan library of cassette tapes (about 2,500 different tapes).

Bible Portions League
Route 3, Box 12
Coushatta, Louisiana 71019
Phone (318) 932-5092

Provides Scripture portions, New Testaments, and religious books for inmates.

The Bridge
Box 3385
Charlottesville, Virginia 22903
Phone (804) 977-4357

Provides a chaplaincy ministry in a few jails in central Virginia.

Christian Jail Workers, Inc.
P. O. Box 4009
Los Angeles, California 90051
Phone (213) 624-3945

Provides chaplaincy services for institutions related to the Los Angeles County Sheriff's Department.

Cincinnati Baptist Association
660 Northland Boulevard
Cincinnati, Ohio
Phone (513) 742-0588

Provides chaplaincy services for correctional institutions around Cincinnati.

Crusaders Club
Winona Lake, Indiana 46590

Provides free Bible correspondence courses for inmates.

Federal Probation: A Journal of Correctional Philosophy and Practice
Administrative Office of the United States Courts
Supreme Court Building
Washington, D.C. 20544

A general journal covering many aspects of the criminal justice system. Subscription free upon request.

Florida Chaplain Service
626 Ashberry Lane
Altamonte Springs, Florida
Phone (305) 420-3016

Provides chaplaincy services for about six Florida jails.

Forgotten Man Mission, Inc.
1108 Leonard Street, N.E.
Grand Rapids, Michigan 49505
Phone (616) 456-5449

Provides chaplaincy services for jails in Michigan.

The Free from Bondage Prison and Youth Outreach Ministries, Inc.
P. O. Box 96
Crystal Beach, Ontario
Canada LOSIBO
Phone (416) 732-5883

Provides correspondence courses and a Gospel team of ex-prisoners for jail/prison ministry.

Full Gospel Business Men's Fellowship International:
Prison Ministry
836 South Figueroa
Los Angeles, California 90017
Phone (213) 489-2828

Establishes FGBM Fellowships within prisons and publishes an occasional magazine, *Convicts for Christ.*

The Gideons
(contact the local Gideon camp)

Will provide services and Scriptures for inmates.

Good News Mission
1036 South Highland Street
Arlington, Virginia 22204
Phone (703) 979-2200

Provides Bible correspondence courses throughout the nation and chaplaincy services for jails and prison units in several states. Conducts an accredited graduate-level course on the correctional chaplaincy each January.

Hope Aglow Ministries
P. O. Box 3057
Lynchburg, Virginia 24503

Provides Christian services in penal institutions.

International Prison Ministry (Chaplain Ray)
P. O. Box 63
Dallas, Texas 75221

Provides Christian literature and tapes for chaplains and inmates and conducts services in institutions throughout the country. Has a nationwide prison ministry radio program and a magazine, *Prison Evangelism.*

Logos International Fellowship, Inc.—Prison Ministry
P. O. Box 191
Plainfield, New Jersey 07060
Phone (201) 754-0745

Provides Christian literature and Christian correspondence for inmates.

Moody Bible Institute
820 North LaSalle Street
Chicago, Illinois 60610
Phone (312) 329-4106

Moody Correspondence School—free popular-level courses for inmates. Moody Literature Mission Department provides literature and films.

The National Council of Churches of Christ (NCC)
475 Riverside Drive
New York, New York 10027

Formerly NCC nomination/approval was required for chaplains in federal prisons. The Department of Pastoral Services maintains an active interest in the chaplaincy.

National Yokefellow Prison Ministry, Inc.
112 Old Trail North
Shamokin Dam, Pa. 17876
Phone (717) 743-4456

Yokefellow Spiritual Growth Groups provide religious comradeship between inmates and those on the outside.

Outreach to Troubled Teens, Inc.
P. O. Box 973
Wilmington, Delaware 19899
Phone (302) 656-8083

Provides religious ministry in Delaware, especially at juvenile institutions.

Prison Inreach Ministries
P. O. Box 1949
Hollywood, California 90028
Phone (213) 461-5811

Provides Bible courses, Christian literature (*Hollywood Free Paper* and other items), and religious services (using Hollywood entertainers who are Christians) in institutions throughout the country.

Prison Mission Association, Inc.
P. O. Box 3397
Riverside, California 92509
Phone (714) 686-2613

Provides Bible correspondence courses, Christian literature, Christian films and tapes, and religious services in many correctional institutions.

"P.S." Ministries
c/o Campus Crusade for Christ
Arrowhead Springs
San Bernardino, California 92414
Phone (714) 886-4118

Provides Christian literature and Bible courses (free for inmates), Christian films, tapes and Campus Crusade for Christ staffers as "para-chaplains" in about a dozen prisons.

The Rock Bottom Evangelistic Assn.
P. O. Box 1717
Turlock, California 95380
Phone (209) 634-7466

Provides Bible Correspondence courses and religious services at a few institutions.

Salvation Army
(use phone book for local address and phone)

Usually will provide a wide variety of social and religious services in correctional institutions. Also provides Bible correspondence courses.

Scripture & Christian Literature Mission
1818 South Summerlin Avenue
Orlando, Florida 32806
Phone (305) 425-6908

Provides Christian literature, Bible courses, and correspondence with inmates.

Scripture Press Ministries
P. O. Box 513
Glen Ellyn, Illinois 60137
Phone (312) 653-5936

Provides *Free Ways* and *Power for Living* papers and religious books for inmates and chaplains.

Source of Light Mission
P. O. Box 8
Madison, Georgia 30650
Phone (404) 342-0397

Provides Bible courses for inmates.

Tarrant County Baptist Association
c/o Chaplain Bobby M. Cox
300 West Belknap
Forth Worth, Texas 76102

Provides chaplaincy services for the Fort Worth Jail.

Tom Skinner Associates, Inc.
185 Montague Street
Brooklyn, New York 11201

Provides Christian services for correctional institutions.

Volunteers in Corrections
550 North Western
Oklahoma City, Oklahoma 73118
Phone (405) 848-4832

Provides a Christian-oriented one-on-one counseling program for Oklahoma prisons.

Volunteers of America
(use phone book for local address and phone)

Often will provide religious and social services for correctional institutions.

World Home Bible League
P. O. Box 11
South Holland, Illinois 60473

Provides Scriptures and Bible correspondence courses.

Appendix E

AEIC and APCCA Certification Requirements

Two professional societies certify correctional chaplains. Their requirements for certification are presented below.

AEIC Certification Requirements

The following is taken from the Constitution of the AEIC, Article V, Section 3, as revised through November 1975:

> The Chaplain category is restricted to ministers who have demonstrated professional competence in the institutional chaplaincy. Therefore, certification is granted not upon the basis of what the applicant might do or plans to do, but upon the basis of what the applicant has done. Moreover, certification requirements must be satisfied from the applicant's recent ministry as institutional chaplain; by "recent ministry," that of the three years preceding the application date for certification (*or its renewal*) is intended. (*A minimum of 500 hours of ministry within the "institution" is required.*) The applicant must possess adequate Biblical and theological knowledge to deal with spiritual problems.
>
> The applicant must demonstrate that he has developed and maintained an acceptable program within his institution(s) of: evangelism, religious instruction and teaching, counseling, appropriate social help, releasee follow-up, and volunteer worker recruitment and training. (*For chaplains not minister-*

ing within an "institution" in the traditional sense of an "institution" [*e.g., a police chaplain*], *comparable programs are required.*)

a. Acceptable relationships with the institution staff and officials (*judges, sheriffs, probation officers, etc.*).

b. Responsible relationships with other religious and social welfare workers within his institution(s).

c. Positive contributions to the institution's rehabilitation program.

d. Effective counseling demonstrated by at least three verified case histories of significantly changed lives, where such change appears to be permanent, which were the result of the Chaplain's ministry.

The applicant must demonstrate that he has good relationships with Christian groups outside his institution(s).

The applicant must demonstrate that he has developed community resources to help in rehabilitation efforts.

APCCA Certification Requirements

The following is taken from the "Procedure and Guidelines for Certification as a Correctional Chaplain" of the APCCA College of Fellows, as revised through August 1975:

Qualifications

Requirements for Certified Correctional Chaplain include:

1. College and theological degree, or such preparation as the endorsing body requires of its chaplaincy candidates prior to ordination.
2. Ordination by church body.
3. Ecclesiastical endorsement.
4. At least three (3) years full time pastoral experience or equivalent.
5. A minimum of three (3) units (33 weeks or 1200 hours) of Clinical Pastoral Education in a center accredited by the Association for Clinical Pastoral Education or such credentials deemed acceptable as equivalent by the National Certification Committee.

6. Submission of materials as required by the National Certification Committee.

7. Satisfactory face-to-face interview before the National Certification Committee.

8. Currently paid-up active membership with good standing in the American Protestant Correctional Chaplains' Association, Inc.

9. Payment of fees as determined by the National Certification Committee.

10. See exception below for clergymen functioning in the correctional area who are certified as full Chaplain Supervisor by the Association for Clinical Pastoral Education.

11. Recommendation by the National Certification Committee and approval by the College of Fellows, APCCA.

Materials

The applicant is required to submit the following materials as indicated:

1. An autobiography.

2. An evaluation of the applicant by his/her Clinical Pastoral Education Supervisor(s) and the applicant's evaluation of his/her training.

3. A letter from the candidate's institutional supervisor describing the role of the candidate in the institution as well as evaluating the candidate.

4. A description and critical evaluation by the candidate of his institution and ministry therein.

5. A paper on one of the following subjects:
   (1) The role of the Chaplain in a correctional setting.
   (2) My personal faith.

6. ACPE Chaplain Supervisors–clergymen functioning in the correctional area who are certified as full Chaplain Supervisor by the Association for Clinical Pastoral Education may be granted certification as a Certified Correctional Chaplain by the College of Fellows upon recommendation of the National Certification Committee and payment of a fifteen dollar ($15.00) application and processing fee. Any or all materials required to be submitted for certification as well as the face-to-face interview before the National Certification

Committee may be waived at the discretion of the Chairman, National Certification Committee.

7. All materials must be submitted not later than sixty (60) days prior to appearance before the National Certification Committee or SubCommittee of the National Certification Committee.

Notes

Introduction

1. For detailed consideration, see K. S. Latourette, *A History of Christianity* (Harper & Row, 1953), especially chapters 30 to 60. The rekindling of the sense of obligation to evangelize all men is illustrated by the 1792 pamphlet of a shoemaker who became a missionary statesman, William Carey: *An Enquiry into the Obligations of Christians to Use Means for Conversion of the Heathens.*

2. *The Nation's Jails* (LEAA:NCJI&SS, 1975), p. 13.

3. *Census of State Correctional Facilities: 1974 (Advance Report)*, (LEAA:NCJI&SS, 1975), p. 30.

4. *Nation's Jails,* p. 13. Implied.

5. "Chaplaincy Services," chapter 29 in *Manual of Correctional Standards,* 3rd ed. (ACA 1966).

6. Some juvenile institutions (e.g., detention centers) are like jails; others (e.g., reformatories and training schools) are like prisons. When the terms *jails* and *prisons* are used in this book, juvenile institutions often are included in the connotation.

7. Some who helped with the chaplaincy course by writing textual materials for it or teaching classes (1972–1976) in it include Myrl Alexander (former Director of the Center for the Study of Crime, Delinquency and Corrections at Southern Illinois University and past president of the ACA), James Bryan (Director of Florida Chaplain Service), Norman Carlson (Director of the U.S. Bureau of Prisons), Elwood Clements (Sheriff of Arlington County, Virginia, and former President of the Virginia Sheriffs' Association), Anthony Delpopolo (college professor and former President of the Correctional Educational Association), Harold DeWolf (Dean emeritus of Wesley Theological Seminary), Carl Hart (CPE Supervisor and

Assistant Director of Chaplaincy for the Home Mission Board of the Southern Baptist Convention), Arnold Hopkins (Assistant Director of the American Bar Association), Dale Keaton (counseling specialist), Burton Kramer (Senior Juvenile and Domestic Relations Judge for Arlington, Virginia), John Melnick (member of Virginia State Crime Commission), Russell Quynn (then Supervisor of Parole and Probation in Virginia and former Secretary of the Virginia Parole Board), Paul Rader (evangelist and former university professor), George Ricketts (Director of Chaplaincy Services of the Churches of Virginia), Fred Silber (then Director of Chaplaincy for the U.S. Bureau of Prisons), Bill Simmer (Director of the Good News Mission and Executive Director of the National Jail Association), John Brabner-Smith (then Dean of the International School of Law), Truman Walrod (Director of Public Relations for the National Sheriffs' Association), William Winston (Chief Judge, Circuit Court of Arlington, Virginia), Eldon Koch (pastor and former seminary professor), and members of the Good News Mission staff.

From 1972 through 1976, some twenty colleges, universities, and seminaries granted credit to their students for the chaplaincy course taught by the Good News Mission in both undergraduate and graduate programs (MA, MDiv, ThM).

From 1972 to 1976, more than a hundred men and women representing about thirty denominations from about twenty states have taken this course. They have included not only pastors and ministerial students but new and experienced chaplains (jail, juvenile, state and federal prison, police, and military), directors of chaplaincy organizations, correctional officials, and a few interested laymen. In 1976, about 70 percent of those who had taken the course were involved full time in ministering to offenders.

The present writer had the privilege of designing the curriculum for this course and has served as coordinator for it each time it has been offered.

This accredited course was the outgrowth of formal training seminars for chaplains and ministerial students organized by the Good News Mission as early as 1969. Many of those involved as instructors in these early seminars also were instructors later in the accredited course.

8. Most of the statistics about chaplains come from the author's doctoral study and are contained in his dissertation, "Contemporary Praxis of the Correctional Chaplaincy" (Luther Rice Seminary, Jacksonville, Florida, 1974). All unreferenced statistics about chaplains presented in this book were drawn from this study.

Chapter 1

9. The Greek word ἔθνος translated "nations" in Matthew 28:19 means a people bonded together by any natural cohesion (racial, linguistic, political, economic, social class, etc.) and is the word from which the Engilsh word *ethnic* is derived. Thus the command of Jesus is to evangelize and disciple

every ethnic group—including the one behind bars. For a detailed discussion of ἔθνος see the article by Schmidt in G. Kittel's *Theological Dictionary of the New Testament* (vol. 2).

10. Approximately 45 percent of jail inmates in 1972 had prearrest annual incomes of $2,000 or less. Only 10 percent of jail inmates in 1972 had prearrest incomes exceeding the U.S. median income of $9,255, *Survey of Inmates of Local Jails 1972: Advance Reports* (LEAA:NCJI&SS, n.d.), p. 4.

11. The eclectic Greek text followed by most modern translations of the New Testament does not include this as part of Luke 4:18. It is included here because it is a part of the prophecy of Isaiah 61 about the ministry of the Messiah. Depression is so great among prisoners that their rates of suicide and attempted suicide are much higher than for the general public. Burton M. Leiser, *Liberty, Justice and Morals* (Macmillan, 1973), p. 217.

12. All incidents reported in this book represent real situations with which the author is personally familiar. Unless the situation is one which has been widely publicized, the description in this book will not provide precise identification and may even change the individual's name to protect anonymity.

13. Gary R. Williams, "The Purpose of Penology in the Mosaic Law and Today," *Bibliotheca Sacra,* vol. 133, no. 549, January–March 1976, p. 53.

14. A high percentage (10 to 30 percent or more) of delinquent girls have had incestuous relationships with their fathers or stepfathers. Howard James, *Children in Trouble: A National Scandal* (Pocket Books, 1970), p. 166.

15. "Nearly every delinquent had had an inadequate home." Howard James, *Children in Trouble,* p. 19. "It is clear that convicted felons characteristically come from severely disordered families." Samuel B. Guze, *Criminality and Psychiatric Disorders* (Oxford University Press, 1976), p. 131.

16. Williams, "Purpose of Penology," p. 53.

17. The reform cry has been raised by many works, among them Ramsey Clark's *Crime in America* (1971), Bagdikian and Dash's *The Shame of the Prisons* (1972), Howard James's *Children in Trouble: A National Scandal* (1971), Jessica Mitford's *Kind and Usual Punishment: The Prison Business* (1973), and Judge Forer's *The Death of the Law* (1975).

18. May Grunhut, *Penal Reform: A Comparative Study* (Oxford Clarendon Press, 1948), p. 253.

19. E. H. Johnson, *Crime, Correction, and Society* (The Dorsey Press, 1964), p. 615.

20. J. Arthur Hoyles, *The Church and the Criminal* (London: Epworth Press, 1965), p. 107.

21. Williams, "Purpose of Penology." In addition, Dr. William L. Simmer of the Good News Mission has also developed a philosophy for the local jail which he presented in a paper at the 1975 Congress of Correction, *Social and Rehabilitative Services—Type and Structure in Local Jails.*

22. Dale K. Pace, *Correctional Chaplains: Shepherds or Hirelings?* (AEIC, 1974).

23. John W. Brabner-Smith, "Who Will Study Justice?" *Christianity Today,* vol. 19, no. 15, April 25, 1975, pp. 9–11.

24. Jessica Mitford, *Kind and Usual Punishment: The Prison Business* (Alfred A. Knopf, 1973), pp. 43–45.

25. In his lecture on the status of reform of the criminal justice system in the Good News Mission correctional chaplaincy course (January 1976), Arnold Hopkins of the American Bar Association stated that thus far fifteen states had reformed their laws restricting employment opportunities for former offenders. Efforts by the American Bar Association included compilation of a comprehensive list of such restrictions, development of model legislation, and encouragement of state legislators to reform their laws.

26. Walter Hooper (ed.), *C. S. Lewis: Poems* (Harcourt, Brace & World, Inc., 1964), p. 135.

27. About 40 percent of jail chaplains and about 90 percent of juvenile and prison chaplains are employed by government agencies.

28. The ACA *Manual of Correctional Standards* (Third Edition) recommends a chaplain for every 300 to 500 inmates in prison. Because of the high rate of inmate turnover in jails and most juvenile institutions, a chaplain is recommended for every 100 to 150 inmates (*daily* population) in those facilities. Currently there are about a quarter million prison inmates: 150,000 to 200,000 in jails, 50,000 to 75,000 in juvenile institutions.

29. The average salary for privately employed (i.e., church-employed) chaplains in 1973 was about $8,000; for government-employed chaplains it was about $12,000. Employer social security, insurance, auto allowance, retirement, etc., increase this another $2,000 to $4,000. Inflation already has upped this another 20 to 30 percent. The experience of the Good News Mission is that it takes about $5,000 in overhead (office, equipment, literature, films, tapes, clerical help, and administrative supervision) for each chaplain. Thus it is reasonable to compute the average cost for a correctional chaplain at a minimum of $15,000 to $20,000 per year.

30. In Matthew 18:6 ff., Jesus warned of the danger of offending others or causing them to fall. The Greek word in this passage is σκανδαλίζω, of the word group from which the English word *scandal* is derived.

31. Some of the problems caused by such obstacles are discussed by Stuart D. Johnson, "The Correctional Chaplaincy: Sociological Perspectives in the Time of Rapid Change," *Canadian Journal of Criminology and Corrections,* 14:173–180, April 1972.

32. Hylon Vickers, "The Place of Religion and a Religious Program in Adult Corrections" (master's thesis, Sam Houston State University, Huntsville, Texas, 1971), p. 45.

33. While such services do provide a "captive" audience, they may encounter distractions such as radio/TV playing, inmates using the toilet,

nearby conversation, even deliberate obscenities and verbal abuse directed at the religious workers. The legality of conducting such services before inmates who do not desire them has not been tested. Because this is the only way for many jails to provide religious services for those who do desire them, the services probably would not be ruled illegal unless they were conducted in a manner that coerced those who did not desire to participate.

34. Constant H. Jacquet, Jr. (ed.), *Yearbook of American and Canadian Churches 1974* (Abingdon Press, 1974).

35. For example, "Crime Wave Hits Churches: Vandalism, Robbery, Arson, and Attempted Rape," *Ministry,* vol. 49, no. 7, pp. 40–41.

36. Most of the points in this discussion come from Dr. John Flanagan, "Imminent Crisis in Prison Populations," *American Journal of Corrections,* vol. 37, no. 6, November–December 1975, pp. 20 ff.

37. Extensive use of probation has a side effect which many neglect. It tends to eliminate the more stable element from the inmate population, leaving a more concentrated collection of callous, often unstable men. This makes both jail/prison administration and Christian ministry in the institution more difficult.

38. While there is much debate about the rate of recidivism, all agree it is high. Most put it at 60 to 70 percent, e.g., *Encyclopaedia Britannica* (1974), vol. 14, p. 1102.

39. "In general, there is little evidence that any method of penal treatment is superior to others, as measured by the numbers of repeaters. . . . No convincing proof of rehabilitative effectiveness has been produced." *Encyclopaedia Britannica* (1974), vol. 14, p. 1100.

40. Such have been the responses of correctional administrators to the growing awareness of the lack of impact of rehabilitation programs on recidivism. Unfortunately, such a response often ignores the fact that many rehabilitation programs were funded explicitly for the purpose of reducing recidivism. For a discussion of the views of prison administrators, see Michael S. Serrill, "Is Rehabilitation Dead?" *Corrections Magazine,* vol. 1, no. 5, (May–June 1975).

41. Most inmates who are helped by prison rehabilitation programs are inmates who (because of the kind of people they are) would not commit more crimes in the future even if they had not been in the rehabilitation program. Most people with substantial experience in corrections can tell which inmates will be coming back and which will not. It is easy to make a rehabilitation program appear more effective simply by allowing only the "cream of the inmate crop" in the program. By such tactics, recidivism can appear to be affected by a program when in reality it has not been.

42. Stories of such conversions may be found in Lewis W. Gillenson's *Billy Graham and Seven Who Were Saved* (Pocket Books, 1968), Tom Skinner's *Black and Free* (Zondervan), and a multitude of books available in any religious book store.

43. Hoyles, *Church and the Criminal*, p. 92.

44. *Ibid.*, p. 98.

45. *Twenty-Sixth Annual Report of the Board of Managers of the Prison Discipline Society* (Boston, 1851), p. 68.

46. *Ibid.*, p. 66.

47. *Ibid.*, pp. 68–69.

48. *Ibid.*, p. 67.

49. H. T. F. Rhodes, *The Criminal in Society* (Drummond, 1939), chapter 9.

50. For examples: Thomas M. Gannon, "Religious Control and Delinquent Behavior," *The Sociology of Crime and Delinquency*, 2nd ed., M. Wolfgang (ed.) (Wiley & Sons, 1970), pp. 499–508; Albert L. Rhodes and Albert J. Reiss, Jr., "The Religious Factor and Delinquent Behavior," *Journal of Research in Crime and Delinquency*, 7:83–98, 1970; Travis Hirschi and Rodney Stark, "Hellfire and Delinquency," in Charles Y. Glock (ed.), *Religion in Sociological Perspective* (Wadsworth, 1973), pp. 75–87.

51. See Appendix C for a theological discussion of conversion.

52. In a large New York jail, the sheriff will allow a maximum of thirty to forty inmates at a time to participate in the Sunday worship services but does not place a similar restriction upon the number of inmates who may attend the jail movies, though they are shown in the same room and are supervised by the same number of correctional officers as the worship services.

Such unnecessary restrictions are not new. In the last century, Chaplain Luckey commented on how "one important opportunity of reclaiming the wayward hearts of our prisoners was lost by the old rule prohibiting the chaplain from conversing on such subjects [i.e., family matters], and confining him exclusively to 'dogmatic theology.'" This rule was designed to "protect" the chaplain from inmate lies about their families and their problems. John Luckey, *Life in Sing Sing State Prison, as Seen in a Twelve Years' Chaplaincy* (N. Tibbals & Co., 1860), p. 76.

53. The reasons for this are varied. Some simply prefer to ignore prisoners. Others see no benefit to the Church by spending time on the "losers" behind bars. Others look down upon chaplains because many jail workers have limited education or entered the chaplaincy after problems in the pastorate.

Chapter 2

54. Vernon Fox, et al., *Introduction to the Criminal Justice System* (Prentice-Hall, 1975). Daniel Glaser (ed.), *Handbook of Criminology* (Rand McNally College Publishing Co., 1974), and Elmer H. Johnson, *Crime, Correction, and Society*, 3rd ed. (Dorsey Press, 1974). The references in these can direct the reader to resources in areas of special interest to him. Two additional works should be mentioned. One had profound effect

in shaping the directions that the criminal justice system has taken in the past decade: *The Challenge of Crime in a Free Society,* A Report of the President's Commission on Law Enforcement and Administration of Justice (U.S. Government Printing Office, 1967). The other is a Christian look at the system: Richard D. Knudten's *The Christian Encounters Crime in American Society* (Concordia Publishing House, 1969).

Every professional worker involved in ministry to prisoners should avail himself of abstracts available through LEAA's National Criminal Justice Reference Service, an international clearinghouse for criminal justice information. Information about this service is available from the U.S. Department of Justice, LEAA, National Criminal Justice Reference Service, Washington, D.C. 20530.

55. Chart 1 is based upon a similar chart in *The Challenge of Crime in a Free Society* (U.S. Government Printing Office, 1967), pp. 8 ff.

56. *Sourcebook of Criminal Justice Statistics 1973* (LEAA:NCJI&SS, 1973), p. 86.

57. *Ibid.*, pp. 23, 86. About 13 percent of the local law enforcement personnel are in sheriffs' departments that have law enforcement responsibilities. The rest are police personnel.

58. *Ibid.*, p. 86.

59. A general overview of LEAA activities through 1976 may be found in the brochure *The Law Enforcement Assistance Administration: A Partnership for Crime Control* (LEAA, n.d.). The need for professionalism in police personnel was pointed out emphatically by Ramsey Clark's observation that "every major riot of the 1960s prior to the widespread violence following the murder of Martin Luther King arose from a police incident." *Crime in America* (Pocket Books, 1971), p. 127. The reader interested in police work should consult John A. Marlo and R. Gene Wright, *The Police Officer and Criminal Justice* (McGraw-Hill, 1970), or some other standard police textbook.

60. Description of these five steps borrowed heavily from materials prepared by Police Captain Alvin Fuchsman for the Good News Mission course on correctional chaplaincy.

61. For simplicity, *police* will be used for all law enforcement personnel from this point on. In most rural jurisdictions, law enforcement is done by the sheriff's department. The sheriff is normally an elected official, whereas chief/commissioner of police is usually an appointed or civil service position. FBI agents or federal marshalls assume police functions in cases where federal laws have been violated.

62. A crime is classified either as a felony or a misdemeanor. Normally a misdemeanor is a crime whose maximum punishment is a year or less in confinement or a fine not to exceed $500 to $1,000. Felonies are more serious crimes and carry heavier penalties.

63. *Miranda v. Arizona,* 384 U.S. 444, pp. 467–473.

64. Except in rare cases, any suspect can be released if the appropriate amount of cash is presented as security to ensure his appearance in court. The suspect can then be released on *bail* with the security known as his *bail bond* or *bond.* If the suspect has adequate financial resources, he simply provides the security. If not, he may choose to use a bail bondsman. A bail bondsman is one whom the court recognizes as surety for the suspect's appropriate appearance in court, charging the bondsman for the bail bond if the suspect fails to appear. Normally, a bail bondsman will charge the suspect 10 percent of the amount of the bail to serve as his surety. Much reform is needed in this area. For example, see Paul Wice, *Bail and Its Reform: A National Survey* (LEAA:NILE&CJ, 1973).

65. Marshall Houts, *From Arrest to Release* (Charles C. Thomas, 1958), p. 83.

66. Grand juries are also used as a screening device to determine who should be charged (indicted) with crimes in general or widespread investigations of suspected wrongdoing. In such cases, the grand jury indictment serves as the basis for an arrest warrant in the same way as a police officer's investigations of a crime.

67. *Nolo contendere* means the charge is not contested, although the defendant does not formally admit guilt. If the *nolo contendere* plea is accepted by the court, it may impose sentence upon the defendant as if he had pleaded guilty.

68. A thorough description of what a presentence investigation report contains and how it is effected may be found in administrative Office of the United States Courts, Division of Probation: *The Pre-sentence Investigation Report,* Publication No. 103 (U.S. Government Printing Office, 1965).

69. For examples, see *A Program for Prison Reform: The Final Report,* Annual Chief Justice Earl Warren Conference on Advocacy in the United States, 1972, or a call for abandoning the parole system by United States Attorney General Edward Levi, *U.S. News & World Report,* March 1, 1976, pp. 65–67. Another point of view is presented by the chairman of the U.S. Board of Parole, Maurice H. Sigler, in "Abolish Parole?" *Federal Probation,* vol. 39, no. 2, June 1975, pp. 42–48.

70. *Sourcebook of Criminal Justice Statistics,* p. 318. Ramsey Clark estimates 90 percent of convictions result from guilty pleas. *Crime in America,* p. 177. Over a third of the inmates in state prisons had been tried. The rest had pleaded guilty. *Survey of Inmates in State Correctional Facilities 1974: Advance Report* (LEAA:NCJI&SS, 1976). This coupled with the preceding implies that many who plead guilty manage to avoid prison by the bargain to which they agree (usually a reduction in the seriousness of the charge).

71. A brief discussion of this subject may be found in James M. Dean, "The Illegitimacy of Plea Bargaining," *Federal Probation,* vol. 38, no. 3, September 1974, pp. 18–23.

72. It is true that some defendants languish in jail long months awaiting

trial only to be found innocent or to have the charges against them dismissed. However, such appear to be a relatively small minority of those incarcerated while awaiting trial. The percentage of acquittals is quite small (e.g., less than 5 percent in U.S. District Courts, *Sourcebook*, p. 318). The percentage of dismissals is much larger (e.g., 10 to 20 percent in U.S. District Courts, *Ibid.*, p. 318), but many of those dismissed were guilty, the government's case just too weak for prosecution. While this author is unhappy when *any* innocent person is incarcerated, it has been his experience that relatively few inmates he has met have been innocent of *all* charges against them, or of some closely related crime. Indeed, many have not been guilty of some of the charges against them.

73. The names for the low and high courts vary: county and circuit courts, lower and superior courts, etc.

74. This is taken with slight modification from material prepared by JDR Judge Burton V. Kramer for the Good News Mission's course on the correctional chaplaincy. It is significant to note also that a very large percentage of juveniles in custody are charged with offenses that apply only to juveniles, such as truancy (in 1971, 23 percent of male and 70 percent of female juvenile inmates were so charged. *Children in Custody: A Report on the Juvenile Detention and Correctional Facility Census of 1971* (LEAA: NCJI&SS, 1971), p. 6. The Church can help the court develop options to institutionalization for some of these youngsters.

75. *The Nation's Jails* (LEAA:NCJI&SS, 1975); *Children in Custody: Advance Report on the Juvenile Detention and Correctional Facility Census of 1972–73* (LEAA:NCJI&SS, 1975); *Census of State Correctional Facilities 1974: Advance Report* (LEAA:NCJI&SS, 1975); and Norman A. Carlson, "The Federal Prison System: Forty-Five Years of Change, "*Federal Probation*. vol. 39, no. 2, June 1975, p. 38.

76. For example, *Sourcebook*, p. 109.

77. Unless noted otherwise, from *The Nation's Jails*.

78. *Sourcebook*, p. 121.

79. *Children in Custody* (1971 Census).

80. *Census of State Correctional Facilities 1974*.

81. For example, a closed prison of 700 to 1,000 inmates had an "education program" but had not graduated a single inmate from its GED (i.e., high-school equivalency) program in the three years prior to the publication of this book.

82. *Census of State Correctional Facilities 1974*, p. 3.

83. Most penal systems also give an inmate credit for good behavior; normally a quarter to half of the sentence can be eliminated in this manner for those who do not make parole or who choose to refuse to be paroled.

84. *Sourcebook*, pp. 127–128.

85. Probation/parole agreements normally require lawful behavior, steady employment, fulfillment of financial obligations (e.g., family support),

regular reports to and interviews with the probation/parole officer, plus his permission for changes of residence, extensive travel, and driving. Special conditions may be added as deemed necessary.

86. For example, Richard Ku, *The Volunteer Probation Counselor Program, Lincoln, Nebraska* (LEAA:NILE&CJ, n.d.).

87. For example, Norman Carlson stated, "Community-based corrections holds great promise," in "The Federal Prison System: Forty-Five Years of Change," p. 40.

88. Over 60 percent of state correctional facilities had work-release programs in 1974, and 35 percent had study-release programs. *Census of State Correctional Facilities 1974,* p. 13. In 1972, slightly over 40 percent of the nation's jails had work-release programs and 46 percent of the jails had weekend-sentence programs whereby sentenced inmates served their time on weekends. *Nation's Jails,* p. 15. In all of these programs, the offender spends a substantial amount of time in the community.

89. Some halfway house programs are specifically oriented toward a particular client population: ex-offenders, drug addicts, alcoholics, etc. Several hundred such facilities are listed in the directory of the International Halfway House Association. In addition, there are many not listed in it. Halfway houses can be classified into two basic categories (regardless of their target populations): friendly shelters and personality-change facilities. For greater discussion, see: *Residential Center: Corrections in the Community* (U.S. Bureau of Prisons, 1971); Benedict S. Alper and Oliver J. Keller, *Halfway Houses: Community Center Corrections and Treatment* (Heath and Co., 1970); or John M. McCartt and Thomas J. Mangogna, *Guidelines and Standards for Halfway Houses and Community Treatment Centers* (LEAA Technical Assistance Division, 1973).

90. For a thorough discussion, see the monograph by Joan Mullen, *The Dilemma of Diversion: Resource Materials on Adult Pre-trial Intervention Programs* (LEAA:NILE&CJ, n.d.).

91. Excellent coverage of this topic may be found in Don M. Gottfredson and Tully L. McCrea, *A Guide to Improved Handling of Misdemeanant Offenders* (LEAA:NILE&CJ, 1974). The antireligious bias of many of the social program professionals shows up in the fact that no mention is made of religious programs in jails although the literature is surveyed extensively in this document; yet the religious programs are found in more than half the nation's jails and make significant contribution to inmate well-being.

92. *Census of State Correctional Facilities 1974,* p. 18.

93. *Nation's Jails,* pp. 47–48.

94. A popular summary of these may be found in David Rudovsky, *The Rights of Prisoners: The Basic ACLU Guide to a Prisoner's Rights* (Avon Books, 1973). More recent and somewhat more detailed discussions may be found in John W. Palmer, *Constitutional Rights of Prisoners* (W. H. Anderson, 1973 with 1974 supplement) or William T. Toal, *Recent Develop-*

ments in Correctional Case Law (South Carolina Department of Corrections, 1975).

95. This can be illustrated by comparing the results of a 1966 survey of jail programs (reported in *Sourcebook,* p. 113) with a 1972 survey of jail programs (*Nation's Jails,* pp. 8–12). The inmate population of the jails was approximately the same (somewhat over 140,000) in both cases. However, the number of social workers, psychologists, psychiatrists, and academic teachers employed in jail programs tripled! The number of custodial staff increased by about a third, and the number of vocational teachers increased by about a half. Similar increases have occurred in penal systems also.

96. See Janet K. Carsetti, *Literacy Problems and Solutions: A Resource Handbook for Correctional Educators* (American Bar Association Clearinghouse for Offender Literacy, 1975).

97. For example, see Judith Wilks and Robert Martinson, "Is the Treatment of Criminal Offenders Really Necessary?" *Federal Probation,* vol. 40, no. 1, March 1976, pp. 3–9, or their extensive review of evaluation studies of the effectiveness of correctional programs, *The Effectiveness of Correction Treatment* (Praeger, 1975).

98. Inmate Jaycee chapters are an illustration of inmates helping themselves and helping other inmates. The past decade has also witnessed a proliferation of ex-convict organizations designed to help other ex-cons and those still in prison. Such expressions of camaraderie were much less frequent before the 1960s.

99. Some of these factors such as limited schooling and poverty may be more characteristic of criminals who are caught and convicted than of criminals as a whole.

100. This particularly becomes a problem in offenses of dubious criminality. For example, it is legal to gamble in a game of bingo at church or volunteer fire department fund-raising endeavors but illegal to gamble by buying a numbers ticket. Moreover, it is relatively clear that much of white-collar crime is learned behavior—whether corporate (such as price fixing or deceptive advertising) or individual (such as embezzling).

101. At the time of their arrest, only 10 percent of jail inmates in 1972 had prearrest incomes above the median income level, and 45 percent had incomes below the official poverty level for an individual with no dependents. *Survey of Inmates of Local Jails 1972: Advance Report* (LEAA: NCJI&SS, n.d.), p. 4.

102. Clark, *Crime in America,* p. 101. Only one in nine of serious crimes reported results in a conviction.

103. See Clark, *Crime in America,* chapter 13; "Prisons: Factories of Crime," pp. 192 ff.

104. The purposes or functions ascribed to prisons are four: (1) retribution or punishment, (2) deterrence, (3) restraint (i.e., removal of the offender from the community), and (4) rehabilitation. It is unpopular

among American criminologists at this time to talk of making the criminal pay for his crime. Yet punishment of the criminal for its own sake is a vital part of penology in the Mosaic law (*see* Gary R. Williams, "The Purpose of Penology in the Mosaic Law and Today," *Bibliotheca Sacra,* vol. 133, no. 529, January–March 1976, pp. 42–55). What evidence there is about the effect of incarceration as a punishment to deter crime at least casts doubts upon its ability to do so (e.g., E. E. Flynn, "Jails and Criminal Justice," in Lloyd E. Ohlin [ed.], *Prisoners in America* [Prentice-Hall, 1973], p. 53). Prisons do fulfill their role of restraint, but rehabilitation is a myth in prisons, at least so far as it affects recidivism (*see* Martinson and Wilks, *The Effectiveness of Correctional Treatment* [Praeger, 1975]). The only punishment with a proved record of reducing recidivism is capital punishment.

105. L. Forer, *The Death of the Law* (David McKay Co., 1975).

Chapter 3

106. J. Arthur Hoyles, *The Church and the Criminal* (London: Epworth Press, 1965) provides a thorough discussion of the relation of Church and state in the ministry to prisoners.

107. From the time of Theodosius the Great (d. 395), heresy was regarded as a civil political crime. The first execution of a "Christian" for lack of orthodoxy by other "Christians" occurred in 385 at Trier. Hans Küng, *The Church* (Sheed & Ward, 1967), p. 250.

108. For discussion of these in detail, see J. Arthur Hoyles, *Religion in Prison* (London: Epworth Press, 1955).

109. Oliver J. Keller and Benedict S. Alper, *Halfway Houses: Community-Centered Corrections and Treatment* (Heath & Co., 1970), p. 7.

110. For example, the letter commending Irenaeus from a group of martyrs. Eusebius' *Ecclesiastical History,* book 5, chapter 4.

111. It has been stated that the early Church "sent evangelistic teams into the prisons and work camps of the Roman Empire. Conversions and revivals took place on such a scale that the Roman government put a stop to the evangelization of prisoners." Bernard Ramm, "Prison: The Solution That Fails," *Eternity,* vol. 23, no. 3 (March 1972), p. 13, from his book, *The Right, The Good, and The Happy* (Word, 1971). However, this author has not been able to confirm the historical validity of such reports.

112. Vernon Fox, *Introduction to Corrections* (Prentice-Hall, 1972), p. 7.

113. A variety of such programs were described in "War on Crime by Fed-Up Citizens," *U.S. News & World Report,* September 29, 1975, pp. 19–22.

114. A thorough description of such a program may be found in Richard Ku, *An Exemplary Project: The Voluntary Probation Counselor Program, Lincoln, Nebraska* (National Institute of Law Enforcement and Criminal Justice, n.d.).

115. A description of a program to minister to all involved in welfare and corrections may be found in Robert J. Carlson, "The Court House Chaplaincy—A Project in Collaboration," *Pastoral Psychology* (September 1972), pp. 18–25.

116. "Florida Corrections Initiates Chaplain-on-Call Program," *American Journal of Correction*, vol. 37, no. 4 (July–August, 1975), p. 34.

117. J. L. Carroll and C. G. McCormick, "The Cursillo Movement in a Penal Setting: An Introduction," *Canadian Journal of Corrections*, 12:151–160, April 1970.

118. For a thorough discussion, see Gerald C. Adams, "Discipleship Training in a Jail," *Journal of the Association of Institutional Chaplains* (July 1976).

119. Literacy and Evangelism, Inc., of Tulsa, Oklahoma, is an example of a structured program, as is the PACE Institute (Programmed Activities for Correctional Education) at the Cook County Jail in Chicago, a program founded by Chaplain John Edwin.

120. To illustrate this, only three cases related to religion behind bars are listed from 1960 or before in "Prisoners' Legal Rights: A Bibliography of Cases and Articles (Second Edition)," a special edition (1974) of the *Prison Law Reporter*, but about ninety cases were listed from 1961–1973.

121. Approximately half of the cases reported in "Prisoners' Legal Rights" (*see* Note 120) were cases that involved the Black Muslim faith.

122. William T. Toal, *Recent Developments in Correctional Case Law* (South Carolina Department of Corrections, 1975), p. 1.

123. John W. Palmer, *Constitutional Rights of Prisoners* (Anderson Company, 1973, with 1974 supplement) provides an excellent summary of the law about religion behind bars.

124. This may become the lever which will cause prisons to stop employing chaplains as they must contend with a growing plethora of religions (including Satan-worship cults and many varieties of Eastern religions) behind bars. The practical problems of abiding by such requirements will be more effective in removing chaplains from prison payrolls than philosophical arguments against state-financed clergy.

125. Liff v. Procunier, 395 F. Supp. 871 (n.d. California).

Chapter 4

126. Kenneth Latourette, *A History of Christianity* (Harper & Row, 1953), p. 231.

127. F. C. Keuther, "Religion and the Chaplain," *Contemporary Correction*, Paul W. Tappan, ed. (McGraw-Hill, 1951), p. 255.

128. The cities of refuge described in Numbers 35:9 ff. illustrate banishment.

129. John T. McNeill, *A History of the Cure of Souls* (Harper Torchbooks, 1951), p. 223.

130. *Ibid.*, p. 224.

131. R. R. Korn and L. W. McCorkle, *Criminology and Penology* (Holt, Rinehart & Winston, 1959), p. 406.

132. J. Arthur Hoyles, *Religion in Prison* (London: Epworth Press, 1955), p. 3.

133. *Ibid.*

134. *Ibid.*, p. 4.

135. *Ibid.*, p. 8.

136. *Ibid.*, p. 9.

137. *Ibid.*, p. 8.

138. *Ibid.*, p. 7.

139. *Ibid.*, p. 11. See *Memoir of the Life of Elizabeth Fry* (Patterson Smith, 1974).

140. Hoyles, *Religion in Prisons,* p. 12.

141. *Ibid.*, p. 15.

142. Appointment of prison chaplains had been authorized by an Act of Parliament in 1773, but another Act in 1814 made the appointment of chaplains in all jails compulsory. Col. Sir Edmund F. DuCane, *The Punishment and Prevention of Crime* (London: Macmillan & Co., 1885), p. 46.

143. W. L. Clay, *The Prison Chaplain* (Patterson Smith 1969 reprint), p. 101.

144. Hoyles, *Religion in Prison,* p. 17.

145. *Ibid.*, p. 64.

146. Henry H. Cassler and George C. Kandle, *Ministering to Prisoners and Their Families* (Fortress Press, 1968), p. 67.

147. Hoyles, *Religion in Prison,* pp. 17–18. Also see, John Howard, *Prisons and Lazarettos* (Patterson-Smith reprint, 1973).

148. *Ibid.*, p. 19. Howard also wanted chaplains who were "Christian" and not just interested in remuneration.

149. *Ibid.*, p. 25.

150. *Ibid.* The chaplaincy was not Clay's first choice for ministry. "He accepted the post in default of one more in accord with his wishes." Clay, *Prison Chaplain,* p. 101. But once he was in the chaplaincy, he gave himself to it totally.

151. The comments about the Reverend John Clay are drawn from Hoyles, *Religion in Prison,* pp. 25–29. The reader interested in a detailed description of John Clay's ministry should consult the Patterson Smith 1969 reprint of Clay's memoirs in *The Prison Chaplain* by his son, W. L. Clay.

152. John Luckey, *Life in Sing Sing State Prison, as Seen in a Twelve Years' Chaplaincy* (N. Tibbals & Co., 1860), p. 359.

153. *Ibid.*, p. 370.

154. The duration of the debate is illustrated by: Lancaster's paper, "Has the Christian Chaplain, as the Minister of Religion, a Rightful Place in All Our Schemes for Character Building Among the Men Committed to Our Care?" in the 1928 Proceedings of the American Prison Association;

Keuther's view that clinical pastoral training saved the prison chaplaincy from extinction as others began to meet social and psychological needs of prisoners, as expressed in his article "Religion and the Chaplain" in the 1951 book, *Contemporary Corrections.* Stuart D. Johnson raises similar issues in a 1972 issue of the *Canadian Journal of Criminology and Corrections* with his article "The Correctional Chaplaincy: Sociological Perspectives in a Time of Rapid Change."

155. While full-time chaplains in 1971 spent an *average* of about two-thirds of their time in religious activities, 31 percent of them spent less than *half* their time in religious activities. Hylon Vickers, "The Place of Religion and a Religious Program in Adult Corrections" (master's thesis, Sam Houston State University, Huntsville, Texas, 1971), p. 32.

156. At one state prison, movies (often X-rated) are shown in the prison mess hall at the same time as the Protestant worship service on Sunday morning. Since such showings began, chapel attendance has dropped from 150 to about 25.

157. CPE was adopted as part of the standards for chaplains by the Ninety-Second ACA Congress of Correction in 1962 and was included in the third edition (1966) of the ACA *Manual of Correctional Standards.*

158. R. Richard Summer, "Correctional Ministry in the Face of Emerging Trends," *APCCA Newsletter & Journal,* vol. 1, no. 1 (November–January, 1975–76), p. 24.

159. *Ibid.*, p. 27.

160. A related question that may come to the front is, Does the "religious program coordinator" need to be a minister if his role is essentially administrative? This author sees no reason a religious program coordinator must be a minister.

161. Hoyles, *Religion in Prison,* pp. 19–20.

162. Keuther describes the situation and says the Federal Bureau of Prisons approached the Council of Churches in 1934. "Religion and Chaplain," p. 256. H. H. Cassler contends that this occurred in 1937 in "Prison Chaplaincy," *Journal of Pastoral Care,* vol. 8, no. 3; 165–168, 1954.

163. Byron E. Eshelman, "The Prison Ministry," *Federal Probation,* September 1968, p. 37.

164. *Reform of the Criminal Justice Systems in the United States and Canada* (Board of Social Ministry, Lutheran Church in America, 1972), p. 37.

165. *Rudd v. Ray,* Civil Case No. 16843, January 8, 1976, in the Eighth Judicial District of the State of Iowa.

166. Masaharu Yanagimoto, "Japanese Penologist Looks at American Corrections," *American Journal of Correction* (May–June, 1966), p. 18.

Chapter 5

167. For example, this breakdown is found in E. F. Proelss, "Reflections on the Social, Moral, Cultural, and Spiritual Aspects of the Prison Chap-

lain's Ministry," *Journal of Pastoral Care,* 12:69–81, Summer 1958, and in Cassler and Kandle, *Ministering to Prisoners and Their Families* (Prentice-Hall, 1968).

168. "Other than medical doctors and nurses, there was no other type of specialized professional person [psychologist, social worker, teacher, etc.] employed in as many as 5 percent of the country's jails." *The Nation's Jails* (LEAA:NCJRS, 1975), p. 11.

169. This insight was presented by the Reverend George Ricketts, Director of Chaplaincy Services of the Churches of Virginia, in his lecture in the 1974 Good News Mission correctional chaplaincy course.

170. The surveys from which the data in this discussion were drawn are described in Appendix B.

171. It is appropriate to ask about the reliability of the data contained in these tables, which came from the study by Pace. The responses to the 1973 surveys of chaplains were adequate in size (about one-third of the full-time correctional chaplains in the nation) and distributed in proper proportions geographically, denominationally, and by type of institution served. The responses to the surveys demonstrated internal consistency and were consistent with other data about chaplains wherever common points were covered.

172. E. M. Bounds, *Power Through Prayer,* chapter 1.

173. The Good News Mission's job description for the position of chaplain uses a nominal sixty-hour workweek and suggests that fifteen of the sixty be spent in prayer and study of the Word, almost double the average for Protestant chaplains.

174. Hylon Vickers, "The Place of Religion and a Religious Program in Adult Corrections" (master's thesis, Sam Houston State University, Huntsville, Texas, 1971), p. 52.

175. H. H. Cassler and G. C. Kandle, *Ministering to Prisoners and Their Families* (Fortress Press, 1968), p. 69.

176. See Table 1 in chapter 4.

177. It is pertinent to remember that the Book of Acts involves teaching (forms of διδάσκω) in evangelism, as in Acts 4:2; 5:42; etc. For a more thorough discussion of this, see Michael Green, *Evangelism in the Early* Church (Eerdmans, 1970). A chaplain with vision for literature distribution will develop both an adequate quantity and variety of tracts (at least several hundred different items).

178. This reflects the greater emphasis upon the laity by Protestants since the number of nonreligious volunteers is very similar for both Catholic and Protestant chaplains.

179. This is the consistent pattern of the New Testament in Ephesians 4:11–16, Acts 14:21–23, 2 Timothy 2:2, etc.

180. Ivan H. Scheier, et al., *Guidelines and Standards for the Use of Volunteers in Correctional Programs* (LEAA: Technical Assistance Division,

1972), p. 53 recommends a full-time program coordinator when a volunteer program has thirty to forty or more volunteers.

181. Most Catholic chaplains ignored the question on the survey asking them to identify themselves theologically. Therefore the theological comparisons are restricted to Protestant chaplains.

182. Charles Y. Glock and Rodney Stark, *American Piety: The Nature of Religious Commitment* (University of California Press, 1968), p. 213.

183. *Ibid.*, p. 221.

184. *Ibid.*, p. 202.

185. *Ibid.*, p. 221.

186. While seminary training does not ensure a chaplain will be good nor its lack prevent one from being a very effective chaplain, a *caveat* is needed. It may be that only exceptional men are able to enter and stay in the correctional chaplaincy without the benefit of seminary training.

187. *Manual of Correctional Standards,* 3rd ed. (ACA, 1966), chapter 29.

188. Vickers, "Religion in Corrections," p. 47.

189. See Appendix E.

190. For illustrations, see the February 1974 or February, March, April 1975 issues of the APCCA Newsletter.

191. The Pace study analyzed administrative capacity by the kinds of weaknesses reported by a chaplain as the three greatest weaknesses of his program. Chaplains were given low marks administratively if the weaknesses were such as could be eliminated by the chaplain. For example, a weakness of too few volunteers could be eliminated by recruiting more volunteers. A chaplain was given a high mark administratively if the weaknesses were outside his control. For example, the weakness of all inmates being confined to their cells for several months while riot-caused damage to the institution was being repaired was considered completely outside the chaplain's control.

192. For example, Daniel Y. Quello, "A Comparative Investigation of the Personality Profiles of CPE and Non-CPE Theological Students," *The Journal of Pastoral Care,* vol. 24 (December 1970), pp. 240–243.

193. Part of the difference may result from the fact that most chaplains with CPE in Table 6 serve prisons, and most chaplains without CPE in that table serve jails. This can only account for less than half the difference in inmate response between the chaplains with CPE and those without.

194. This liberal bias is explicitly expressed by Jenny Yates Hammett, "A Second Drink at the Well: Theological and Philosophical Content of CPE Origins," *Journal of Pastoral Care,* vol. 29, no. 2 (June 1975), pp. 86–89.

195. *Ibid.*, pp. 87–88.

196. Edward E. Thornton, *Theology and Pastoral Counseling* (Fortress Press, 1964), p. 132. The hostility has decreased since the 1950s.

197. John L. Florell, "After Fifty Years: Analysis of the National ACPE Questionnaire 1975," *Journal of Pastoral Care,* vol. 29, no. 4, December 1975, p. 231.

198. *Reform of the Criminal Justice Systems in the United States and Canada* (Board of Social Ministry, Lutheran Church in America, 1972), p. 73.

199. For example, see Dale K. Pace, "Programs ARE Possible," *National Jail Association Newsletter*, May 1975, pp. 1–4.

200. A man entering the correctional chaplaincy after years in the pastorate undergoes a great deal of "cultural and occupational shock."

201. It should be noted also that some of the most effective chaplains have been men who were forced into the chaplaincy by circumstances. For example, John Clay, whom Arthur Hoyles calls almost the "patron saint" of prison chaplains, "would never have spontaneously chosen the office of assistant chaplain to a prison: he accepted the post in default of one more in accordance with his wishes." W. L. Clay, *The Prison Chaplain* (Patterson Smith reprint, 1969), p. 101.

202. Several of the most effective chaplains known personally by this author are men who became chaplains without pastoral experience. But all of them were mature men when they entered chaplaincy.

203. Whether a new chaplain comes with years of pastoral experience or none, he needs thorough orientation and much supervision during the first year of ministry as a chaplain for his ministry to be most effective.

Chapter 6

204. This section draws heavily from the article by Dr. William L. Simmer in the textual materials used by the Good News Mission for its course on the correctional chaplaincy, "Characteristics Desired in a Chaplain," in Dale K. Pace (ed.), *Notes on the Correctional Chaplaincy* (Good News Mission, 1972).

205. Leon Morris's insight here is helpful. "The really essential thing about the New Testament view of the ministry is that the one basic ministry is that of Christ Himself. Ministers in the church are never regarded as exercising a ministry by virtue of any inherent power or right of their own. All that they do they do only because of what Christ has done for them." *Ministers of God* (Inter-Varsity Fellowship, 1964), p. 25.

206. The literal idea of the Greek word νεόφυτος (*novice* in the King James) is that of "newly planted." Its literal use in the Septuagint often implies immature plants, i.e., those not yet in the fruit-producing stage of development.

207. John Bunyan, *The Pilgrim's Progress*.

208. To illustrate, in the Good News Mission each chaplain ministers under the supervision of a Regional Coordinator and reports to him weekly on his activities. In addition, each chaplain's ministry is evaluated (once or twice a year) by a Supervisor Chaplain. This evaluation is extensive, lasting several days and covering all aspects of the chaplain's ministry: programs within the institution, administration, public relations, volunteer

recruitment and training, personal goals and professional growth, family relationships, follow-up of releasees and inmate families, etc. The purpose of the evaluation is to help each chaplain achieve his full potential.

209. Vickers' 1971 survey of chaplains reported the following race breakdown: black (8), brown (3), semitic (16), white (271), yellow (1). This included part-time and full-time chaplains. Hylon Vickers, "The Place of Religion and a Religious Program in Adult Corrections" (master's thesis, Sam Houston State University, Huntsville, Texas, 1971), p. 34. Pace's 1973 survey of chaplains reported 97 percent were Caucasian males.

210. Pace study and Vickers, "Religion in Corrections," p. 34.

211. Pace study and Vickers, "Religion in Corrections," p. 52.

212. From Pace study. The data from Vickers's 1971 survey are very similar: 92.5 percent of full-time chaplains reported seminary-level training ("Religion in Corrections," p. 37). Because his survey considered only chaplains serving penal institutions, Vickers' CPE figures were higher than those in Table 12, namely 84 percent for full-time Protestant chaplains and 71 percent for Catholic chaplains (Vickers, p. 39). About 80 percent of Protestant prison chaplains responding in the Pace survey of 1973 reported having CPE, again confirming that the data from the two surveys are consistent.

213. These data are consistent with Vickers' 1971 survey, which reported an average of 3.2 dependents for Protestant chaplains, p. 35.

214. "Chaplaincy Services," *Manual of Correctional Standards,* 3rd ed. (ACA, 1966), chapter 29.

215. Henry H. Cassler and George C. Kandle, *Ministering to Prisoners and Their Families* (Fortress Press, 1968), p. 78.

216. Vickers, "Religion in Corrections," pp. 47–48.

217. This section was taken with only minor changes from Dr. Eldon W. Koch, "The Chaplain's Relation to Local Churches," in Dale K. Pace (ed.), *Notes on the Correctional Chaplaincy* (Good News Mission, 1972).

218. This discussion draws freely upon the article by Chaplain William E. Austin for the Good News Mission's correctional chaplaincy course, "The Chaplain's Personal Well-Being," in Dale K. Pace (ed.), *Notes on the Correctional Chaplaincy* (Good News Mission, 1972).

219. *Power Through Prayer* by E. M. Bounds cannot be too highly recommended. It should be read at least yearly by everyone in the ministry.

220. Charles Ryrie, *Balancing the Christian Life* (Moody Press, 1969), p. 31.

221. The present writer has a penchant for the historical and has benefited much from writings in this vein by patristic authors such as Clement of Alexandria (*Stromata*), medieval mystics such as Bernard of Clairvaux and Bonaventure, Anabaptist and other Reformation writings (especially Luther's letters of spiritual counsel), Puritan writings such as John Bunyan's *Holy Life,* and John Owen's. It is hoped that chaplains and other

Christians will not restrict their devotional reading to contemporary authors but will also read from God's men of the past.

222. It has been this author's goal to read biographies on nearly every major leader of evangelical Christianity. There has been great value in the challenge and stimulation of reading how God worked through such varied men as Count Zinzendorf (Moravian Brethren), John Wesley, Watchman Nee (Little Flock of China), Bakht Singh (of India), and Billy Graham. Perhaps the most challanging biography this author has read is Norman Grubb's *Rees Howells: Intercessor.*

223. For information about enrolling, write to the National Criminal Justice Reference Service (NCJRS), U.S. Department of Justice, Law Enforcement Assistance Administration, Washington, D.C. 20530.

Chapter 7

224. Too few of the chaplains responding to the 1973 survey spent *any* time in this area to permit development of a statistic by denomination, institution, or other chaplaincy parameters.

225. *Philosophy and Religion,* vol. 32 of *Comprehensive Dissertation Index 1861–1972* (Ann Arbor, Michigan: Xerox University Microfilms, 1973).

226. Most textbooks on corrections or the criminal justice system make only very brief mention of chaplains and religious programs.

227. The conditions are ripe for such a history. A number of pertinent works have been reprinted (e.g., Clay's *The Prison Chaplain*). The extensive bibliography prepared by this author for publication in the December 1976 issue of the AEIC Journal provides the first step in beginning such a study.

228. Hylon Vickers, "The Place of Religion and a Religious Program in Adult Corrections" (master's thesis, Sam Houston State University, Huntsville, Texas, 1971), p. 42.

229. Albert Edward Bailey, *The Gospel in Hymns* (Charles Scribner's Sons, 1950), p. 313.

230. The majority of Christian educational materials are designed for white middle-class America. At times, these inadvertently create trouble when they are used. For example, the Christian film *Barabbas: the Robber* looks at the trial and crucifixion of Jesus through the eyes of Barabbas, and does a very fine job of it. However, only one black person appears in the film: a young boy who plays the slave who brings Pilate a bowl of water in which to wash his hands of guilt in Christ's condemnation. Reaction to this by black inmates normally is intense and vociferous, destroying the impact and message of the film.

231. "Procedure and Guidelines for Membership as a Fellow in the College of Fellows of the APCCA."

232. This writer was shocked by these findings. He had expected superior performance from APCCA-certified chaplains and leaders.

233. *The Church and the Prisoner: The Report of the Prisons Commission to the Church Assembly* (Westminster, England: The Church Information Office, 1960), p. 31. Their recommendation was for an appointment of seven years' duration with the possibility of extending it to ten years in exceptional cases (p. 22).

234. *Ibid.*, p. 10.

235. Comparison of the AEIC and APCCA membership lists in mid 1976 revealed that less than 10 percent of the total number of people they represent belong to both the AEIC and APCCA.

236. *Reform of the Criminal Justice Systems in the United States and Canada* (Board of Social Ministry, Lutheran Church in America, 1972), p. 73.

237. Chaplain Services of the Churches of Virginia has provided chaplains for Virginia's penal system since the 1920s.

238. This can be illustrated by the comment of two "political prisoners," Howard Levy and David Miller, in their book *Going to Jail* (Grove Press, 1971): "The men and women who are provided by prison authorities to look after the spiritual welfare of inmates . . . actively support the present system or are silent." (p. 65).

239. In *Gittlemacker v. Prasse,* the court pointed out that to "suggest the Free Exercise Clause demands that the state not only furnish the opportunity to practice one's religion, but also supply the clergyman, is a concept that dangerously approaches the jealously guarded frontiers of the Establishment Clause." Cited by John W. Palmer, *Constitutional Rights of Prisoners* (W. H. Anderson Company, 1973), p. 63.

240. Palmer, *Constitutional Rights,* pp. 64 ff., discusses this subject.

241. *Ibid.*, p. 71. A popular discussion of this may be found in David Rudovsky, *The Rights of Prisoners: The Basic ACLU Guide to a Prisoner's Rights* (Avon Books, 1973), chapter 4.

242. Thus far the courts have ruled that government-paid chaplains do not violate the Establishment Clause of the First Amendment because it has been felt that failure to provide chaplains would restrict inmate rights to the free exercise of religion. Such opinion may change if the church demonstrates that it can and will minister adequately to allow inmates free exercise of religion without the necessity of government-paid chaplains. A January 1976 ruling in an Iowa court followed this line of reasoning: "There has been no showing that the religious needs of inmates would not, or could not, be met if tax-supported chaplains were unavailable. The record does indicate that ready access to chaplains or ministers might be more difficult, yet this goes to quantity of religious assistance, a criteria that so far as known, the courts have not yet accepted as a justification for tax-supported ministers, or chaplains." *Rudd vs Ray,* Civil Case No. 16843, January 8, 1976, Eighth Judicial District of the State of Iowa. The court then banned the payment of chaplain salaries because the Iowa constitution specifically pro-

hibited the use of tax monies to pay ministers. The decision was appealed and has not been decided at the time this book went to press. It should be noted that most of those involved thus far in litigation seeking to eliminate tax support for chaplains have been persons hostile to Evangelical Christianity.

243. An illustration of this may be found in Levy and Miller, *Going to Jail,* pp. 70–71, where they describe the efforts of a prison chaplain to circulate a petition to exonerate prison officials charged with an abuse of discipline. Several writers on the chaplaincy have repeated the theme that chaplains are hindered in their ministry when on the payroll of the institution. For examples, see Harvey L. Long, "The Church's Mission and Delinquents," *Federal Probation,* December 1963, pp. 26–31, and S. G. West, "The Crisis in the Correctional Chaplaincy," *Canadian Journal of Corrections,* 10(2): 327–331, 1968.

244. For example, see Charles R. Tolson, "The Marriage Issue in Corrections: A Position Paper," *The APCCA Newsletter & Journal,* May–July, 1976, pp. 51–53.

245. During the early 1970s, a number of chaplains have become wardens, superintendents, or administrators at other levels of correctional units. A large number of counselors in penal institutions are former ministers. The options thus available to chaplains would be many, particularly since the number of chaplains involved would be small—only a few in each state.

246. "Christian-Muslim Prison Service Due," *Richmond News Leader,* July 2, 1976, p. 11.

247. Howard J. Clinebell, Jr., *Basic Types of Pastoral Counseling* (Abingdon Press, 1966), p. 299.

248. Clyde M. Narramore, *The Psychology of Counseling* (Zondervan, 1960), p. 114.

249. This author cannot speak about CPE-trained ministers as a whole, but the characteristics presented in this section are typical of the chaplains with CPE whom he knows. Of course, there are exceptions to the pattern. Part of this blurring of the opportunity for soul-winning in counseling comes from liberal confusion about evangelism, which has found its way into CPE. For example, "evangelism in our day is finding one's way to people and demonstrating concern and affection for those people." Russell L. Dicks, *Principles and Practices of Pastoral Care* (Fortress Press, 1963), p. 36. Such is not evangelism, either from a biblical perspective or from the theology of Evangelical Christianity.

250. Jenny Yates Hammett, "A Second Drink at the Well: A Theological and Philosophical Context of CPE Origins," *Journal of Pastoral Care,* vol. 29, no. 2, June 1975, p. 87.

251. Wayne E. Oates, "Introduction: Evangelism and Pastoral Psychology" in Simon Doniger (ed.), *Evangelism and Pastoral Psychology* (Pastoral Psychology Press, 1956), p. 6.

252. Until the late 1940s, CPE supervisors "shared a common hostility against seminaries" and "often they directed their hostility against leaders of the institutional church as well." Edward E. Thornton, *Theology and Pastoral Counseling* (Fortress Press, 1964), p. 132. Such hostility still seems to manifest itself against theological conservatives.

253. This may explain why there are so few Plymouth Brethren chaplains employed by the state (one, to this author's knowledge, in 1976) compared with the number of Plymouth Brethren chaplains supported by Church and private organizations (about half a dozen or more in 1976).

254. Ministers from religious groups outside the usual denominational structure (groups such as Plymouth Brethren, independent Baptists, etc.) appear to hold less than their numerical proportion of the government-supported chaplaincy positions. Whether this has resulted from a disinclination on their part to seek such jobs or a reluctance on the part of correctional institutions to employ them is unknown at present.

255. Cf. Hammett, "Second Drink."

256. See Table 4.

Chapter 8

257. Samuel B. Guze, *Criminality and Psychiatric Disorders* (Oxford University Press, 1976), p. 131.

258. *Ibid.*, p. 42.

259. *Ibid.*, p. 41.

260. *Ibid.*, pp. 40, 86. *Survey of Inmates of Local Jails 1972: Advance Report* (LEAA:NCJI&SS, n.d.), p. 3. *Survey of Inmates of State Correctional Facilities 1974: Advance Report* (LEAA:NCJI&SS, n.d.), p. 3.

261. Guze, *Criminality*, pp. 40–41.

262. Peter Barton Hutt and Partricia M. Wald, *Dealing With Drug Abuse: A Report to the Ford Foundation* (Praeger Publishers, 1972), p. 31. *Inmates of State Correctional Facilities*, p. 6.

263. Helen Erskine, *Alcohol and the Criminal Justice System: Challenge and Response* (LEAA:NILE&CJ, 1972), pp. 8–9 points out that about one-fourth of violent crimes are committed while the culprit is intoxicated (alcohol consumption is a factor in about two-thirds of homicides), and there are in addition the problems of the drinking drivers and the drunks. Guze, *Criminality*, pp. 45, 87, lists about half of the felons in his study as having a serious problem with alcoholism.

264. There is evidence that imprisonment may start or reinforce drug use, Hutt and Wald, *Drug Abuse*, p. 32. Even the best drug treatment programs have limited success, *Ibid.*, pp. 24–25. About 14 percent of inmates in state prisons have tried drug treatment programs. *Inmates of State Correctional Facilities*, p. 7. Burns claims AA and comparable drug programs (e.g., Teen Challenge) have a cure rate of about 70 percent for those who want to stop their addiction—but admit that only one in ten addicted to

alcohol or drugs really wants to stop. John Burns *et al., The Answer to Addiction* (Harper & Row, 1975). Drug abuse tends to decrease with age, and even many heroin addicts "mature out" in their thirties and forties. A. E. Wilder Smith, *The Drug Users* (Shaw Publishers, 1969), p. 115. It has also been noted that there is a "striking reduction in recidivism associated with increasing age." Guze, *Criminality*, p. 137.

265. *Inmates of Local Jails*, p. 15 and *Inmates of State Correctional Facilities*, p. 2.

266. Janet K. Carsetti, *Literacy Problems and Solutions: A Resource Handbook for Correctional Educators* (American Bar Association Clearing House for Offender Literacy, 1975), p. 2.

267. *Inmates of Local Jails*, p. 4. From twenty to fifty percent of inmates were unemployed at the time of their arrest. *Ibid.;* Guze, *Criminality*, pp. 40, 85; and *Inmates of State Correctional Facilities*, p. 2.

268. Guze, *Criminality*, p. 40. About a third have been fired at least once, and a third have not been able to hold a job as long as a year.

269. *Sourcebook of Criminal Justice Statistics 1973* (LEAA:NCJI&SS, 1973), p. 322. Over 70 percent of inmates in state prisons have served two or more sentences. Over half have been sentenced at least twice for the same offense. *Inmates of State Correctional Facilities*, p. 12.

270. Guze, *Criminality*, pp. 47, 79, 103.

271. *Ibid.*, pp. 42 ff. and 87 ff.

272. *Inmates of Local Jails*, p. 3, and *Inmates of State Correctional Facilities*, p. 1.

273. For example, see *Attica: The Official Report of the New York State Special Commission on Attica* (Bantam Books, 1972), p. 105.

274. Guze, *Criminality*, pp. 41, 100.

275. *Children in Custody, A Report on the Juvenile Detention and Correctional Facility Census of 1971* (LEAA:NCJI&SS, n.d.), p. 6.

276. *Inmates of State Correctional Facilities*, p. 10.

277. This factor should also be remembered when the program's success is evaluated–how much was due to the program and how much due simply to participant selection? Also, it is important to recognize that the later stages of the program may not do as well because the participants were not screened as tightly. The lower "success" rate of the program later may not be a reflection upon the quality of the program at all, but may simply reflect that more people were allowed into the program.

278. Because jails and prisons are not always the cleanest places, it is wise to wear clothes that will not be damaged if soiled. Inmates react adversely to ministry of those overly concerned about their clothes. Many inmates who had formerly rejected a chaplain's ministry have become receptive to him and his message after he sat on the cellblock floor next to them and talked with them.

279. For a description, see Dale K. Pace, "Programs ARE Possible," *National Jail Association Newsletter*, May 1975.

280. A number of states have instituted state offices on volunteerism. Voluntary action centers abound around the country. There is an extensive government management force overseeing Volunteers in Service to America (VISTA) programs, etc.

281. Ivan H. Scheier, *Guidelines and Standards for the Use of Volunteers in Correctional Programs* (LEAA Technical Assistance Division, 1972), pp. 26 ff.

282. Many helpful suggestions in these areas may be found in Scheier, *Guidelines and Standards.*

283. *Ibid.*, pp. 6–7, 28 ff.

284. *Ibid.*, pp. 187 ff.

285. Many one-on-one counseling programs are frustrating for Christian volunteers because of total lack of spiritual structure. The Good News Mission program includes a structured Bible-study and sharing emphasis along with supportive counseling and social help.

286. Only 14 percent of jail chaplains reported having inmate clerks, as contrasted to 87 percent of prison chaplains.

287. Although the general consensus is that chaplains should minister to staff as well as inmates, in discussion of the role of the chaplain, Dr. George Beto, then-director of the Texas Department of Corrections, stated that the chaplain should not be chaplain to the staff "but only to the inmate population." "Summary," *Proceedings: ACA 1962*, p. 43.

288. While the precise definition of "the doctrine of Christ" in 2 John 9 is uncertain, it no doubt clearly excludes from fellowship or spiritual association such as have knowingly rejected the divinity of Christ and His vicarious atonement. Yet such chaplains exist, and some are or have been part of the APCCA and other ecumenically oriented religious groups.

289. Occasionally the official church program of the institution will be so bad that the serious Christian must withdraw from it both for his own well-being and for his testimony. For example, a small penal unit in the mountains had church services conducted by a religious group that was blatantly racist. In addition, some of the inmates participating in them were extensively involved in the pornographic and drug activities of the unit. When asked about the situation by a Christian inmate, the author advised him to disassociate himself from the group.

290. The releasee without past church ties can simply be directed to a good evangelical church. Usually it is wisest to encourage the releasee with past church ties of a positive nature (personal or family) to become involved in that church (even if not too evangelical), trusting the Lord to lead him away from it later should that be God's will. The reason for this is simply to enlist every resource in helping the releasee become actively involved in the Church.

291. The Gideons have a great potential for such follow-up and should be used whenever possible. With Gideon camps in most communities, the prison ministry leader of the local Gideon camp can become the contact point to get an evangelical Christian in touch with the releasee in a distant community.

292. Whenever many of the inmate families live a great distance from the institution (as is the case with most prisons), it is helpful if the chaplain is available for counseling with them on visiting days. Otherwise, he limits his ability in this area of follow-up.

293. About a third of the eight to ten thousand students on the Good News Mission's Bible correspondence course are relatives of inmates. Most of the other two-thirds are inmates and releasees.

294. The dispute between Paul and Barnabas (Acts 15:36–41) resulted in two missionary teams going forth instead of one.

Chapter 9

295. It should not disturb the chaplain that some inmates come to him merely because they hope to exploit his help. Some of these may even get saved as the chaplain helps them, even though they came to him initially only for secular or mundane reasons. God's Spirit often will catch a prisoner by surprise.

296. Volunteers should always channel complaints about the institution through the chaplain. They should not speak directly to the institution staff or others about problems *except in most unusual cases.*

297. Telephone calls to inmate families and visits with them, helping to make arrangements for special visits, etc., demonstrate the genuineness of the chaplain's interest in inmate welfare and will increase their interest in his ministry.

298. Those recommended by this author are A. Berkeley Mickelson's *Interpreting the Bible* (Eerdmans, 1963) and the classic by Milton S. Terry, *Biblical Hermeneutics* (Zondervan reprint, 1961), Merrill F. Unger's *Principles of Expository Preaching* (Zondervan, 1955), Andrew W. Blackwood's *The Preparation of Sermons* (Abingdon, 1948), and especially Charles W. Koller's *Expository Preaching Without Notes* (Baker Book House, 1962). One final book must be added because its emphasis pales the techniques of these other works into a place of secondary importance. It should be read and pondered carefully by all who preach or teach the Bible. It is Watchman Nee's *Ministry of God's Word* (Christian Fellowship Publishers, 1971).

299. The King James translation uses the term *Mars' hill* for Areopagus. The Greek text of Acts 17:23 lacks the article *the* of the King James "TO THE UNKNOWN GOD."

300. See Appendix A.

301. Many of the lessons and messages of Jesus were impromptu, initiated

by a question or incident (e.g., the parable of the good Samaritan was a response to a lawyer's question, Luke 10:25–37).

302. Dr. B. S. Brown of the National Institute of Mental Health found the average IQ of more than 50,000 inmates to be 95 (compared with 100 for the nation's population in general), and 40 percent of the inmates had IQs below 85 (compared with only 16 percent in the national population).

303. Protestant chaplains reported in 1973 that about 8 percent of the inmates in the institutions which they served were enrolled in Bible correspondence courses.

304. A good collection of these are in Donald Grey Barnhouse's *Teaching the Word of Truth* (Eerdmans). Though designed for children, the materials in this book are very helpful for adults also.

305. See Appendix D.

306. Condensed from Dr. Paul Rader's "Preaching/Teaching for Decisions" in Dale K. Pace (ed.), *Notes on the Correctional Chaplaincy* (Good News Mission, 1972).

307. The Dwight Moody incident comes from materials belonging to the Rader family. Dr. Rader's uncle was a former pastor of Moody Church in Chicago.

Chapter 10

308. A 1967 survey of eighteen Protestant chaplains in Federal prisons revealed that the chaplains saw counseling as their most important task and gave most of their time to it. E. M. Clarke, "Expectations and Role Performance of Chaplains in Federal Penal Instittuions," *Journal of Pastoral Care*, 24:135–139, June 1970.

309. Russell L. Dicks, *Principles and Practices of Pastoral Care* in the *Successful Pastoral Counseling Series* (Fortress Press, 1966), p. 18.

310. The significance of such vested interest must not be overlooked. As Richard Stuart noted, it is the primary reason for the irrational response to scientific studies that show the statistical ineffectiveness of psychotherapy: "Treatment has not worked; therefore expand it!" *Trick or Treatment: How and When Psychotherapy Fails* (Research Press, 1970), p. 200.

311. This includes both group and individual counseling and is in marked contrast to the chaplains without CPE, who spend about 25 percent of their workweek in counseling.

312. Results from a survey of over 1,200 CPE-trained ministers revealed that three times as many placed individual counseling as their top priority as considered worship their top priority. John L. Florell, "After Fifty Years: Analysis of the National ACPE Questionnaire 1975," *Journal of Pastoral Care*, 39:221–232, December 1975.

313. William A. Clebsch and Charles R. Jaekle, *Pastoral Care in Historical Perspective* (Harper Torchbooks, 1967), p. 80.

314. *Ibid.*, p. xvi.

315. For a discussion of this, see Bernard Berelson and Gary A. Steiner, *Human Behavior: An Inventory of Scientific Findings* (Harcourt, Brace & World 1964). The one who brought this problem to the forefront is Dr. H. J. Eysenck, "The Effects of Psychotherapy: An Evaluation," *Journal of Consulting Psychology,* 16:319–324 (1952) and *The Effects of Psychotherapy* (International Science Press, 1966). That this still is the case can be seen in the extensive review of the question of psychotherapy's effectiveness by Stanley Rachman, *The Effects of Psychotherapy* (Pergamon Press, 1971). His conclusion after reviewing more than 750 research projects and studies was simply, "We do not have satisfactory evidence to support the claim that psychotherapy is effective." He goes on to suggest that "psychotherapy does no more than provide the patient with a degree of comfort while [his] disorder runs its natural course."

316. The evidence for this conclusion is overwhelming. For examples: Herman Schwartz, "The Myth of Rehabilitation," *The Prison Journal,* vol. 3 (Spring–Summer, 1972); Stuart Adams, *Evaluative Research in Corrections: A Practical Guide* (LEAA:NILE&CJ, 1975); *A Program for Prison Reform* (the final report of the Annual Chief Justice Earl Warren Conference of Advocacy in the United States, 1972); or the extensive study by Dr. Robert Martinson (with Douglas Lipton and Judith Wilks), *Effectiveness of Correctional Treatment—A Survey of Treatment Evaluation Studies* (Praeger Publishers, 1975).

317. Berelson and Steiner, *Human Behavior,* p. 613.

318. Clebsch and Jaekle, *Pastoral Care,* p. 76. This is especially so of CPE training, as noted by J. Y. Hammett: "Clinical pastoral education, under the influence of pragmatism and liberalism, emphasized from its inception scientific or empirical method, but not theological content." Hammett goes on to state, "Although CPE went through the era of a developing neoorthodoxy and a developing existentialism, it appears not to have changed its basic liberal orientation of scientific method over theological content." Jenny Yates Hammett, "A Second Drink at the Well: Theological and Philosophical Context of CPE Origins," *Journal of Pastoral Care,* 39: 86–89, December 1975.

319. This author knows that God works in the lives of people when they obey His Word. While a pastor, a member of my congregation had been subject to seizures at least monthly for over a year and a half as a result of a brain tumor operation. While continuing to seek medical treatment, this man approached the church leadership about obeying the instructions of James 5:14–15. We obeyed. The seizures ceased and have not returned. Since then, he has been active in the Christian ministry and carries a heavy load of responsibilities and duties.

320. Jay E. Adams, *Competent to Counsel* (Presbyterian and Reformed Publishing Co., 1970). It is of interest to note the conclusion of the review of this book by Quentin L. Hand in the *Journal of Pastoral Care,* 39:141, December 1975. He writes, "This book takes a theological position and

maintains it in developing a method of 'counseling.' As such, it offers the quite conservative clergyperson a ready model. It challenges other pastoral counselors to be equally diligent in developing the theological basis of their counseling." Presumably by "other pastoral counselors," Hand means CPE-oriented counselors. Yet earlier in that same issue of the *Journal of Pastoral Care,* on page 88, Hammett had commented, "Throughout the history of the [CPE] movement there have been repeated attempts and failures to formulate any common theological doctrine."

321. See Frederick C. Kuether, "The Council for Clinical Training," *Pastoral Psychology* (October 1953) or Albert L. Meiburg, "The Heritage of the Pastoral Counselor" in Wayne E. Oates (ed.), *An Introduction to Pastoral Counseling* (Broadman Press, 1959).

322. Charles B. Truax and Robert R. Clarkhuff, *Toward Effective Counseling and Psychotherapy: Training and Practice* (Aldine-Atherton, 1967). They observe that while counseling as a whole cannot be proved effective, some counselors are definitely helpful and others definitely harmful. A brief discussion of this in Christian terms may be found in Andre Bustanoby, "Without These, Don't Start" in "The Minister's Workshop," *Christianity Today,* vol. 17, no. 21 (July 20, 1973), pp. 32–33 and vol. 16, no. 23 (August 31, 1973), pp. 38–39.

323. Most issues of psychological counseling journals such as *Counseling Psychologist* or *Journal of Counseling Psychology* contain at least one article related to the development of such characteristics in counselors.

324. While this author does not disparage formal counseling training, he has many questions about the appropriateness of much of it, since (1) the suicide rate is significantly higher among psychiatrists than for those in any of the other sixteen specialty groups listed by the American Medical Association as part of the medical profession (Bulletin of Suicidology, December 1968); (2) Howard James cites a complaint from administrators of juvenile institutions that this author has heard from many in prison administration: "Administrators constantly complain that the psychologists and social workers they hire have more problems than the kids!" *Children in Trouble* (Pocket Books, 1970), p. 111; and (3) several CPE supervisors known to this author *have* to have weekly visits with their psychiatrists in order to function normally.

325. Restitution is an essential part of dealing with guilt, although it has been neglected and not emphasized by many pastoral counselors. The essence of the principle of restitution may be found in Matthew 5:23–24. Until restitution is made, the brother will have something against the guilty one. This prohibits the guilty one's communication with God. Restitution brings reconciliation and opens the way for communication with God. Zacchaeus illustrated this principle when he said, "If I have taken any thing from any man by false accusation [the use of εἰ plus the indicative verb implies such was the case], I restore him fourfold" (Luke 19:8). Interest in restitution as a part of the rehabilitation process is growing; *see also*

Marvin Marcus et al., *Victim Compensation and Offender Restitution: A Selected Bibliography* (NCJRS, 1975).

326. The counseling suggestions in the last section of *Ministering to Prisoners and Their Families* states this well.

327. For a more thorough discussion of prayer in counseling, see H. Dale Keeton, "The Role of Prayer in Counseling," *Journal of the Association of Evangelical Institutional Chaplains,* July 1976.

328. Howard J. Clinebell, Jr., *Basic Types of Pastoral Counseling* (revised, Abingdon Press, 1966), p. 28.

329. *Ibid.,* p. 224.

330. *Encyclopaedia Britannica* (1974), vol. 14, p. 148.

331. Jessica Mitford, *Kind and Usual Punishment: The Prison Business* (Alfred A. Knopf, 1973), p. 123.

332. An examination of the empirical, practical, and ethical issues pertaining to the use of behavioral modification may be found in C. J. Braukmann, D. L. Fixsen, E. L. Phillips, and M. M. Wolf, "Behavioral Approaches to Treatment in the Crime and Delinquency Field," *Criminology,* 1975, pp. 299–331. Stephen H. Braun argues for a code of ethics to govern the application of behavioral modification in "Ethical Issues in Behavior Modification," *Behavior Therapy,* vol. 6, no. 1 (January 1975), pp. 51–62. This problem was emphasized by an editorial in the *International Journal of Offender Therapy and Comparative Criminology* which stated, "Today we tend to ignore the vital issues of morality," in "Conclusions: Rehabilitation—Morality—and the Forming of New Habits," vol. 17, no. 3, 1973, p. 308. For a discussion of legal issues involved, see William T. Toal, *Recent Developments in Correctional Case Law* (South Carolina Department of Corrections, 1975), section 15 on "Rehabilitation."

333. "American Criminal Law Review Examines Behavior Modification," *American Journal of Correction,* vol. 37, no. 6, November–December 1975, p. 10.

334. A comprehensive history of AA is contained in *Alcoholics Anonymous Comes of Age* (Harper & Brothers, 1957).

335. Information about the Yokefellows may be obtained from National Yokefellow Prison Ministry, Inc., 112 Old Trail North, Shamokin Dam, PA 17876.

336. Thomas A. Harris, *I'm OK—You're OK* (Harper & Row, 1967), p. xiv.

337. For example, M. James, *Born to Win: Transactional Analysis With Gestalt Experiments* (Addison-Wesley Publishing Co., 1971).

Chapter 11

338. Donald McGavran, *Understanding Church Growth* (Eerdmans, 1970), has a valuable chapter, "Indigenous Church Principles and Grow-

ing Churches," that traces the history of the indigenous church principle and discusses proper limits upon its application.

339. Both of these works by Allen should be read and studied carefully. Their practical usefulness is great in spite of their age.

340. Roland Allen, *The Spontaneous Expansion of the Church* (Eerdmans Reprint, 1962), p. 19.

341. *Church Growth and Methods of Evangelism in Asia–South Pacific* (Missions Advanced Research and Communication Center, 1970), p. viii.

342. Allen, *Spontaneous Expansion,* p. 34.

343. Throughout this chapter, *paternalism* will be used to describe the attitude that only the missionary (or chaplain) is *fully* qualified to be in charge, i.e., he is the only one truly qualified for spiritual leadership.

344. Allen, *Spontaneous Expansion,* p. 35.

345. *Ibid.,* pp. 30–31.

346. *Ibid.,* p. 5.

347. For illustrations, see Harold R. Cook, *Historic Patterns of Church Growth* (Moody Press, 1971).

348. Allen, *Spontaneous Expansion,* p. 10.

349. *Ibid.,* p. 32.

350. David Fuller (ed.) *Valiant for the Truth: A Treasury of Evangelical Writings* (McGraw-Hill, 1961), p. 257.

351. George H. Williams, "The Ministry in the Ante-Nicene Church (c125–315)" in H. Richard Niebuhr and Daniel D. Williams (ed.), *The Ministry in Historical Perspectives* (Harper & Brothers, 1956), pp. 29–30.

352. "The Epistle of Ignatius to the Trallians" (longer version), *The Ante-Nicene Fathers* (American Reprint of the Edinburgh Edition, 1885), vol. 1, p. 68. Most scholars feel that the longer versions of Ignatius' letters are interpolations of his writings, although such were made in the early centuries of the Christian era.

353. Allen, *Spontaneous Expansion,* pp. 20–21.

354. *Survey of Inmates of State Correctional Facilities 1974: Advance Report* (LEAA:NCJI&SS, 1976), p. 9, and *Survey of Inmates of Local Jails 1972: Advance Report* (LEAA:NCJI&SS, n.d.), p. 5.

355. This may be illustrated by the Protestant chaplains serving the Federal Bureau in 1973. At that time, one of the requirements for a Protestant chaplaincy position was nomination from the National Council of Churches. Consequently, more than 80 percent of the federal prison Protestant chaplains were from denominations affiliated with the National Council of Churches, even though the membership of the National Council of Churches denominations accounted for less than 60 percent of American Protestants. Also, only 10 to 20 percent of federal prison Protestant chaplains came from denominations which Stark and Glock had identified from a mass of empirical data as effective in reaching what they called the "unchurched" (the most common religious background of inmates). Charles Y.

Glock and Rodney Stark, *American Piety: The Nature of Religious Commitment* (University of California Press, 1968). Details of the above may be found in Dale K. Pace, "Contemporary Praxis of the Correctional Chaplaincy" (doctoral dissertation, Luther Rice Seminary, Jacksonville, Florida, 1974), pp. 116–119, 143.

356. Each form of church government lays claim to being the biblical pattern, and the arguments may be found in standard texts on church polity. Each form of church government has some biblical support for it, but none so strong that it excludes the other two. Thus other considerations must serve as determining factors for which form of church organization is most appropriate in a given situation.

357. Court rulings prohibited the mailing of sermons for inmate ministers of The Church of the New Song to inmates in other institutions.

358. When a group decides to organize an indigenous church inside an institution, the following steps are suggested. First, the idea should be discussed thoroughly with the chaplain and administration of the institution, enlisting their cooperation and assistance if possible. Second, correspondence with the National Fellowship of Congregations Behind Bars can provide a sample constitution (for organizational purposes) and advice (if desired). Third, the exact shape of the congregation's organization and activities should be adapted to the needs and requirements of that particular institution. And finally, *do* it. The entire process should be conducted with much prayer and sensitivity to the guidance of God the Holy Spirit.

359. The idea of unordained inmate leaders baptizing and serving Communion may offend some whose theology is strongly sacerdotal, but it should not be any more offensive than the fact that many religious bodies outside prisons have unordained leaders that do the same—unless one has an unbiblical bias against offenders.

Chapter 12

360. Many Evangelical Christians have reacted adversely to the fossilization of much of the "organized church," developing an antiorganizational bias in religious matters, and have turned almost exclusively to informal fellowship with other Christians as the total expression of their faith.

The problem is not organization. To organize is simply to "put into working order" (*Webster's Dictionary*). Lack of organization implies one is either disorganized (i.e., "thrown into disorder," *Webster's Dictionary*) or unorganized (i.e., "having no system or order," *Webster's Dictionary*). Both of these conditions are contrary to God's plan for His people. The apostle Paul commanded the church at Corinth to "let all things be done decently and in order" (1 Corinthians 14:40), because confusion is not from God (*see* 1 Corinthians 14:33).

Organization is not contrary to dependence upon God's Spirit for guidance. The Spirit of God can guide one's prayerful planning as completely as He can direct one's impulses of the moment.

In the Old Testament, God's organizational plan for the religious activities of His people is explicit, extensive, and detailed. He specified the designs for the tabernacle (Exodus 25 ff.) and for the temple (1 Chronicles 29–2 Chronicles 7; note 2 Chronicles 3:3). He specified the feasts, offerings, etc. (e.g., the entire Book of Leviticus). The Old Testament development of the religious organization of God's people is more detailed than that in the New Testament because the people had no existing structure upon which to build. They had just been delivered from Egyptian slavery. They were starting with a *tabula rasa,* a blank slate. They required explicit, detailed organizational instructions. Not so for the Church in the New Testament. It could build upon the structure of the Jewish synagogue, and it did.

Consequently, the organizational instructions of the New Testament for God's people are relatively few and general: spiritual requirements for leadership (1 Timothy 3; Titus 1); the principle of peace, decency, and order from 1 Corinthians 14 mentioned above, etc. Unfortunately, some have misconstrued the New Testament's limited, general instructions in this matter to imply that organization is not needed by Christians. This conclusion ignores the habitual silence of the Scriptures on matters already understood by its original audience.

361. At present (1976), at least 500 to 600 correctional institutions in this country have adequate inmate populations to justify at least one full-time chaplain: about 250 jails, 100 to 150 juvenile institutions, and 150 to 200 penal units. About half of these currently employ full-time chaplains. A significant number of these institutions are large enough for several full-time chaplains, e.g., 10 to 20 percent of the nation's inmate population are housed in institutions of 2,000-plus inmates. A few institutions are large enough to justify as many as a *score* of full-time chaplains (e.g., Los Angeles County Central Jail). These comments are based upon inmate/institution statistics published by NCJI&SS from surveys and censuses in the early 1970s and ACA and AEIC recommendations and standards regarding the number of chaplains needed for adequate ministry to inmates.

362. This author prefers the term *cross-denominational* to describe a correctional ministry which is not limited by denominational boundaries but which crosses them freely. This term avoids the untoward connotations on nondenominational, undenominational, interdenominational, etc.

363. Two examples of such organizations ministering primarily to offenders would be the Good News Mission and the International Prison Ministry. Two examples of such organizations which minister to offenders as only a part of their activities are the Salvation Army and the Greater Minneapolis Association of Evangelicals (sponsors a full-time chaplain for jails and a

prison, another full-time chaplain to work with police, plus volunteer police chaplains. See *Power for Living*, July 25, 1976, from Scripture Press).

364. Denominational ministries include Bible correspondence courses plus a few full-time and a larger number of part-time chaplains serving correctional facilities.

365. Some halfway houses are operated by individual congregations. A number of congregations have programs at correctional units that are identified as a ministry of that congregation. However, this author knows of no single congregation which provides a chaplain with a total ministry for an institution of any size. There are two basic reasons for this: First, a correctional administrator is reluctant to place control of the religious activities in his institution in the hands of a chaplain identified only with a single congregation. That has great political dangers. Second, the demands of a comprehensive religious program for even a modest-size institution exceed the manpower and money resources of most congregations. For example, a jail or juvenile detention center with a daily population of only thirty inmates will probably process more than a thousand prisoners during the course of a year. Thus several hundred Bibles and several thousand pieces of Christian literature can be distributed profitably each year in this small institution. Up to fifty Christian films could be shown annually. If a follow-up program were a part of the ministry in this institution, from fifty to one hundred man-hours of ministry *per week* would be required for a comprehensive program.

366. For example, this was the stated opinion of editor Manford Craig in the *APCCA Newsletter & Journal*, vol. 1, no. 3, May–June 1976, p. 6.

367. As expressed earlier in this book, this writer has questions about the propriety of government-employed chaplains but recognizes that many government-employed chaplains are dedicated men of God, serving Christ faithfully, and he praises God for their ministries. The problem is that professional clergy who are not true servants of the Living God have also become government-employed chaplains and are as detrimental to God's work among offenders as were the sons of Eli and Samuel among Israel (*see* 1 Samuel 2:22–25; 8:1–3).

368. Such support functions provide an excellent opportunity for a local church to minister to offenders, maintaining its identity as a local church. For example, a church might supply the special award-study Bibles given to inmates who complete a prescribed course of Bible study in the jail or prison, with an appropriate inscription in the Bible identifying its source and purpose.

369. The several thousand small correctional institutions in this country offer an ideal situation for a minister to be a chaplain on a part-time basis (five to twenty hours a week) while continuing his primary duties as pastor, associate pastor, or denominational official. The costs of his ministry could be financed through his church or denomination. His position as chaplain

could be augmented and strengthened not only by an official appointment as chaplain from the institution but by a cross-denominational advisory board with cognizance of his ministry within the institution. Interested denominations could provide part-time chaplains in this way for many correctional institutions in rural settings by hiring pastors of small parishes to serve them, and the cost to the denomination would be relatively slight.

370. Especially those institutions in which the Salvation Army or the Gideons minister.

371. God is able to supply every need of His servants, and can do so for organizations ministering to offenders—with or without IRS recognition. However, God expects His people to use wisdom and not to place unnecessary obstacles in the way of normal support for His work.

372. Denominational broadness and community influence should not be secured at the cost of doctrinal or spiritual commitment. *Everyone* on such a board should be in full agreement with the basic doctrinal position of the organization and should be a dedicated man of God.

373. A few organizations, e.g., the Salvation Army, draw financial support from businesses which they operate (e.g., Salvation Army Thrift Stores) and may receive funds from the United Givers Fund (UGF). Organizations receiving UGF monies must normally agree to certain restrictions on their other fund-raising efforts and may not be able to openly maintain a clear evangelical stance.

374. The *faith promise* is a form of pledge whereby an individual formally promises to contribute a specified amount which he believes God wants him to give to the organization. Often it is emphasized as giving in addition to one's normal support for his local church.

375. At a prison road camp in Virginia, the responsibility for Sunday services rotated among three churches. Two of the churches did a fine job. The third church (responsible for fourth and fifth Sundays of the month) sometimes showed up with half a dozen people to conduct the service, sometimes with only one or two, and occasionally not at all. This indifferent performance had a most discouraging impact on the spiritual atmosphere of the camp.

376. Analysis of chaplain time-use and activities under chaplain supervision that were reported in Pace's 1973 survey of chaplains *implies* that most chaplains themselves serve as the cadre, suggesting that chaplains have failed to develop cadres and delegate authority to them.

377. For example, at the Henrico County Jail (Virginia), a team of ten to twelve men provide the Sunday worship services. Five or six of these are present each Sunday, each man coming twice a month. Thus this ministry does not become a burden to these volunteers. The rotation is staggered so that half the team from the preceding Sunday is present each week.

378. For example, Ivan H. Scheier, *Guidelines and Standards for the Use of Volunteers in Correctional Programs* (LEAA, Technical Assistance Division, 1972).

379. At a jail where different church groups provided the Sunday services each week, three men mingled one Sunday with the group of eight to ten men from the church and started to enter the jail with them. The leader of the church group called the jailer aside and told him that the three men were not part of his group. The men were found to have a number of hacksaw blades, a substantial amount of drugs, and other contraband in their possession. It was later discovered that a mass escape was in the planning, and these items were to have been smuggled to certain inmates at the church services.

380. There are a number of religious malcontents who do not have a wholesome relationship to their own churches yet want to minister to prisoners. In general, those who do not have a wholesome relationship in a congregation will not be an asset to a ministry to offenders. The mere presence of questions about one's relationship to the local church on the application form will have the benefit of dissuading many unsuitable applicants from even submitting their applications.

Conclusion

381. *On Penitence.* In William P. LeSaint (tr.), *Tertullian, Treatises on Penance* (Newman Press, 1959).

382. "The tendency to use the term 'theologian' only in relation to the specialist theological scholar is regrettable. For it implies that other ministers and other Christians have no obligation to be theologians." Seward Hiltner, *Preface to Pastoral Theology* (Abingdon, 1958), p. 34. At least some chaplains and pastors should qualify as theologians as well as the professors in Bible colleges, seminaries, and theological schools.

383. The Scripture never advises or commends simple sorrow for wrongdoing. It always requires total correction (e.g., Matthew 5:23–24).

Appendix C

384. Many Evangelicals prefer the view that man is a dichotomy instead of a trichotomy. The trichotomic conception of man was common among the second- and third-century Greek Church Fathers but lost favor after Christianity became the official religion of the Roman Empire. The trichotomic position began to be reasserted by a number of German and English theologians in the nineteenth century and was widely popularized in this century among American Evangelicals by the notes of the Scofield Reference Bible. The dichotomic view blurs that awful distinction between lost men and saved men and may encourage some to believe that the new birth is not absolutely essential for salvation, causing them to rely upon their good lives, church membership, etc., instead of depending solely upon the precious blood of Christ.

The trichotomic view undergirds O. Hallesby's helpful and practical book on the varieties of Christian experience, *Temperament and the Christian Faith* (Augsburg Publishing House, 1962), pp. 2–3. In it, "temperament is the soul's (i.e., the personality's) *essential response to its surroundings*" (p. 10).

385. In describing man, the Scripture constantly sets forth man's unity and uses such a variety of terms, many of them with several levels of meaning, that some despair of drawing conclusions about man's nature. Along this vein, see the discussion in G. C. Berkhouwer, *Man: The Image of God* (Eerdmans, 1962).

386. The vigor of the new life in converts varies, as noted long ago by Archibald Alexander, first professor of Princeton Seminary and an acute observer of Christian experience: "As in nature, some children as soon as born are active and vigorous and healthy, and let all around know quickly that they are alive and have strong feeling too; whereas others come into the world with so feeble a spark of life that it can hardly be discerned whether they breathe or have any pulsation in their heart and arteries; and when it is ascertained that they live, the principle of vitality is so weak and surrounded with so many untoward circumstances and symptoms, that there is a small prospect of the infant reaching maturity; *just so it is in the new birth*" (emphasis added). *Thoughts on Religious Experience* (Banner of Truth Trust, 1967 reprint of the third edition originally published in 1844), p. 23.

387. This can be illustrated by Paul's command in Ephesians 4:28. The verb construction clearly implies that the converted thief was still stealing—and Paul said to cease. See A. T. Robertson, *Word Pictures in the New Testament* (Broadman, 1931), vol. 4, p. 541.

Selected Annotated Bibliography *

This bibliography concentrates on the Christian ministry behind bars. The reader interested in the criminal justice system, its ailments and the remedies proposed for them will find a few references in the notes on chapters 1 and 2. Single copies of most of the LEAA-related publications are available without charge, especially those from NILE&CJ and NCJI&SS. A brief bibliography on counseling is presented at the conclusion of chapter 10. In general, brief anecdotal articles appearing in magazines have been omitted.

Annotation often has been omitted for entries whose titles provide an adequate indication of content. Because each issue of the following publications is concerned with ministry to offenders, references to individual articles have been excluded from this bibliography: the journals and newsletters of the AEIC and the APCCA, The *Chap-Lett* (publication of the American Catholic Correctional Chaplains' Association), and *The Prison Chaplains' Journal* (England). Likewise, the regular publications of organizations listed in Appendix D about their ministries are excluded. Consequently, booklets such as *Miracles in Prison Cells* from International Prison Ministry have been omitted.

* This bibliography was drawn from a more comprehensive one prepared by this author for publication in the December 1976 issue of the *Journal of the Association of Evangelical Institutional Chaplains*.

Books and Pamphlets

Asmuth, Robert C. *Preacher with a Billy Club.* Logos International, 1971.

Story of a Florida minister who worked as a volunteer chaplain with police for fifteen years.

Ball, B. P. H. *Prison Was My Parish.* Hernemann, 1956.

Barth, Karl. *Deliverance to the Captives.* Harper, 1961.

Prison sermons.

Baulch, Lawrence. *Return to the World.* Judson Press, 1968.

Conversion in prison and ministry of the director of the Yokefellow Prison Ministry.

Booth, Maud Ballington. *After Prison—What?* Revell, 1903.

Early efforts of the Volunteers of America in prison ministry.

Burke, Carl. *God is for Real, Man.* Association Press, 1966.

By a jail chaplain.

Cassler, Henry H., and Kandle, George C. *Ministering to Prisoners and Their Families.* Prentice-Hall, 1968.

Well-balanced description of prison life, the legal process, and how both chaplain and pastor can and should be involved.

Church and the Prisoner, The: The Report of the Prisons Commissions to the Church Assembly. The Church Information Office (Westminster, England), 1960.

Analysis of the prison chaplaincy for the Anglican Church. Strongly recommends against indefinite (i.e., permanent) civil service employment of chaplains. Proposes a limit on chaplaincy service of a maximum of seven to ten years because chaplains become ineffective with longer service.

Clay, W. L. *The Prison Chaplain: A Memoir of the Rev. John Clay, B.D., Late Chaplain of the Preston Gaol, With Selections from His Reports and Correspondence, and Sketch of Prison Discipline in England.* Patterson Smith 1969 reprint. Originally published in 1861 by the son of John Clay.

Arthur Hoyles said John Clay could almost be called the "patron saint" of prison chaplains.

Eschelman, Byron E., with Riley, Frank. *Death Row Chaplain.* Prentice-Hall, 1962.

Finley, James B. *Memorials of Prison Life.* Arno Press 1974 reprint. Original by Swormstedt & Poe, 1855.

Provides a good description of the experiences and ministry of a nineteenth-century chaplain at the Ohio penitentiary.

Garmon, William S. *Who Are the Criminals?* Broadman Press, 1968.

A challenge to Christians to accept responsibility for the rehabilitation of criminals.

Grant, Fern Babock. *Ministries of Mercy.* Friendship Press, 1962.

Harvey, T. E. *The Church and the Prisoner in English Experience.* Epworth, 1931.

Hoyles, J. Arthur. *The Church and the Criminal.* Epworth, 1965.

Discusses all major aspects of the relation of the church and the secular state in dealing with criminals.

———. *Religion in Prison.* Epworth, 1955.

Very helpful history of the Protestant ministry to prisoners in England and America.

Institutional Chaplaincy, The. Atlanta, Georgia: Division of Chaplaincy, Home Mission Board, Southern Baptist Convention, 1969.

Jervis, Eustace. *Twenty-Five Years in Six Prisons.* Unwin, 1925.

Knudten, Richard D. *The Christian Encounters Crime in American Society.* Concordia Publishing House, 1969.

Discusses rehabilitation from sociological and political perspectives. Almost ignores the correctional chaplaincy.

Levy, Howard, and Miller, David. *Going to Jail.* Grove Press, 1971.

Chapter 8 on "Religion" presents a disparaging view of chaplains by two former "political prisoners."

Lincoln, C. E. *The Black Muslims in America.* Beacon Press, 1973 (rev. ed.).

The most important book about the Black Muslims.

Luckey, John. *Life in Sing Sing State Prison, as Seen in a Twelve Years' Chaplaincy.* Tibbals & Co., 1860.

Luckey's ministry also included extensive follow-up with releasees.

Luttrell, Mark. *Behind Prison Walls.* Broadman, 1974.

By a former Commissioner for Corrections (Tennessee). Includes a chapter "What Christians Can Do for Prisoners."

Memoir of the Life of Elizabeth Fry. Patterson Smith, 1974.

Contains extracts from her journal and letters. Reveals much about her activities with prisoners.

Message to the Church and a Statement of Policy and Practice Concerning the Churches in Indiana and State Institutions, A. The Department of Institutional Ministers of the Indiana Council of Churches, 1975.

Morrish, R. *Christ With the C.I.D.* Epworth, 1953.

Neale, Erskine. *Experience of a Gaol Chaplain.* AMS Press reprint of the 1849 edition.

Pace, Dale K. *Correctional Chaplains: Shepherds or Hirelings?* AEIC, 1974.

An essay identifying major areas of failure in the chaplaincy.

——— (ed.), *Notes on the Correctional Chaplaincy* (Good News Mission, 1972). Used as text for the Good News Mission's chaplaincy course 1972–1976.

Pean, C. *Devil's Island.* Hodder and Stoughton, 1939.

Story of the ministry of a French Salvation Army chaplain on the notorious Devil's Island.

Reform of the Criminal Justice Systems in the United States and Canada. Board of Social Ministry, Lutheran Church in America, 1972.

Role of the Chaplain in New York City Correctional Institutions, The. Board of Correction Task Force on the Church and the Prison, Final Report, 1972.

Very well done discussion of the needs and role of the chaplaincy in New York City Jails.

Thomas, Nancy White. *A Year in Jail.* Richmond, Virginia: Printed by Whittet and Shepperson, 1970.

Experiences of a volunteer working with females in jail.

———. *Five Years in Jail.* Richmond, Virginia: Printed by Whittet and Shepperson, 1973.

Tucker, Park. *Prison Is My Parish. The Story of Park Tucker as Told to George Burnham.* Revell, 1957.

Tucker was chaplain at the federal prison in Atlanta, Georgia.

Articles

Abbott, W. J. "The Prison Chaplain," *Prison Service Journal* (Liverpool), 7:21–31, 1968.

Examines the role of the prison chaplain in England in the light of regulations, by opinions of chaplains, and historically.

Abramson, M. "Priest Within Cole Prison Walls; Father Francis J. Lane, Elmira Prison," *Catholic Digest,* 12:12–16, June 1948.

Bates, E. A. "The Woman Chaplain." *Christian Century,* 79:83, January 17, 1962.

Beane, R. "Shepherd of the Stray Sheep." *Friar,* 23:39–43, April 1965.

Bennett, James V. "The Role of the Modern Prison Chaplain." *News Bulletin of the Osborne Association,* 8, December 6, 1937.

———. "The Role of the Chaplain in Federal Correctional Institutions." *Progress Report, The Prison Chaplain,* April–June 1963.

Bloom, Herbert I. "Religion as a Form of Institutional Treatment." *Proceedings: American Correctional Association, 1963.*

Bonaker, Ralph D. "The Training School Chaplain as Counselor." *Federal Probation,* April–June 1944, pp. 12–15.

Bosco, A. "Action Before Attica: Dismas Committee." *Columbia,* 53:14–23, January 1973.

Brevis, H. G. "Counseling Prison Inmates." *Pastoral Psychology,* 7:35–42, February 1956.

By a rabbi who served Attica prison as a visiting chaplain.

Bromfield, J. "The Prison Chaplain and His Captive Audience." *Liguorian,* 61:51–54, May 1973.

Carlson, Robert J. "The Court House Chaplaincy—A Project in Collaboration." *Pastoral Psychology,* September 1972, pp. 18–25.

Describes the program in Harvey County (Kansas) to minister to all involved in welfare and corrections, using half a dozen clinical pastoral trainees as the main source of manpower.

Carroll, J. L., and McCormick, C. G. "The Cursillo Movement in a Penal Setting: An Introduction." *Canadian Journal of Corrections,* 12:151–160, April 1970.

Describes results from two marathon group encounters (three days each) in a Canadian jail, conducted along the lines of a Cursillo retreat (i.e., a short course in Christianity or human interaction).

Carter, S. "A Woman's Self-Affirmation in the Ministry." *Pastoral Psychology,* 23:45–50, March 1972.

Brief account of her entrance into the correctional chaplaincy in a woman's prison in South Carolina.

Cassler, H. H. "The Prison Chaplaincy." *Journal of Pastoral Care,* 8, No. 3:165–168, 1954.

Explains why the National Council of Churches serves as a clearinghouse on chaplains for the Federal Bureau of Prisons and why a prison chaplain must be able to function interdenominationally.

Cederleaf, J. L. "The Chaplain's Role with Delinquent Boys in an Institution." *Federal Probation,* March 1954.

———. "The Therapeutic Role of the Chaplain with Delinquent Boys." *Journal of Pastoral Care,* 6, No. 3:17–25, 1952.

Clarke, E. M. "Expectations and Role Performance of Chaplains in Federal Penal Institutions." *Journal of Pastoral Care,* 24:135–139, June 1970.

Summarizes the findings of an eight-page survey answered by eighteen Protestant chaplains in federal penal institutions in 1967.

Cole, W. E. "The Social Worker and the Chaplain: Institutional Team Mates." *Pastoral Psychology,* 23:31–38, March 1972.

Coogan, John E. "The Myth Mind in an Engineer's World." *Federal Probation,* March 1952, pp. 26–30.

Discusses the question, Is religion of decreasing importance in correctional work?

———. "Religion and the Criminologist." *American Catholic Sociological Review,* 6:154–159, October 1945. Same in *Catholic Mind,* 44:277–281, May 1946.

———. "Religion: A Prevention of Delinquency." *Federal Probation,* 18 (December 1954), pp. 29–35.

"Cursillo at Collins Bay Penitentiary." *Federal Corrections* (Ottawa), 8:3–4, 1969.

Description of a Cursillo retreat.

Devlin, W. J. "The Diagnostic Role of the Chaplain with Delinquent Boys." *Journal of Pastoral Care,* 6, No. 3:11–16, 1952.

Doyle, Barrie. "Prison Ministry: Jesus in Jail." *Christianity Today,* vol. 18, no. 20, July 5, 1974, pp. 44–46.

Descriptions of ministries of Bill Glass Evangelistic Association in prison and of the Good News Mission.

Edmonds, Leonard S. "The Place of Religion in the Treatment of the Offender." *Federal Probation,* September 1951, pp. 14–17.

Erwin, John R. "Cook County Jail's Short-Term Education Program." *American Journal of Correction,* March–April 1970, pp. 14–17.

Description of an education program in a jail by its Protestant chaplain.

Eschelman, Byron E. "The Prison Ministry." *Federal Probation,* September 1968, pp. 37–41.

"Florida Corrections Initiate Chaplain-on-Call Program." *American Journal of Correction,* July–August 1975, p. 34.

French, P. "The Minister and the Delinquent." *Journal of Religion and Health,* 3:271–275, April 1964.

Gannon, Thomas M. "Religious Control and Delinquent Behavior." In M. Wolfgang (ed.), *The Sociology of Crime and Delinquency,* 2nd ed. Wiley & Sons, 1970, pp. 499–508.

Discusses a study which investigates the effect of religious influence on delinquent boys.

Gavin, John A. "Summary of Rehabilitation Through Administration and Religion." *Proceedings: ACA,* 1962.

Gladych, E. "SIG Members Don't Come Back: Father F. Prange, McNeil Island Penitentiary." *Catholic Digest,* 28:118–120. August 1964.

Grandstaff, Earl-Clayton. "The Power of a Purpose." *Proceedings: ACA,* 1964.

Hager, Don J. "Religion, Delinquency, and Society," *Social Work,* 2 July 1957.

Hart, A. C. "The Institutional Chaplain: and Ye Visited Me." *The Baptist Program,* November 1970, pp. 6–7.

Heller, M. S. "Psychotherapy and the Prison Chaplain." *Journal of Pastoral Care,* 8, No. 3:160–164, 1954.

Hiltner, Seward. "The Function of the Prison Chaplain." *News Bulletin of the Osborne Association,* 9, June 1, 1938.

———. "The Role of the Prison Chaplain in Relation to Parole." *Federal Probation,* August–October 1940, pp. 34–36.

Presents an ideal relationship.

Hirsch, Travis, and Stark, Rodney. "Hellfire and Delinquency." In Charles Y. Glock (ed.), *Religion in Sociological Perspective: Essays in the Empirical Study of Religion.* Wadsworth, 1973, pp. 75–87. Also in *Social Problems 17,* No. 2 (Fall 1969).

"Is the Christian sanctioning system of hellfire for sinners and heavenly glory for the just, able to deter unlawful behavior even among those who are firm believers? . . . Evidence on the question is mixed" (p. 76).

Home Missions. November 1972. Home Mission Board, Southern Baptist Convention.

The entire issue is devoted to corrections and the Christian ministry to those involved. Very well done.

Hubble, B. "That Untold Prison Story." *Moody Monthly,* July–August 1972, pp. 36–37, 53–55.

A few highlights of the correctional chaplaincy from various institutions.

Jabay, E. "The Institutional Chaplaincy." *Reformed Review,* 19:12, March 1966.

James, Thomas. "Christ, the Christian and the Criminal." *The Niagara Anglican,* March 1973. Also in *The Prison Chaplains Journal* (England), Spring 1974.

A Roman Catholic chaplain's contention that a chaplain's ministry as prophet and pastor flows from his ministry as priest.

———. "Philosophy, Theology and the Correctional Process." *The Canadian Journal of Corrections,* 9, No. 2, 1967.

Jarvis, T. A. "Early Life of a Prison Chaplain; Father A. F. Carlyle" (Abridged). *Catholic Digest,* 11:74–77, August 1947.

Jelinek, R. "Prison Chaplain: Men and Work." *Christian Family,* 52:26–30, September 1957.

Jiskoot, D. "Evangelism in Prison." *Reformed Review,* 24:42–45, Autumn 1970.

Johnson, Stuart D. "The Correctional Chaplaincy: Sociological Perspective in a Time of Rapid Change." *Canadian Journal of Criminology and Corrections,* 14:173–180, April 1972.

Reviews the activities of the correctional chaplaincy and discusses problems created by current religious turmoil.

Kannwischer, A. E. "The Role of the Protestant Chaplain in Correctional Institutions." *American Journal of Corrections,* 19:12 ff., January–February 1957.

Keuther, Frederick C. "What the Federal Chaplain Does About Parole." *Federal Probation,* November–December 1940, pp. 31–33.

———. "Religion and the Chaplain." *Contemporary Corrections,* Paul W. Tappen (ed.). McGraw-Hill, 1951.

Sees clinical pastoral training as saving the prison chaplaincy from extinction as other professionals in corrections meet social and psychological needs of prisoners.

Kirkpatrick, A. M. "The Church in Corrections." *The Canadian Journal of Corrections,* 7:2, April 1965.

Knudten, R. D., and Knudten, M. S. "Juvenile Delinquency, Crime and Religion." *Review of Religious Research,* 12:130–152, Spring 1971.

Bemoans the lack of empirical data. Extensive references.

Lancaster, R. V. "Has the Christian Chaplain, as the Minister of Religion, a Rightful Place in All Our Schemes for Character Building Among the Men Committed to Our Care?" *Proceedings: American Prison Association,* 1928.

Contends the chaplain must first and foremost be a religious minister or he is not needed.

Long, Harvey L. "The Church's Mission and Delinquents," *Federal Probation,* December 1963, pp. 26–31.

Incidentally, the author comments that correctional chaplains "would be even more effective if they were employees of the church instead of the state" (p. 27).

McCallion, W. "Prison Chaplain at Work," *Homiletic and Pastoral Review,* 63:307–313, January 1963.

McGiffert, A. C., Jr. "In Prison and Ye Came," *Christian Century,* 59: 245–249, February 25, 1942.

McHahon, John F. "The Work of the Volunteers of America in the Field of Correction." *American Journal of Correction,* May–June 1963, pp. 24–29.

Maxey, D. R. "Swinging Prison Priest; Chaplain for the Five D.C. Prisons in the Washington Area." *Look,* 28:24–29, December 29, 1964.

Miller, Marshal E. "The Place of Religion in the Lives of Juvenile Offenders." *Federal Probation,* March 1965, pp. 50–53.

Very valuable.

Morris, Albert. "The Comparative Opinions of Commissioners, Wardens, Prison Psychologists and Chaplains on Conditions and Trends in Correctional Systems: A National Opinion Poll." *Institutions of Massachusetts Correctional Association,* 1966.

———. (ed.). "What's New in the Work of the Church and the Chaplain in Correctional Institutions?" *Correctional Research Bulletin No. 11* from the United Prison Association of Massachusetts, November 1961.

Oliver, John W. "To Whom Should the Prison Chaplain Minister?" *Federal Probation.* March 1972, pp. 19–22.

As social and psychological workers take over the duties that formerly had fallen to the chaplain, he should expand his ministry to the outside community, enlisting volunteers needed for inmate rehabilitation programs.

Pace, Dale K. "Programs ARE Possible." *National Jail Association Newsletter.* May 1975, pp. 1–4.

Description of programs under a jail chaplain's supervision.

———. "I Was in Prison, and Ye–." *Foresee,* January–February 1976, p. 4.

Comparison of chaplaincy with pastorate.

Pike, Burlyn. "I Was in Prison and Ye Came Unto Me." *Federal Probation,* June 1949, pp. 29–33.

A good example of community involvement in corrections.

Plott, David L. "Counselling the Drug Abuser: A Christian Approach." *International Journal of Offender Therapy and Comparative Criminology,* vol. 18, no. 1, 1974, pp. 62–67.

Advocates directive counseling as developed by Dr. Jay Adams.

Powers, George E. "Prevention Through Religion." In William E. Amos and Charles F. Wellford, *Delinquency Prevention: Theory and Practice.* Prentice-Hall, 1967, pp. 99–127.

Powers, Sanger B. "The Role of a Chaplain in a State Correctional System." *Proceedings: ACA,* 1964.

Prestor, R. A. "God's Gleaner." *Pastoral Psychology,* 10:20–26, May 1959.

General discussion of the chaplain's task.

"Prisons, Punishment and the Christian." *Eternity,* March 1972.

Proelss, E. F. "The Ministry of a Prison Chaplain." *Princeton Seminary Bulletin,* 55:25–36, September 1961.

———. "Reflections of the Social, Moral, Cultural, and Spiritual Aspects of the Prison Chaplain's Ministry." *Journal of Pastoral Care,* 12:69–81, Summer 1958.

Valuable, balanced description of the ministry of a Protestant chaplain by the Episcopal chaplain of the New York City Prison on Rikers Island. Discusses the tasks of the chaplain: (1) ministry of the Word and sacrament, (2) ministry of religious education, and (3) ministry of pastoral care.

Rees, Lloyd L.. "The Church and the Prisoner." *Prison Service Journal,* 5(19):21–24, 1966.

"Religious Freedom in Prison." *Albany Law Review,* 36:416–428, 1972.

Rhodes, Albert L., and Reiss, Albert J., Jr. "The Religious Factor and Delinquent Behavior." *Journal of Research in Crime and Delinquency,* 7:83–98, 1970.

Reports that subjects with no church affiliation have the highest rate of delinquency.

Ridgeway, J. M. "Some Attitudinal and Motivational Changes Among Heroin Addicts Involved in a Religiously Oriented Program of Rehabilitation." *The Drew Gateway,* 43:47–48, Fall 1972.

A dissertation abstract.

Rothstein, R. J. "Corrections is Based on the Dignity of Man." *Federal Probation,* 34:38–40, 1970.

By a chaplain but contends that treatment of inmates with human dignity is more important than religious activity.

Ryan, Gerald J. "The Role and Contribution of a Chaplain to a Community Police Department." *Law and Order,* September 1971, pp. 86–87.

Sartain, G. "Mending Broken Lives: Seminarians at Rikers Island," *National Council,* 7:9–10, 1957.

Scarlett, William H. "I Was in Prison and Ye Visited Me: The Story of the Salvation Army," *American Journal of Correction,* November–December 1965, pp. 8–12.

Shanahan, L. "Portrait of a Prison Chaplain: Father Thompson of Los Angeles Jail." *Saint Joseph Magazine,* 65:7–10, January 1964.

Shedron, Mark. "The Religious Program in a Correctional Setting." *Federal Probation,* March 1958, pp. 42–44.

Sheehy, D. "Baptism in a Prison Parish." *American Ecclesiastical Review,* 151:298–306, November 1964.

Summer, R. R. "The Gospel and Prisoner Rehabilitation." *Lutheran Quarterly,* 23:240–250, August 1971.

Describes the program at the federal youth center in Morgantown, West Virginia.

Tilden, Paul L. "The Role of the Chaplain in Correctional Institutions." *Prison World,* January–February 1953.

Wallace, J., Jr. "Prison Redeemer and Hero." *Coronet,* 32:128–130, September 1952.

Weaver, C. E. "Christian Vocation in the Institutional Chaplaincy." *Brethren Life and Thought,* 4:45–48, Summer 1959.

West, S. G. "The Crisis in the Correctional Chaplaincy." *Canadian Journal of Corrections,* 10(2):327–331, 1968.

Discusses the negative effect on the chaplaincy of religious disunity and lack of interest by major religious bodies. Also concludes that the chaplain should not be paid by the correctional system.

Weir, E. "A Chaplain's Solution to the Problem of Crime." *Proceedings: American Prison Association,* 1936.

Society shows little interest in religious programs in prisons.

Yancey, Philip. "Paper Chains." *Campus Life,* February 1976.

The story of John Erwin, senior chaplain at the Cook County Jail.

Youmans, Robert O. "Group Counseling in a Jail." *American Journal of Correction,* May–June 1968, pp. 35–37.

A rehabilitation program conducted under the chaplain of the sheriff's department in San Diego, California.

Zahn, Franklin. "Lay Visiting in a Correctional Institution." *Federal Probation,* September 1957, pp. 29–31.

Unpublished

Carter, Thomas Edwin. "The Counseling Role of the Protestant Chaplain in an Adult Male Correctional Institution." PhD dissertion, Southwestern Baptist Theological Seminary, Fort Worth, Texas, 1966.

Pace, Dale K. "Contemporary Praxis of the Correctional Chaplaincy." ThD dissertation, Luther Rice Seminary, Jacksonville, Florida, 1974.

See Appendix B.

Vickers, Hylon. "The Place of Religion and a Religious Program in Adult Corrections." Master's thesis, Sam Houston State University, Huntsville, Texas, 1971. See Appendix B.

Topic Index

The topic index provides a few references to the notes as well as indexing the text of this book.

Scripture Index

(Does not include Appendixes or Notes)